TREATING SEVERE DEPRESSIVE AND PERSECUTORY ANXIETY STATES

TREATING SEVERE DEPRESSIVE AND PERSECUTORY ANXIETY STATES

To Transform the Unbearable

Robert Waska

KARNAC

First published in 2010 by
Karnac Books Ltd
118 Finchley Road
London NW3 5HT

British Library Cataloguing in Publication Data

A C.I.P. for this book is available from the British Library

ISBN-13: 978-1-85575-720-2

Typeset by Vikatan Publishing Solutions (P) Ltd., Chennai, India

Printed in Great Britain

www.karnacbooks.com

CONTENTS

ACKNOWLEDGEMENTS

I wish to thank all my patients for their willingness to learn and change, sharing their intimate struggles with me and allowing me to learn and grow as a clinician. All identities have been disguised and details of each case have been modified to protect the personal details involved.

My thanks go out to my wife who is always ready to lend a hand in whatever way is needed, providing feedback and gentle guidance with my writing endeavours.

Finally, I appreciate the permission to reprint particular material that has been previously published in journal form. Chapter Two has appeared in Issues in Psychoanalytic Psychology (1), Chapter Six in the Bulletin of the Menninger Clinic (2), Chapters Three, Seven, and Eight in Psychoanalytic Psychotherapy (3), Chapter Ten in Psychodynamic Practice (4), and Chapter Eleven in the American Journal of Psychotherapy (5).

1. Waska, R. (2008). When suffering never ends: The internal experience of the paranoid and depressive worlds colliding. *Issues in Psychoanalytic Psychology*, in press.

2. Waska, R. (2008). Session-by-session report of a low frequency Kleinian psychoanalysis with a borderline patient. *Bulletin of the Menninger Clinic, 72*(2): 85–108.

3. Waska, R. (2007). When patients face the dual threat of depressive and paranoid phantasies. *Psychoanalytic Psychotherapy, 21*(4): 315–329.
Waska, R. (2008). A Kleinian view of psychoanalytic couples therapy: Part one. *Psychoanalytic Psychotherapy, 22*(2): 100.
Waska, R. (2008). A Kleinian view of psychoanalytic couples therapy: Part two. *Psychoanalytic Psychotherapy, 22*(2): 118.

4. Waska, R. (2008). Why won't the voices leave me alone? Patients who live in a world of persecutory anxiety. *Psychodynamic Practice, 14*(2): 193–206.

5. Waska, R. (2008). Using the counter-transference: Analytic contact, projective identification, and transference phantasy states. *American Journal of Psychotherapy, 62*(4): 1–1.

PREFACE

This Book serves two purposes. First, it provides the psychoanalyst or psychotherapist with a more flexible method of practicing psychoanalysis. This is the clinical approach of Analytic Contact, a technical stance in which more patients can be reached in a deeper and more helpful manner. Analytic Contact is an operationally robust Kleinian approach for the real world of private practice and targets the combination of internal and external factors that are consistently at play with all patients.

The second aim of this book is to examine specific groups of patients that present unique challenges to the psychoanalyst. These populations are examined and new and creative ways of working with them are introduced.

Building on the work of his last two books, the author invites the reader to discover the clinical value and technical utility of Analytic Contact. Analytic Contact is a psychoanalytic therapeutic approach that brings the healing possibilities of psychoanalysis to the more disturbed patients that tend to fill our private practice offices. In addition, Analytic Contact enables the clinician to reach populations that are not usually considered easily treatable by the psychoanalytic method, such as once a week sitting up patients, psychotic patients, couples who are seeking help with marital issues, and chronic borderline and narcissistic individuals.

In the first portion of the book, extensive case material is provided to show the reader a set of patients who suffer from both paranoid and depressive anxieties. They are caught within pathological phantasies without any viable defence and therefore experience chronic fragmentation, fear, and despair. Without any viable psychological shelter, they tend to act out and stage difficult transference and counter-transference climates highlighted by intense projective identification processes.

In the second portion of the book, analytic contact is shown to be useful in working with patient groups not usually discussed in the psychoanalytic literature as within the scope of cure. Low-frequency patients who are within the borderline and narcissistic spectrum and are caught with this combined paranoid and depressive emotional dilemma are examined with detailed case reports. Couples who are seeking resolution of long-standing conflicts, often on the brink of separation or divorce, are shown to be reachable through the process of analytic contact and specific psychoanalytic ways of working with the often paranoid-schizoid situations the couples present with. Finally, psychotic patients and patients utilizing rigid manic defences are both shown to be viable candidates for psychological transformation through analytic contact.

In the third portion of the book, counter-transference is examined. Numerous case reports are used to illustrate the demands put on the analyst through projective identification-based transferences and the resulting counter-transference confusion.

This book highlights various difficult and resistant patients and offers the clinician hope and therapeutic direction through the clinical concept of analytic contact. Analytic contact embodies the core elements of a Kleinian psychoanalytic approach without the rigidity of external criteria such as frequency, couch, duration, or diagnosis. Instead of being tied to external factors, the treatment is based on internal elements such as transference, defence, phantasy, and unconscious conflict. This intra-psychic focus is consistent with Freud and Kleins' directive to understand and modify the patient's internal world. Through analytic contact, underlying psychological patterns of pathology can gradually be altered. Learning, change, and choice become possible and lasting healing and new perspectives unfold.

INTRODUCTION

In **Chapter One**, the concept of Analytic Contact is presented as a therapeutic process that is clinically based rather than defined by extrinsic matters. The immediate, in the moment, interpretation of transference, defence, and conflict is central to the practice of analytic contact and the Kleinian base it rests upon. Using analytic contact to reach acutely troubled patients, the author demonstrates a psychoanalytic technique that focuses on transference, internal conflict, and phantasy states, regardless of pathology, frequency of visits, phase of or duration of treatment.

In fact, the case material deliberately investigates analytic encounters with patients whose intense internal struggles with both persecutory and primitive depressive anxieties often bring about premature termination. This Chapter begins a multi-chapter investigation of work with patients suffering with both paranoid and depressive anxieties, often creating difficult transference standoffs based on their internal experience of being haunted by persecutory and depressive phantasies without any psychological retreat or resolve available to them.

Chapter Two continues to explore the many individuals who function within psychological combinations of paranoid and depressive experiences. Rather than successfully shifting from one state to another without much inner fragmentation, these individuals are trapped with the worst of both worlds. They operate within an immature, distorted view of the more dreadful and out of control versions of these two mental perspectives.

As a result, the transference as well as the general trajectory of their psychoanalytic treatment tends to be rocky and chaotic. The nature of these patient's anxieties is apt to be so catastrophic that they cling to whatever shred of predictability they have and see change as traumatic. Analytic contact can be difficult to establish. The combination of intense persecution and unreachable, irreparably damaged objects leave the ego without hope. Transference states of deadness, helpless agony, angry resentment and entitlement, avoidance of separation or autonomy, dread of change, severe guilt, obsessive demand for perfection, constant longing for love and caretaking, and resistance to contact and closeness all weave together in confusing and challenging ways.

Because of all these factors, growth, separation, and autonomy are considered dangerous. Faith in being an independent entity able to safely rely on others who in turn can be tolerant, dependent, and understanding is rarely reached. Clinical material will be used to show the more severe aspects of these clinical issues and this material will be contrasted with those patients using pathological organizations or psychic retreats to deal with such issues.

In **Chapter Three**, the focus falls on patients who enter psychoanalytic treatment appearing to suffer from depressive anxieties in which they fear harming their objects, so they try to make amends and find a peaceful solution to perceived conflicts.

However, over time these same patients reveal a deeper and darker form of internal chaos in which they are experiencing a combination of paranoid and depressive phantasies of an overwhelming nature. As outlined in the previous Chapters, primitive experiences of loss combine with persecutory feelings to bring about unbearable states of mind. Projective identification and splitting are used defensively but also increase this pathological internal situation. Attempts at reparation fail, leaving the ego to eternal loss and life without forgiveness. Dead and destroyed objects return for revenge, replacing hope with dread. These patients have an immature foothold in the depressive position while still struggling with paranoid conflicts. Rather than finding refuge in pathological organizations or regressing from one position to another, they face the constant threat of both paranoid and depressive experiences without any reliance on good internal objects to soothe, save, or guide them. Melanie Klein's theoretical discoveries in this area are discussed and extensive clinical material is used to illustrate the gradual establishment of analytic contact in such choppy clinical waters.

Chapter Four provides more clinical material to show the intricate and rocky moments involved in establishing analytic contact with patients facing a combination of paranoid-schizoid and depressive position phantasies. In a sense they have the worst of both worlds, as neither position is fully worked through and neither state stands in mature form. Rather, they suffer with brittle and precarious states of persecution, guilt, grief, and abandonment. With unresolved conflicts in both arenas, the normal psychic resolutions of object relational compromise are distorted, over-used, or unavailable. The transference with such patients is predictably unpredictable, with transference conflicts shifting abruptly and precariously from one collection of depressive and paranoid phantasies to another.

In **Chapter Five,** the details of these patients' internal struggles continue to be illuminated. These individuals attempt to develop and engage with both the internal and external world from a place of rigid uncertainty, and emotional demand. They have intense phantasies of the inevitable breakdown of all valuable attachment. They try to move forward psychologically to navigate the depressive world of whole objects, trust, and reciprocal relationships. But, they are handicapped by their paranoid-schizoid phantasies of primitive loss, emotional deprivation, and persecution. Again, these internal phantasy states create significant roadblocks to successful psychoanalytic treatment but analytic contact is still possible.

Guilt, separation, dependence, and other elements of the depressive position become overwhelming, contaminated, or perverted by paranoid states of mind. Unlike some patients who retreat into pathological organizations meant to avoid any paranoid or depressive experiences, these patients are trying to traverse the rocky road of grow and change, but bring intense dual object relational pathology to the journey. So, the depressive position that usually brings a more active and flexible state of mind that provides a sense of healing and hope actually feels more like unbearable suffering, unfair demand, and brutal injury to both self and object.

So, most of these patients continue to long for and search for their object even though it is a disappointing and disappointed object that seems to eventually turn into a rejecting, angry object bent on injury or withholding. In the transference, this becomes more obvious as a cycle of aggression, guilt, and persecution that further promotes some patients to even more aggression, anxiety, guilt, and flight. Thus, working through and exploration of the transference and phantasy states are difficult and slow, but certainly necessary for any lasting psychic change.

Chapter Six provides an in-depth clinical example of the flexible and technically useful concept of analytic contact. While the psychoanalyst's ideal private practice is filled with nothing but neurotic, classical psychoanalytic patients seen on the couch five times a week for years at a time, this is certainly not the clinical reality for the majority if not all of the profession. However, there is virtually no literature regarding the psychoanalytic treatment of patients with less than three times a week frequency other than those articles that include the word psychotherapy in the title.

Even though more lenient positions are taken in public forums and between colleagues, there is still a vast political split between what is considered kosher psychoanalysis and "that other procedure" of psychotherapy with no middle ground to be found. The leading publication for psychoanalysis worldwide, the International Journal of Psychoanalysis, now includes articles on psychoanalytic psychotherapy. It is remarkable, but never mentioned, to notice how the cases and clinical process written about are usually indistinguishable from the cases and clinical process in all the other papers concerning psychoanalysis.

This book presents material based on the belief that if a consistent pattern of transference analysis has taken place along with regular exploration of phantasy and defence, then regardless of frequency, analytic contact can take place. This is then regarded as "true" psychoanalysis. In other words, psychoanalysis becomes defined by clinical process rather than external criteria.

This Chapter uses a case of a borderline patient, Nancy, to illustrate the process of analytic contact in low-frequency Kleinian psychoanalysis. By concentrating on the basic tenets of analytic contact, which include phantasy, defence, transference, containment, and interpretation, the author worked to help this patient find resolution to a severe internal conflict and lack of ego integration.

The author worked in the more classic Kleinian direction, which, as Segal (1973) has outlined, involving interpretations of the complete or total (Joseph, 1985) transference. These interpretations are not limited to here-and-now moments of transference exploration but also include the analysis of the patient's daily life and external interactions, the parallel between those factors and the original parental relationship, and the link between internal figures and external ones.

Even though this is a Kleinian approach, it is very much in agreement with Couch's (1995) paper in which he sees classical Freudian analysis as including internal, external, past, present, and the reality of daily life. Rangell (1995) has also noted that the external realities of a patient's life as well as their upbringing cannot be separated from the internal structure psychoanalysis usually works on. Analysts from different theoretical perspectives seem to have this common clinical approach regardless of the political and territorial disputes they become embroiled in.

Chapter Seven investigates the central elements of psychoanalytic couple's treatment. The role of analytic contact is discussed and the importance of each party of the couple being witness to the other party's response to analytic contact is discussed. Emphasis will be placed on issues of thinking, projective identification, and the concept of container-contained. This Chapter will focus mainly on theoretical issues and utilize one clinical case to illustrate some of the theoretical points.

Many if not most psychoanalysts see couples as a regular part of their private practice. Certainly, couple's therapy can be conducted in a very non-analytic manner by manipulating the transference, giving advice, and making decisions about the relationships that are beyond the power of anyone but the couple. However, couple's therapy can truly be a psychoanalytic process in which analytic contact is the goal with working through of phantasy, transference, defences, and unconscious conflict as the aim. Using the theoretical and technical guidelines of Freud and Melanie Klein, this is one more way the profession is able to help those in emotional need.

Chapter Eight continues to explore the psychoanalytic treatment of couples. Since most couples enter treatment operating in a more primitive paranoid-schizoid stance, the author contends it is best to initially focus on each partner's pathological projections and have the other partner witness their struggle to overcome personal issues that contaminate the couple's unified psychology. With continuous working through, the couple can gradually find a more depressive, integrative footing within themselves and as a couple. The value of "witnessing" and working through individual defensive reactions against thinking, pathological projective identifications, and the breakdown of the container-contained function are all examined in the clinical presentations. All these clinical elements are part of the establishment of analytic contact first with each party as individuals and later as a unified couple.

Chapter Nine takes a look at patients who exhibit an overly rosy outlook on life that serves to shield them from the painful realities of external life as well as internal life. Historically, these patients report family experiences in which they felt their primary objects were unable or unwilling to serve as comforting or supportive containers for their childhood anxieties. In fact, these patients typically experience their primary objects as actively refusing to serve as supportive containers for their core fears and conflicts. A concurrent phantasy often encountered is that of an object overwhelmed and burdened by the ego's needs or worries.

As adults, these patients repeat and relive this psychological situation by ignoring their own fears and needs out of a sense of guilt and anxiety. This is expressed in their adult relationships as well as in the transference and creates a pseudo-pleasant therapeutic climate that neutralizes any conflict or dependency. Projective identification is one major factor in the overly optimistic view of important objects, situations, or life in general. This use of projective identification can be useful in coping with overwhelming anxieties and guilt, but also creates a cycle of idealized objects and phantasies of hopeful, fulfilling objects that ultimately disappoint or abuse.

Optimism can be part of a pathological organization or defensive system certain patients rely on to ward off unbearable phantasies of an either paranoid or depressive nature. Often, it can be a chaotic mix of both persecutory and depressive phantasies. Establishing analytic contact with these patients can be very difficult due to the very rigid manner in which they utilize optimism to relate to their objects.

Akhtar (1996) has noted certain patients use pathological optimism as their primary defence, creating idealized objects and a reliance on denial as a way to cope with various anxieties. Klein (1952) discussed the role of positive projective identification and how it can be used as a defence to protect the self from an unavailable object that is not what one needs or wishes for and a defence against aggressive feelings that could harm the object.

Case material with patients in various levels of depressive conflict (Espasa, 2002) shows the clinical situations in which optimism can emerge as part of the transference and the manner in which guilt and persecutory fears can shape the nature of the patient's view of self and object. Several cases are presented to illustrate how analytic contact was achieved or not achieved and how different forms or levels of optimism were the central theme of the analysis.

Chapter Ten examines those patients who reveal a great degree of anger and spite towards the object, feeling disappointed by it and constantly devaluing it as unnecessary or useless. This anger is usually a narcissistic response to feeling unloved or rejected. One way this appears clinically is a harsh superego that leaves the patient constantly and cruelly wanting to achieve a state of self-contained perfection. This is the result of projective identification processes in which the desire and demand for an ideal object is put into the object and experienced as both conscious and unconscious judgement, rigidity, and expectation. Naturally, this means the patient is always failing themselves and attacking themselves or others for being less than ideal.

One case of a psychotic patient seen in low-frequency psychoanalysis will be explored to understand certain aspects of this problem. Analytic contact was successful. The patient was able to reach significant integration and reduce his borderline experience of self and others.

In the course of psychoanalytic treatment, there are some patients with whom it is difficult to locate, understand, and interpret their transference state. **Chapter Eleven** examines the use of the counter-transference to assist in making analytic contact in these vexing clinical situations. The concept of analytic contact is once again explored, positioning it as the more clinical definition of psychoanalysis. With the goal of analytic contact being the identification, understanding, and working through of core object relational phantasy states, counter-transference can be valuable in helping the analyst find their way to the transference, especially when the transference is exclusively shaped by projective identification processes. Case material is used to show work with patients exhibiting difficult to access transference states primarily determined by projective identification-based phantasies.

The influence of projective identification is an integral aspect of most psychoanalytic treatments, especially with more disturbed patients but also with higher- functioning neurotic individuals. Projective identification involves both internal relational phantasies of self and object as well as external interactions with the environment. Both elements shape the transference. Continuous cycles of projections distort the ego's image of the object, causing bias introjections that saturate the ego with guilt, anxiety, and envy, creating even more radical projections in reaction. Consequently, the counter-transference is repeatedly stimulated in an evolving or devolving manner (Clarkin, Yeomans, & Kernberg, 2006).

This Chapter uses case material to illustrate the constant interplay between projective identification, transference, and counter-transference as well as the utility of counter-transference in making the most helpful interpretations. The concept of analytic contact is shown to be the vehicle of optimal psychological transformation. Rather than an emphasis on frequency, diagnosis, use of couch, or mode of termination, the focus is more on the clinical situation and the moment-to-moment work on internal conflict, unconscious phantasy, destructive defences, analysis of the transference and extra-transference anxieties, and the gradual integration of core object relational experiences. Regarding a more clinical rather than theoretical definition of psychoanalysis, Sandler (1988) states that what truly defines a treatment as psychoanalytic is the analyst's attitudes towards his patient, his willingness to contain and make the effort to patiently understand the patient's unconscious conflicts and reactions to internal phantasy states, the humane detachment and lack of judgement, and the maintenance of a comfortable and safe setting in which the transference can unfold. This definition is certainly similar to the elements of analytic contact.

Use of the counter-transference is crucial in finding a path into the patient's projective identification processes, which in themselves often hold the core phantasy states that the patient most struggles with. These phantasies shape his experience of the analyst and the world around him. Melanie Klein thought that phantasy was an essential aspect of the mind from birth onwards, with love, hate, and the quest for knowledge being innate, yet also influenced by external events that then recast the phantasy and the patient's reaction and perception of those external situations (Spillius, 2007). Klein's belief that phantasy is so much the bedrock of human experience has led the Kleinian school to conceptualize the transference as being constant and all pervasive, and therefore not something that arises at selected times in the treatment. In other words, there is no differentiation between the transference and the working alliance.

So, if the analyst is consistently on the alert for manifestations of the transference, he or she may be able to help the patient identify and work through their phantasy conflicts. However, the transference, even through a constant phenomenon, may elude the analyst, for many reasons. Projective identification dynamics are often the culprit, in that base transference phantasies are hidden, discharged, communicated, acted out, camouflaged, or traded off in projective identification interactions with the analyst. It is here that the counter-transference, a similarly constant element in the treatment setting, can be most useful in relocating the transference phantasies. Then, the analyst can begin to explore them, rather than be a part of the patient's denial, destructive acting out, or gratifications.

As the counter-transference is better understood, the analyst can begin to more properly contain, translate, and ultimately interpret the core phantasy states so as to help the patient feel more in control of them. So, it is this ongoing emphasis in working within the transference/projective identification/counter-transference matrix that gradually brings clarity to the analyst who can share that knowledge as an interpretive proposal. Then, the patient can potentially use it to build greater psychological freedom, emotional stability, and personal choice.

Chapter Twelve explores how projective identification is often a pivotal component of a patient's transference mode of relating. This projective-based transference climate easily triggers a wide variety of counter-transference reactions. Similar to the previous Chapter, this Chapter uses case material to examine the cycle of transference→projective identification→counter-transference and to explore the benefits of utilizing the counter-transference to better understand, manage, and ultimately interpret the patient's underlying phantasies and conflicts. Along the way, acting out is expectable by both parties. However, if the analyst tries to be in a state of constant curiosity regarding the way projective identification may be acting as a bridge between transference and countertransference phenomenon, what could be destructive or a repetitive enactment can instead be more of a map to the patient's unconscious defences, communications, anxieties, and hopes. The technical process of analytic contact is again shown to be the most clinically relevant method of working with the core conflictual phantasy states at the heart of all analytic treatments.

PART I

COMBINED PERSECUTORY
AND DEPRESSIVE TRAUMA

CHAPTER ONE

Psychoanalysis as defined by the clinical situation: Establishing analytic contact with acutely troubled patients

In psychoanalytic treatment, we strive to identify, understand, and work with the core unconscious phantasies that shape, distort, or constrict the patient's experience of themselves, others, and day-to-day existence. We seek to analyse the phantasies that create imbalance or anxiety in the patient's internal and external world. In order to perform this work, we strive to create the best conditions to learn about and change these psychological issues. This clinical situation is best described as the successful establishment of analytic contact (Waska, 2006; 2007).

This is a therapeutic process that holds the transference as the primary vehicle of change, but also considers the elements of containment, projective identification, counter-transference, and interpretation to be critical to therapeutic success. Dream-work, genetic reconstruction, analysis of conflict and defence, and extra-transference work are all seen as valuable and essential. The concept of analytic contact is not so much tied to external factors such as use of couch or frequency of visits as it is to building a clinical forum for the understanding and modification of the patient's deepest phantasies. Analytic contact is about finding a foothold into the transference and as well as into the core phantasy states that are

3

having the greatest impact on the patient's feelings, thoughts, and actions.

In working to establish analytic contact, I employ a combination of classical and contemporary Kleinian approaches to better reach the patient at his current internal experience of self and object. Again, this involves the consistent exploration and interpretation of all conflictual self↔object relational states and the struggle between love and hate within those states of mind. Counter-transference is vital to finding the often jumbled threads of transference and to understand the nature of projective identification communications or attacks that are so frequent in most treatments.

Working to achieve analytic contact involves utilizing the clinical perspective of contemporary Kleinian approach but without the constraints of frequency, couch, diagnosis, or duration of treatment as a primary element of working with the unconscious. In fact, the essential core focus is always on the internal conflicts, phantasies, and defences within the transference and extra-transference climate, regardless of how often the patient is attending or what the diagnostic profile might be.

Rather than wait for a "positive transference" to develop or a "therapeutic alliance" to form, the Kleinian-based concept of analytic contact technically moves on the premise that careful compassionate psychoanalytic work can and must be part of the treatment from the first moment of engagement. While some contemporary Freudians, Relationalists, or those influenced by Kohut or Winnocott would wait to cultivate some sort of reparative link with the patient and see the immediate and ongoing interpretive style of analytic contact as counterproductive or even aggressive, I advocate the more contemporary Kleinian trend towards moment-to-moment interpretive work on the total transference situation (Joseph, 1989). It has been my experience, illustrated by the case work in this Chapter, that this cornerstone of analytic contact helps alleviate the patient's more intense persecutory and depressive anxieties, thereby clearing the way for the integrative work of transference, defence, and phantasy analysis.

To summarize, analytic contact is a way to newly define the process of psychoanalysis from a purely clinical perspective, a process aimed at reaching the core phantasies and conflicts a patient unconsciously struggles with which they often demonstrate through projective identification acting out and other transference-related communications. Analytic contact holds as its goal to discover, investigate, and work through the repetitive, destructive archaic experiences of self↔object. Ideally, this takes place within the transference matrix and provides a new and healing experience of new, healthy, and creative self↔object experiences. This in turn leads to gradual integration of a less hostile, more hopeful internal view and the ability to function in the world in a more balanced and holistic manner. The patient can begin to feel more securely grounded in a more robust internal world of whole objects and fortified versions of self.

Case material

In day-to-day psychoanalytic practice, one encounters a number of patients who seem to share similar phantasies regarding the desperate longing for a loving object as well as the dread of being rejected by that same object. Hoping to please the object as a way to being loved factors large in their life, but equally important in their internal experience is the counter-phantasy of always disappointing the object, leading to combinations of primitive loss, abandonment, and persecution. These are complex conflicts involving paranoid and brittle depressive or pre-depressive phantasies that create tricky if not outright treacherous treatment situations.

Making analytic contact with such patients can be difficult and fraught with setbacks. In treating these individuals, the internal struggles with persecution, primitive loss, and fragmentation emerge quite quickly and need to be addressed as they unfold. The patients highlighted in this paper certainly have phantasies of injuring or destroying the needed and loved objected. But, they do not have the stable or enduring capacity for faith, hope, and trust in the recovery, reconstitution, and reunion with the lost or destroyed object.

The following case material illustrates very early presentation of such conflicts that necessitate immediate interpretation and exploration.

Case 1

Klein (1963) wrote about how the superego is actually made up of projected or split-off aspects of the ego. These cruel parts of the self deny forgiveness. Instead, they simply demand a lack of all things aggressive or destructive without any compromise or understanding (Klein, 1963). This separation from any human mix of good and bad creates unbearable loneliness and a sense of emptiness that this first case illustrates.

Bill was a man in his early twenties who had dropped out of college after feeling "depressed all the time and overwhelmed at never fitting in or finding a way to connect with people." He worked at a fast food restaurant and "felt like an alien, with his coworkers." He had broken up with his girlfriend several months before treatment when "things just fizzled out and faded away." Bill told me he felt "clueless to know how to socialize and wanted to sort out his feelings because he felt he was going no where and was very depressed."

Bill appeared extremely anxious when meeting with me and I interpreted that he might not be sure how to relate to me and was trying hard to fit in with me but didn't know how to connect. He replied, "That is pretty much on target. I am dreading these moments of silence after I say something and you respond. I am sure I am supposed to say something next but I don't know what that is so I feel terrible and on the spot. I am sure you are just waiting for me to respond so I feel like I am freaking out." I interpreted that he was trying to appease me and dreaded disappointing me. Bill said "that was so" and that he felt he was always "one inch away from looking like a fool."

He had been raised in an extremely religious family where sin and punishment were preached in the home and at church services. Bill told me he "has turned away from that way of thinking and is seeking something more spiritual in life." I interpreted that he may still be operating at that sin-sinner-banishment level that leaves him afraid of how others judge him, including his analyst. Bill associated to being a teenager and masturbating. He said he felt very guilt about being such a sinner but he did it anyway and thought he could pray for forgiveness later. But, then he became frightened that he would forget to ask God for forgiveness and end up going to hell. Or, more commonly, he imagined a giant meteor would fall from the sky and kill him before he had time to pray. During his teenage years, he "constantly worried about the meteor."

I interpreted that Bill felt something would always get in the way of forgiveness. I said he may still feel that he is blocked from the compassion and understanding of the object, left to suffer as a sinner in the object's eyes. He said he "totally agreed" and added that he "always feels without a soul, empty and hollow, like there is just wind blowing through a huge abandoned warehouse." I interpreted that he hopes I will help him find forgiveness and acceptance from others, so he feels less like a sinner. I said he must feel very anxious being so hollow and he must hope we can find a way to feel make him feel more solid, stable, and safe. Bill associated to "wild punk rock shows where I feel solid and alive when I dive into the crowd when fights are going on. I throw myself into the middle of the violence and am surrounded by angry people kicking and punching. I get hit and bloody all over and suddenly feel alive and connected. I look in the mirror the next day and see myself bloody and bruised and feel happy I was a part of something." I interpreted that he was in a real conflict because he felt connected to others and solid inside himself if he voluntarily chose to be beaten and attacked. But, I interpreted, that same aggressive bliss was what left him scared of others in situations where he felt he was not in control. In other words, I was starting to interpret the projective identification process with me and others in which he felt he would be emotionally beat with judgement and rejection without warning. I said perhaps this related to the guilt he felt. The beatings at the show were a form of penance that left him solid and forgiven. Otherwise, he felt guilty and unworthy, soon to be sent to hell without hope of forgiveness or understanding. Bill said my comments "make a great deal of sense and he wanted to figure it out so he could feel better."

This analytic contact was established in the span of the first three sessions of Bill's treatment. It remains to be seen how things will unfold in the future, but a difficult patient with profound anxiety and persecutory conflicts has begun to work with his analyst in the realm of transference and phantasy.

Case 2

As Klein (1948) has noted, many of our more troubled patients have experienced a great deal of external hardship, deprivation, and even abuse in their early family years. Klein (1948) explains how this painful external environment combines with the aggressive and fearful internal conflicts and phantasies to produce a more toxic experience of life. In some cases, this leads to an adult life punctuated by confusion between internal and external and generates many unresolved paranoid and depressive conflicts. I would add that, through projective identification, the most troubling internal struggles become predictably acted out interpersonally.

Betty was a nineteen-year-old woman who came to me with full knowledge she could only have three visits because she had no money or family support and her college had provided for several free visits to a mental health worker of her choice. Betty was overweight and rather plain, but she exuded such sexuality that she seemed like the prettiest of women. This seductive presentation was combined with an extremely deferring, apologetic manner that immediately made me feel she was my love slave.

I told her she seemed overly eager to be polite and thankful. She said she "only wanted to make sure I was willing to see her and not kick her out." I interpreted that she already saw us in a very specific relationship and understanding that might help us. She agreed and said she was like that with everyone because "she never knew who liked her and she needed people to like her." I said it seemed she felt very anxious about being rejected and left alone. Betty said, "I hate myself so I need others to love me enough to counterbalance that."

Betty went on to tell me she was a drug addict and frequently used a combination of opiates, cocaine, marijuana, alcohol, and various pills. The main reason she had elected to start treatment was that she had recently stolen money from her mother, whom she lived with, to buy drugs with. They got into a fight that became physical and her mother told her to "get help or get out." Betty had been to three other therapists in the last two years. She said that one "was useless," one was "so troubled by my situation that she kept crying every time we met," and the last one "just tried to tell me what to do and wanted me to stop using drugs right away and I couldn't do that." I commented, "I think you might want to stop for yourself some of the time, but having someone else tell you to might be a whole different thing." Betty said, "Yes, I need to want to do it."

Betty's family experiences were troubled. Her parents divorced when she was five years old and she was shuttled back and forth for years. Her father is an alcoholic and I immediately wondered if she had perhaps been sexually abused by him given her seductive transference stance. Now that she wasn't getting along with her mother,

Betty was staying with her father but told me, "its hard since he hasn't worked in years, is drunk most of the time, and he is completely broke." Betty's only other sibling lived in another state and had been in jail for a year from several drunk-driving arrests. Betty's mother worked at a local clothing store and barely made enough to pay the monthly bills, let alone help Betty out. Betty had been working for about a year at a bar but she was fired for showing up under the influence. She had been attending college for almost two years, but the first year was a series of failed classes due to the drugs. Now she was trying to "hang in there but was unsure how to pay for it" since she had no money and would be asked to leave within weeks. What was striking about her school problems was that she seemed very interested in obtaining a degree in science and when she put her mind to it, she was able to make good grades and said she "enjoyed it and really felt like she was doing something that felt right to her."

This was one of several moments where I not only felt sorry for her but thought that this was someone who really deserved a break in life, as she seemed like a person with a good heart living a dark tragedy and wanted better. I made note of this feeling because I also considered it a counter-transference feeling that gave me some insight into how Betty seemed to want a fatherly figure that would be supportive and believe in her. I made such an interpretation and she said she had never had such an experience, but was eager "to find that." I interpreted that she wanted that from me but also wanted it to be in a very dependent way where I called the shots and told her what to do. So, it was a wish for a caring father but also it seemed like she felt she had to make a bargain with her ideal object that in exchange for that feeling of guidance and love, she would have to give up her identity and rely on the object in a more sadomasochistic manner.

I made this interpretation and Betty told me it "made her realize something about how she relates to men." She said she routinely had sex with random men in exchange for drugs and often would have sex with multiple partners even if they didn't give her any drugs but simply "acted nice and asked her to come home with them from a bar." She went on to tell me that she "feels good when they pay attention to me and like me, even though I know they only want sex and will forget about me later. I really like it when they seem to value me and show me they care by giving me drugs and telling me I am pretty. I feel like I finally have what I have been looking for, I feel content. But, I know it is bad and I am ruining myself, which is why I want to work with you to stop all this. I know it isn't really me but I have been doing it so long it has become me."

Betty tried to use this sexualized way of finding a loving parental figure in several ways with me. One example was when she was explaining how she might have to move out of her father's house and her mother would not let her return to live with her either. Betty said, "If that happens, I will have to live with a butch of guys I know in their place. It would be me and four or five guys. They love to party so there would be gangbangs and heavy sex all the time. Can you imagine me involved in a gangbang with four or five different men?" While she was saying this in a desperate way, relating her anxiety about her living situation and lack of money, it was clearly a very seductive manoeuvre to turn me on. I said that to Betty and she replied, "Oh, you got me! I am sorry. You are right. But, it just comes right out. I can't help it. I am sorry. That is exactly what I need to learn not to do." So, this led us to discuss how she felt unable to reach me or see me as a helpful male figure in her life without giving herself over to me sexually and in the process controlling and manipulating me.

When she said she really wanted to "stop that stuff and find a way to change," I interpreted that I believed she wanted to change but it was a confusing situation for her because it was unclear how much she wanted to change for me to please me and how much she simply wanted to change for herself. I interpreted that she may be reluctant to change for herself because that means she is establishing her own identity, separate from the object and that may feel threatening or frightening. She replied, "I don't know if anyone will want me or see me as important if I just follow my own path." I interpreted that she wanted to be special to me because she imagined I would consider her own true self to be inadequate or useless. So, she had to imagine what I might want and adapt to that in order to be special. This left her only temporarily fulfilled as it was an attack on herself and a cloning of my desires to preserve our relationship, not a genuine pursuit or expression of her own wishes, needs, and desires. Betty replied that she "wanted to learn how to do what I said, but isn't sure how to stop being what others want." This psychological problem is similar to what Bass (2007) outlined in his exploration of the as-if character from a Kleinian perspective. Betty was unsure of her own self because she tried to be what others wanted. Indeed, she was frightened of the consequences of freeing herself from this emotional slavery. If I was able to continue working with Betty, I would pursue the exploration of her projected aggression, dependency, and envy because it seemed that this was at the root of her struggle. In other words, she projected her envy of the object's ability to have an identity and have needs and then she felt threatened by that object in a "if you dare to be yourself we will punish you or leave you" way. Her dependency was so aggressive she felt she would crush the object so she needed to deny any personal needs.

So, here we were facing her core anxiety and phantasy of becoming abandoned, alone, and without value if she was to be separate or different from the object. To please the self was to displease the object in a manner that left her with a primitive sense of loss, attack, and rejection. This persecutory phantasy had more to do with her fear of survival than her concern for the object. As Segal (1994) has noted, in order to deal with internal or external chaos, the ego projects its good aspects into the good object. With pathological reliance on projective identification, this led to the ego being stripped of its own resources and potential. Betty seemed to need to prop others up in the hopes they would be able to finally parent her and love her in the way she felt denied. However, this projection was bound up with her aggressive view of the object as a disappointing, abusive, and weak entity so she had to sacrifice herself to prop up the object in the hopes of it now being able to provide her with the aid she so desperately needed.

Of course, this was a vicious cycle in which she felt more and more empty and desperate and her objects became more and more unreliable and false. In the counter-transference, I immediately had these types of feelings and phantasies, which when developed into interpretations, were confirmed by Betty's associations. As Brenman (2006) points out, some patients, such as Betty, need to distort their view of themselves and of the object in order to avoid unbearable emotional pain and to prevent what they perceive to be a constantly imminent relational catastrophe in which the self suffers emotional desolation. This was the condition Betty was in when she sought help from me. Sadly, it was the condition she left in as well. I think she may have been able to take in some of our work as a new type of introject that may eventually bring her back for more help in the future or at least offer a feeling of security in her moments of pain.

Case 3

Frank was a plumber in his late twenties when he sought help for his "rocky relationship." He was a nervous looking man who was undereducated and talked in a rough manner that at first suggested he would not be able to relate psychologically or symbolically. However, he was very motivated to have things improve in his life and seemed willing to look within himself in a way he had never tried.

Frank has smoked pot almost everyday for the last fifteen years. He would usually smoke after work and as a result, he would show up for his sessions intoxicated. In addition, he was drinking to the point of drunkenness every weekend and often on weekdays. Most weekends, he would "hook up with running mates" and take large quantities of cocaine, opiates, and ecstasy. He would come close to crashing his car, spend enormous amounts of money, and have to call in sick to work frequently.

Frank agreed with me that he had a problem but wasn't sure if "he wanted to stop or could stop." I told him I would help him try and understand why he needs to depend on drugs and alcohol and if he wanted to reduce or stop using I would aid him in that as well. It was important with Frank to not tell him he must stop as that would be part of a counter-transference acting out. Instead, I frequently pointed out that he must have a difficult time relating to me without being high and I told him I was interested in finding out more about that.

I have met with Frank for almost two years now and in that time he has made considerable progress. However, there is a great deal of acting out and resistance to change for Frank, as change means danger and loss in a most primitive way.

Frank was raised in a family where his father was an alcoholic and a drug addict. His parents fought with each other most of the time and divorced when Frank was eight years old. Frank's father was a brutal man, an ex-boxer, who raised Frank in a chaotic, violent manner. There were beatings and threats and when Frank disagreed with his father as a teenager, his father made him put on boxing gloves and fight with him. Through his upbringing, Frank was made to smoke marijuana, drink beer, and watch his father's friend's have sex with prostitutes so "he was educated about the ways of the world." Most of his father's conversations had to do with how "all women are whores and just need to be handled with a strong hand," "nothing beats a good night drinking," and "if someone fucks with you, you fuck them up good."

While this view of the world was most certainly frightening and confusing, another aspect of Frank's experience with his father was more sad than scary. During most of Frank's life, his father was barely working and in the last ten years, he didn't work at all. This was because of his drug addiction to cocaine and pain pills as well as his alcoholism. In the last few years, he had managed to not use drugs except for weekends and he now had a part-time job. But, when Frank goes over to visit him in the mornings, they frequently share several beers for breakfast since his father drinks every morning "to get the motor running."

The way Frank described this made me interpret that he felt sorry for his father, seeing him as someone who had fallen off the path and wasn't able to care for himself. Frank agreed and said he wished his father would take better care of himself but "that just wasn't who he is." I immediately had the sense that Frank was seeing himself as slowly becoming more of an independent, competent man than his father and I thought this might leave him feeling very conflicted. I made this interpretation and Frank said he had never thought of anything like that but it sounded "kind of right and makes him think a bit."

Frank barely finished high school, telling me he wasn't able to concentrate on the reading. He said he never read any books but just listened to the lectures and passed most of the tests. He had actually achieved some of the best scores in his senior class on a college preparation test, but never applied to any schools upon graduation. He went on to work in a plumbing company and quickly mastered the most complex of projects, showing a real talent and creativity, as well as being able to fix most any thing by hand.

Much of the first six months of his analytic treatment was spent discussing his relationship with his girlfriend of five years. He told me about how they lived in different cities and she would never make the effort to visit him so he was "always shelling out for gas and having to shuffle my ass up to her place, like I don't have anything better to do than to sit in traffic for two hours." Once he was at her place, he felt obligated to take her out to dinner and give her money to cover her bills. He said he loved her and enjoyed spending time with her but "hated that she is never in the mood for sex, is always depressed about something, and never really wants to talk." It was the last part of what Frank said that caught my ear. Over time, I interpreted that he wanted to have an equal, predictable relationship with her in which he could depend on her and talk about his and her emotions, finding a resource in each other. Instead, he felt a guilty obligation to please her and keep the peace. He agreed and said it was important to him to be able to communicate and know what was wrong with her if she was depressed. He also said he felt guilty if "he did his own thing and didn't visit her." I also interpreted that he felt sorry for her and felt like he would be abandoning her if he wasn't "there for her," especially when she seemed depressed, working in a dead-end job, and always complaining about her life. Also, his drug use was something he felt he was always hiding and if he left her it would be "not right given I have been high behind her back most of the time, so I would be betraying her twice."

After about six months, he did in fact break up with her after they had started spending less and less time together. He had suspected that she was interested in a mutual friend and found out that was true. From my perspective, it seemed that she had become unhappy with his drinking and pot smoking, was depressed about her own life, and found someone else who seemed to pay more attention to her. He seemed to have been unhappy with not being able to openly communicate with her, was tired of feeling obligated to make her happy, and was tired of lying to her about his drug use. For a month or two, he seemed to feel very guilty about the impact of his drug use on the relationship and later became angry that she had started seeing someone else behind his back before they broke up. I interpreted that while those feelings were true, I thought he also was very angry that he had to care for someone who didn't seem willing or able to accept his more emotional side and would not share theirs either. I related this to the same possible feelings he had towards his father. Frank said he "agreed and wished she had been able to hear him when he wanted to be real, but he also felt crappy for being loaded so often instead of being there for her." So, we worked with those feelings for awhile.

Regarding the transference, I made interpretations about how he also tried to please me, how he felt obligated to always show up and be on time, and how he felt guilty when reporting his latest drug binges. I commented on how he was quick to see us in that particular type of relationship.

In investigating his chronic drug use, it became evident that Frank needed to be high most of the time to avoid what he called, "a bad case of the what nows." In exploring what he meant by this, we found that he was extremely anxious about being around new people, scared of making new friends, and "clueless about how to meet a girl." Over the course of about the first year, I had the distinct impression, through how he acted, how he related to me, and what he talked about, that Frank wanted a fuller life than what he had grown up with and that he wanted to differentiate from his father. Indeed, Frank knew how to act like his father but it wasn't really him. I made that interpretation and Frank told me, "Yeah, that isn't really me but I don't know what is." This came out in Frank telling me about how his father "scored drugs for him" and how they frequently got high together, but also how, "it is a little on the uncomfortable side when I am out with my friends and my father starts cursing and talking about all his racial shit and then chugging down his whiskey and hounding my friends to get him some blow." So, I interpreted that he felt sorry for his father and also wanted to separate and become his own person, but felt guilty and scared. Here, I was pursuing what I felt to be his phantasy of primitive loss (Waska, 2002; 2005) in which the object is destroyed without hope of repair and in its place rises up a persecutory figure bent on revenge without chance of forgiveness or compassion. This is in line with what Klein (1948) stated about how paranoid anxiety deforms ego integration and cancels out depressive capacities. As a result, the "loved injured object may very swiftly change into a persecutor and the urge to repair or revive the loved object may turn into the need to pacify and propitiate a persecutor" (p. 121). This persecutory guilt (Bicudo, 1964; Rosenfeld, 1962) is more about a demanding, punitive object than an understanding, guiding parental figure.

When I made such interpretations, Frank told me he feared hurting his father's feelings and was anxious about his father's retaliation. He said, "I don't want to do him wrong, he has done his best with me. And, there could be hell to pay if I cross paths with him." So, at first, it was more a depressive concern of disappointing and abandoning his father. But, it quickly changed to being scared of being punished. I told Frank, "I think you want to find your own identity and be your own person, but you feel like you would be lost in a wilderness if you are different than him." He said, "I have no clue how to be that other person, but it might be nice. Or, I could end up in a dead end. Maybe his way isn't so bad." I said, "It sounds like change makes you very nervous so it feels safer to go with what you know instead of ending up on a deserted island by yourself." He nodded in agreement.

I brought up these issues by making such transference interpretations as, "I think you want to relate to me in a new way and see me like a father who could guide you and understand you. But, I think that is also very confusing and scary. Perhaps that is why you show up stoned to your sessions. It helps you have to not face it or feel it." Frank said, "I do like being able to relate in a different way. It is a one-way street with my father and pretty much the same with my friends. Sometimes, I could talk like this with my old girlfriend, so that is one reason I miss her. And, every once in a while, I can talk to my mother this way. But, pretty much this is it, when I come to see you. Feelings and shit are not considered cool to talk about in my family."

So, I interpreted that Frank longed for a reliable understanding object who would love him for who he was, not a fragile or even pathetic object that demanded allegiance and saw growth as betrayal and difference as criminal. Frank felt an unbearable paranoid guilt and schizoid anxiety that made him feel obligated to please the object and do as they wished as the only way out.

So, we explored the manifestations of this in the transference in which he was initially very guilty if he was late or on occasion forgot to come, but quickly this shifted to a fear of my displeasure and even anger. In working with this transference anxiety, he discovered that he was locked into the same sort of relationship with his friends. In the course of two years, Frank was able to acknowledge to himself and to me that many of his friends "were simply dope heads and users who didn't work and relied on him to give them drugs, money, and a ride." Gradually, this insight led Frank to drop some of these friends and focus on the ones who seemed to respect him and who allowed him to be more himself. We discussed the pain involved in this move because he felt he was letting them down and "leaving them behind." I interpreted that this feeling was a part of his overall fear of growing past his father and leaving him behind.

This new but uncertain way of experiencing the world also came about in how he perceived women. Now, he rarely parroted his father in talking about them. Before he would say, "I hope I can grab a piece of ass at the bar tonight. A man has to get his rocks off you know!" Now, he would say, "I am trying to figure out where to meet women outside of the bar scene. But, I am nervous about what to say if I do meet one." Now, we explored his fears about how to be himself if he wasn't copying his father's behaviour. And, this led to more discussion about how he wanted to relate to me as a father who didn't curse, drink, threaten, or ignore him and in doing so he could be more himself and less of a clone of his father. He told me, "it is kind of refreshing to not always refer to the women I know as *the whores*." In the counter-transference, I felt a warm affection for a man who was trying hard to be himself within an internal world that barely permitted such a breach of tradition. I kept in mind that this counter-transference experience was also likely to be part of some projective identification process that I was not yet full aware of.

During the second year of his analytic treatment, Frank reduced his drug and alcohol intake. He still smoked pot almost everyday, but would put together several days in which he didn't. We discussed how he seemed to "survive it," including meeting with me on occasion without being high. He also greatly reduced his drinking and would only take opiates, LSD, or cocaine on "special occasions." We also talked about how this was sometimes an effort to please me and to prevent me from being angry. Again, this was a more primitive combination of depressive and persecutory fears. But, he was also honestly interested in "turning a corner" in his behaviour, realizing "it is a real dead end most of the time." As we explored his drug use, we found it to be a complicated issue. One aspect was his identification with his father. Another was drugs as a buffer between his paranoid and depressive phantasies regarding his father and other authority figures. Still another was the use of drugs as an emotional defence against the great anxiety he felt when wanting to strike out on his own and grow into his own person. This included learning to relate to others in a new way, without needing to take care of them, please them, or be frightened of them.

Unlike Case 2, he was not quite as overwhelmed with phantasies of complete annihilation, emptiness, loss, and abandonment and therefore Frank felt somewhat more courageous in daring to dream for more in his life and actually take steps towards changing his view of himself and his objects. He was also more willing to disappoint, hurt, or anger the object in his hopes to change and grow. And, in seeing me as a potential new and different type of father object, he was able to relate to me in a slightly more sophisticated, whole object manner. One way to differentiate the level of guilt and persecutory dread between the cases of Betty and Frank is to use Espasa's (2002) categories of depressive conflict. Both Frank and Betty suffered from para-psychotic phantasies regarding the object's health and exist-ence, but some of the time Frank was also able to achieve a more Para-Depressive state in viewing his relationships.

However, Frank still was caught in a fearful transference of primi-tive dependency and guilt in relationship to me and others. Frank was extremely talented and motivated to excel in his job, but we discovered that this was also a safe arena for him to have more of an identity because he reported to a father/boss and was ultimately doing what he was told rather than what he wanted to. I interpreted that his pride in his work was such that he may dream of being his own boss someday, but that might also be frightening because he isn't sure how I, his father, or others might react to his independ-ence. I interpreted that being drug free might hold the same fright-ening independence that he longed for but dreaded. Frank said he did want to own his own business one day and thought he could "pull it off" but added that "I think I need to get my shit together quite a bit before I will be able to do it." He added, "I do worry what you guys think of me. We are cool, right?" We spend time discussing his sudden fear about our stability and his anxiety over causing any conflict with me.

As I mentioned earlier, there were times in which I felt sad for Frank. He obviously wanted more in his life, but he had always felt held back. He was unable to pursue literature, the arts, hobbies, or any sort of creative outlet that would allow new knowledge and experience. His life was narrow and restricted, fenced in by fear and obligation. In these moments of feeling sorry for Frank, I had to examine myself and take note of how much of this feeling was part of Frank's desire for an understanding and compassionate father in me. As Brenman (2006) notes, through projective identification, our patients frequently bring us in touch with particular beliefs or ways of thinking about them, which must be understood as transference communications and then interpreted as such. So, I consistently brought up his desires for a new father and the ways he related to me that actually repeated his current master-slave relationship with his father than to build a more equal relationship where difference is respected.

As mentioned, Frank struggled with primitive guilt and phantasies of persecutory loss. This is a state in which there is a fundamental resentment concerning the sense of obligation in having to please and prop up the weak but rabid object. This is in line with what Grinberg (1964) has noted about persecutory guilt and was present in how Frank resented his father and his "loser friends." But, it is also different in that Frank experienced great anxiety about the result of his abandonment or betray of his father and friends. Frank was sure it meant he was deliberately harming the object as well as a guarantee of retaliation from that object without any hope of reconciliation. So the guilt is more of a fear of abandoning the object to cruel collapse that would lead to a sense of personal desolation and debilitating uncertainty. This phantasy combines with a fear of object's revenge. The phantasy is that if separation occurs and individuation begins, there will be abandonment and attack. This is similar to Klein's (1957) notion that if envy is too excessive in the infantile ego, the object of the ego's guilt becomes a persecuting assailant. However, instead of envy, Frank felt more of an emotional hunger for something better: a better father, a chance to grow into his own person, and a desire to have a more fulfilling experience with his objects. This hunger was a combination of anger, fear, guilt, anxiety, and confusion and led to the same result Klein mentioned. At the same time, not only is there this multiple anxiety about leaving the object behind, but the projected anxiety makes the concept of a new object and new self uncertain and scary as well: "will anyone like me if I change, who will I be, and what do I do if I give this stuff up?"

An example of current progress in these matters involves Frank's search for a girlfriend. If he finds a girl, he said he is even "willing to just be friends so we could talk. If it goes further than that, it's cool."

When he said this, it was in opposition to his father's advice to "just get those panties off and stick it in."

When Frank finally said hello to a woman he was interested in on his bus ride to work, he told me, "The next step is to ask her to do something. Holy shit, I don't know what to do or say! But, I can figure it out, we will find a way!" Here, Frank was showing off the new initiative he felt despite the fear of rejection he felt. And, even though he wanted me to tell him what to do or say, from our work together he knew it was up to him and indeed he now felt that was possible. Later, he told me he walked this woman from the bus to her workplace and told her he would like to do that again the next day. This led to him summoning the courage to ask her to dinner and even though he ended up feeling like she wasn't really his type, he felt proud and fulfilled with having asked her and having been able to spend the evening talking with her without feeling over-whelmed with panic or dread. And, Frank deliberately chose to not get high prior to the date. He did drink a fair amount at the dinner, but he said he was "pretty much all there, sailing the ship on my own recognizance." He had found a way to be his own self, an indi-vidual capable to making it in the world without fear or guilt. Part of the success in this story was that unlike other relational situations in the past and even in the early transference situation, he did not project all of his strength and goodness into her, making her ideal and stripping himself of identity and personality (Segal, 1994).

Analytic contact is the therapeutic process in which the analyst attempts to assist the patient in getting in touch with and gradually reach an emotional and intellectual understanding of their warded off unconscious phantasies regarding the relationship of self and object. This insight provides the vehicle for subsequent working through and change, but does not solve the issue of resistance to that change. This is the arena of the ongoing analysis of transference, defences, anxieties, and internal gratifications.

Regarding the concept of analytic contact, more and more clini-cians within the psychoanalytic field are concluding that this is the more honest definition of what is psychoanalysis in that it is about the clinical process. Fossege (1997) believes there is no real distinc-tion between psychoanalysis and psychoanalytic psychotherapy and therefore proposes that the best definition of psychoanalysis is that it is an investigatory science searching for the best understanding of the patient's experiential world. This is in line with my concept of analytic contact being the therapeutic process of clarifying and modifying the patient's core conflictual phantasy states. And, analytic contact contents that the transference→projective-identification→counter-transference→interpretation climate is the best possible venue to achieve that goal.

The focus of analytic contact is the working through of phantasies and the multiple manifestations of love, hate, and knowledge that involve anxiety towards self and/or other. Projective identification is very often the primary climate in the analyst situation. The interplay between projective identification and transference can be intense and constant in particular treatments, regularly triggering counter-transference feelings and thoughts. Many clinicians including myself (Waska, 2005; 2006; 2007) have extended Klein's (1946) intra-psychic concept of projective identification to include the interpersonal and interactional aspects of the analytic situation. This is certainly in agreement with Blum's (1982) ideas about the various levels of important analytic work necessary in every treatment setting, including the interpersonal, the interactional, and the intra-psychic.

The cases presented in this Chapter represent difficult (Waska, 2005) but not unusual patients for the average psychoanalyst's practice. While not necessarily meeting the external requirements often associated with psychoanalysis, such as frequency, use of couch, diagnosis, or length of treatment, each was a treatment in which analytic contact was achieved. In that sense, psychoanalysis was taking place. The concept of analytic contact defines psychoanalysis by what takes place clinically. This is in line with Fine's (1979) statement concerning the work with difficult and more disturbed patients, "inasmuch as these therapists attempt to work out the transferences and resistances, they are doing analysis by Freud's definition, even if other parameters are introduced. Whether one calls this psychotherapy or psychoanalysis seems to be a matter of semantics" (p. 517).

CHAPTER TWO

When suffering never ends: The internal experience of the paranoid and the depressive world colliding

This Chapter continues to show how some of our most difficult analytic patients suffer from being trapped in a psychic state in which both paranoid and depressive phantasies have not been successfully or amply negotiated. Rather than having both internal developments as a positive, strong psychological foundation, the patient is caught within a world of dual conflicts and destabilizing phantasies.

In this fragile internal place, aspects of the depressive position are present, guilt is felt, and the desire to make restitution occurs. But, the reason to make amends is not to heal the object out of guilt but to protect the self. In this immature depressive mode, forgiveness, restoration, compassion, tolerance, and negotiation are not seen as existing in the object. So, mistakes are fatal. Therefore, pathological compromises and destructive object relationships are not easily given up as they represent the only thread holding back the eternal banishment, the infinite destruction, and the final separation.

Within this combination of paranoid and depressive experiences, there is a sense of guilt that is not present in the paranoid-schizoid mode. However, it is delicate and not fully formed. So, it is more of a feeling of I have done something to offend and hurt you AND now you will hate me, reject me, and hunt me down. The guilt comes from not only remorse for injuring the object but terror of the object wanting payback.

Many of these ideas are similar to those of Rey (1994), in which he examines a pre-depressive mode where reparation is stunted or contaminated by paranoid phantasies. This leads to pathological states of mourning (Tarnopolsky, 2000) in which excessive aggression, desperate need, and envy of what could and should have been (Grotstein, 2007) create unbearable guilt and corrupt the working through of the depressive position.

Normal states of loss and mourning are experienced over the lifespan from the frustrations of weaning to the acceptance of death. However, when internal and external object relational conflicts are still unresolved within the paranoid position and the ego has only a delicate and immature foothold in the depressive position, the ability to deal with mourning is severely handicapped. Through projective identification, the object is experienced as unable to tolerate the ego's needs, assertiveness, and aggression. In phantasy, an incurable, unforgiving dead object is the result. Guilt shifts to fear and restitution is replaced by persecution. Creative thought, desire, hope, and symbolic endeavours all are casualties to this condition. Segal (1952) has noted that creativity involves the symbolic substitution for the lost object and the creation of a new object that can sustain the tie to the old. This is not possible if loss is experienced as more of an irresolvable catastrophe (Waska, 2002) and autonomous thought, personal identity, and feelings separate or different from the object must be killed off to preserve the harmony and therefore wellbeing of the relationship between self and object.

Rey (1994) states that it is very difficult to build a stable ego if the normal introjective identification process is tainted by persecutory feelings based on projected envy, greed, or rage. I would add that the lack of a stable external object complicates this issue greatly.

In this brittle world of brittle objects and a formless self, forgiveness, compassion, and acceptance of flaws are hard to find and impossible to maintain. Rey (1994) discusses this as a psychic state in which reparation is only concrete and used as a desperate effort to keep dead objects alive until some type of cure can be found. But, none is forthcoming. Rey (1994) rightly points out that genuine reparation is by its nature flawed but part of normal development.

Omnipotent magical acts of reviving dead objects are destined to backfire, with the dead object now a zombie-like figure that can easily turn on its creator. Healthy depressive mourning and reparation include the restoration of attachment, but also acceptance of a now scarred and eternally changed object. Time does heal wounds, but scars remain. This is a concept too frightening to integrate for some patients, who feel that old wounds can easily open up again and lead to fatal infection.

In my experience, the most challenging patients in psychoanalytic treatment tend to exhibit a combination of paranoid and depressive anxieties to which they feel no solution to. Indeed, they may try many defensive manoeuvres to escape this emotional nightmare, but they never find any sufficient or lasting way to defend against it. Instead of finding a psychological foxhole, or psychic retreat (Steiner, 1989), I am highlighting patients who always feel in the midst of an emotional crossfire, a battleground with no refuge. So, they are constantly attempting to avoiding, guarding, and suffering from the agonies of both psychological states. Without the full knowledge of how to heal the injured object, they live in dread of their beloved objects dying and returning as angry stalkers. They are always faced with this fear of loved ones becoming contaminated and destroyed by their needs and desires. Then, they return from the grave as a treacherous zombie-like creature, unable to forgive, soothe, or understand. This is often the result of internalizing an external object that was weak, unavailable, or abusive object and infusing it with the ego's own aggression, desire, and anxiety.

The healthier patients in this group I am examining manage to put their dead, contaminated objects into a sort of suspended animation, through various sadomasochistic compromises in which they are eternally on the watch to keep the delicate object happy and healthy, as they wait desperately for the cure to be found. As Rey (1994) and Bartner (2007) note, many of our patients come into treatment specifically in search of this cure. However, these patients present very difficult transference states due to their dual conflictual experiences of the object. They want to change but also see change as deadly to both self and object.

The desire to bring back or resuscitate the dead object and prevent it from becoming the dreaded vicious zombie searching out revenge is based on idealistic phantasies of creating an object and a childhood that never was. So, the combined paranoid and depressive states these patients exist in are a bit like the Frankenstein tale. It is an idealistic quest to avoid flaw, loss, and death by building the perfect beast. But, the perfect beast can easily turn into the monstrous beast. Instead of normal mourning and acceptance of loss, difference, and separation, which would bring back a scarred, blemished object from the grave but one that is still available to love and depend on, these patients attempt to mould a faultless and untarnished object cleansed of resentment, injury, or mistakes. This is part of a projective identification cycle of envy, control, and aggressive hunger for constant love and the ideal parenting experience. Anything short of this is felt to be bad and brings about phantasies of fallen objects, intense disappointment and rage, and the fear of persecution. Again, this is often a mixture of internal pathology and a history of neglect or trauma that creates a vicious cycle of projective guilt, anxiety, and fear. In wanting such an ideal parent, the ego is left with a very fragile object that can quickly crumble into a vision of abandonment, primitive loss, severe guilt, and unrelenting persecution. Thus, the ego is captured by dead object bend on revenge.

Case material

In his sixth year of psychoanalytic treatment, on the couch, Mark said, "I was born to manage and maintain my mother's mental health. I was raised as a caretaker for her sanity. She put her lifeless empty shell into me." I interpreted, "you feel lifeless and empty and look to me to bring you back to life." Mark replied, "In the past, I think I would have been clueless to what you just said. But, today I do understand and I think you are right. But, knowing that makes me furious and so pissed that I keep myself in this little fucking box!"

A few months later, Mark began the session by saying how bad the traffic had been that morning. Since the highway he took to my office had been under construction for three months with predictable traffic jams every morning, I was interested in what this meant. So, I said "it was bad today, but it has been bad for several months now. I wonder what was different." As I said it, I realized my tone might be a bit strict or direct. I imagined Mark might take it that way and feel angry and want to talk back to me or correct me. In the past, I have sometimes reacted to his distant, unattached manner by speaking in an irritated way, which we later were able to discuss and explore.

Mark said, seeming to address me indirectly, "I blew up with my father twice in the last week." Then, he fell silent as he often does. I said, "Maybe you are angry right now." He said no, "I feel nothing." But then he mentioned that he might be angry, because he "suppresses everything in his life, including anger." This comment was an example of his real progress over the course of our analytic work. In the beginning of his treatment, Mark was never able to think of himself as having any unconscious agency. Rather, he saw himself as a passive victim to life and if he contained any emotional identity, it had been put there by someone else.

Over the course of many years, we continue to understand and slowly modify his depressed view of himself as well as his anxious and distorted view of the world. However, he is firmly resistant to a more basic shift in his relationship to others. Mark is reluctant to approach women, even though he desperately longs for their company. He is so unwilling to be autonomous and self-expressive that he hasn't worked in over five years. And, this complete disengagement from the world is reflected in his distant, warded off transference as well.

It has been a difficult therapeutic journey with Mark, as he reacts to multiple phantasy states that often switch abruptly or coexist and overlap in a confusing and overwhelming manner for both of us. We have discovered several strands of thought and feeling that rule his life.

From a more paranoid perspective, he worries that without his tie to mother, he will be lost, a "train wreak waiting to happen." Also, he feels "she just wants to suck the life out of me, like a vampire. One of us will die. Either she will kill me with her control and passive aggressive bullshit, keeping me on a leash until I choke to death. Or, I will kill her to gain my freedom."

Mark also fears "being on my own and realizing I have no idea how to relate. It is like I will finally break free from my jail cell, leaving her to rot on her own, only to not know how to survive on my own." These anxieties combine a persecutory phantasy of being lost in a strange land without any knowledge of how to survive and no one there to help and his guilt over breaking free of mother's clutches. This more depressive phantasy of being sent to a barren loveless land for abandoning his needy mother has a treacherous flavour to it in that the guilt and loss shift into more of a vision of exile without chance at redemption or change. It is a vision of escaping one prison only to find himself in another equally painful form of entrapment without hope of parole.

As he described, Mark sees himself as mother's emotional caretaker, without whom she would perish, wither, and die. This primitive depressive phantasy contains no reparative element or hope of eventual resolution. Mourning is absent. To effectively grieve the loss of his wished for attachment to mother, he would have to concede the failure of that bond. And, for Mark, that still feels like a catastrophic descent into despair, rejection, and guilt for his murderous envy and contempt. The concept of pining, Klein's (1940) idea of sorrow, concern, and effort to find and regain the good but injured object is beyond Mark's reach at this point. This is due to the immature and brittle nature of the depressive position, perhaps caused by the lack of healthy dependence on a caretaker object able to fend for herself without looking to Mark to be a caretaker in return.

In addition, his unresolved paranoid issues in which the quest for an ideal object and the resulting anger when denied creates a dangerous bad object that must be avoided or destroyed. These lingering anxieties make the unstable depressive position easily fragmented and prone to collapse. Indeed, Mark would often scream, "I am going to kill that bitch one day. I have no life of my own. I have forsaken my life to keep her propped up. She always needs me and I can't move on and be myself. I have no idea what it would mean to be myself. I have become her servant and nursemaid. She has controlled me from the beginning and taken my soul away. I think she will literally die if I leave her, but you know what? I don't care! I just want a life of my own. But, I can't figure out how to make that happen. Who am I?"

This outcry was a combination of his persecutory fears and his depressive guilt of causing her death if he were to break free and live his own life. So, it was always a confusing combination of who would die first, who would suffer the most if the other were to detach or become independent, who was benefiting more from this parasitic fusion, and who would suffer more from its breakup.

One of the many ways this emerged in the transference was Mark's passive and detached relationship to me, while keeping a constant presence in my life at the same time. So, when I would suggest that he consider attending more times each week, he always said no. I was left to always offer, to then eventually feel rejected, and finally to feel a sense of apathy and detachment. However, he would surprise me at how consistent and reliable he was in attending when he did. Just when I began to feel a real lack of meaning or attachment in our relationship, he would sort of remind me or reassure me by showing up like clockwork and make a genuine effort to explore his troubles. By my writing about him, it is evident that he holds a strong place in my mental life, even though it is like shifting sands in its form.

The parasitic nature of the immature depressive position involves concerns and controls over the object to keep it safe and happy, but not for the sake of the object so much as for the sake of the self. That is one reason I think I never feel sure if Mark is truly rooted in his analytic treatment.

In other words, he feels that without the care of the object he is thrown out to perish and he feels the same is true for his mother if he were to stop caring for her. So, Mark is chained to the role of mother's caretaker so as to not forsake her and destroy her by gaining his own identity and freedom, just as he imagines he would perish if he separated from her and sought out his own life. No one is allowed a different, separate, unique expression of their own mind and heart without it somehow severely damaging another and without it causing severe retribution. There is no negotiation or allowance in this matter. It is a rigid, no win situation.

However, with slow, hard work Mark has begun to find a small faith that he will be able to make his own way in life and if his mother cannot function without him, that will be sad and tragic, but not a final death sentence for either one of them. So, he has recently begun attending parties and actually speaking to women. He is now exercising, seeing his body as important and a part of his identity. Internally, he has started to see himself as having value and form, without that value and form creating immediate threat to self and object.

Steiner (1987) has discussed patients who seek to avoid the pain and anxiety of both the depressive and paranoid positions. The two cases discussed in this paper are representative of patients unlike Steiner's (1987) cases. His patients have successfully found a refuge or psychic retreat from both depressive and paranoid anxieties, abet a pathological solution. The patients examined in this paper have either been unable to reach Steiner's psychic retreat or if they have, their retreat has collapsed. Rather than being sealed off from both paranoid and depressive states, they are constantly at the mercy of both psychological storms.

Case material

To illustrate the difference between Steiner's patient group and the group I am exploring, I will briefly present a case in which I believe there was a psychic retreat utilized, which immobilized the treatment. Doris was a middle-aged patient who initially came for help with stress in her job. She was "nervous about how her manager viewed her and how the manager 'could end up reprimanding her or even firing her for what she had done'." In asking for details, it turned out that over a weekend, Doris had taken a computer and some files home to work on a project she was behind on. She had started to worry that this was a violation of company policy and that her manager might find out. According to her, it was in fact a company policy that no one was to bring home company computers or files. However, it was clear other workers occasionally did, no one would probably ever find out, and that the reason Doris had "committed this violation" was not to hurt the company but to try and complete an important company project.

I began to interpret that she had taken the project home not because her manager had asked her or because she had been told she was behind, but because she started to feel anxious about being behind. I commented on how she was already deciding she was "in violation" by being behind schedule, that she was feeling pressured by her schedule. I asked if perhaps she was being hard on herself and feeling guilty over not meeting her own expectations. Without much thought or reflection on my question, Doris quickly told me it was simply "a concern about the company policy." "They told us to not do what I did. So, I am simply worried about getting caught. Anyone would worry about it. What is strange about that?"

This concrete response to my attempt at exploring her emotional experiences was a prelude to many such impasses over the next two years. Over and over, Doris would present concerns about a situation in which she would feel exposed to something dangerous that she needed to avoid or control, a circumstance in which she believed she put someone else in harms way, or a situation in which she felt she had violated the rule of some authority and feared the consequences. Often, she was very anxious about something that combined all of these elements.

In one example, she told me about how she had put her cigarette out on the ground after lunch, and later thought there was a chance it was still lit and could create a fire that might burn the building down and injure others in the process. Doris worried about this and called various friends to query them about the risk factors. Later that day, she felt compelled to leave work early to go by the site and make sure she had not caused such destruction. When we discussed it, Doris said, "I know this might be part of my obsessive compulsive disorder that I went to therapy for last time, but actually I think this was a genuine thing to be concerned about. I wasn't sure the cigarette was out and I don't want it to catch on fire. What is wrong with that?"

I began to take two directions with Doris. One, I interpreted the transference in which she seemed to need to control things between us to make sure we stayed on a safe and predictable track. Emotions were to be eliminated. Second, I interpreted that she must feel very guilty and very vulnerable at all times, so she had to always be on watch to protect herself and protect others. She needed to always be ready to keep the peace and provide restitution for her deeds. I linked this to her strict code of how things had to be and the consequences that followed any infraction of any rules. Here, I was interpreting her aggression and control that left her with both injured or dead objects as well as angry and vengeful objects.

Doris told me she intellectually understood what I meant, but didn't agree with it. She said she "felt nothing like that" and simply thought "rules are there for a reason." So, theoretically, I saw Doris as plagued by intense depressive guilt for disappointing and hurting the object but also feeling haunted by persecutory phantasies of revenge, retribution, and punishment. There was no sense of give and take or understanding and tolerance, from her or from her objects.

Another example of these dynamics was the time Doris thought she might have left the stove on before she left for vacation. She had to call the fire department every day to check and see if her house had burnt down. I interpreted that she might have feelings about the vacation that she was uncomfortable with, such as guilt about taking the time off and thus she would be punished for it. She said it was simply a safety issue. I mentioned that she might also be troubled about the consequences of going away from her analytic treatment and the consequences of that. She said she had never given it any thought. I asked her to explore the fact that she claims to have no thoughts or feelings whatsoever about her treatment and her relationship to me. She said "ours is simply a medical situation, a doctor-patient relationship."

Each of these moments in which I tried to access the transference and develop a window into her phantasies hit a wall. Doris seemed to have constructed a rigid psychic retreat that protected her from both depressive and paranoid anxieties. This created a psychological barricade that prevented any analytic contact (Waska, 2007) from emerging in the treatment. Analysis of the transference and exploration of her phantasy world was near impossible most of the time because of this sealing off from emotional experience. As a consequence, Doris felt in control and at a safe distance from these dual dangers, but she was in a sealed psychic envelope that kept her from growth, change, or meaningful relationship to herself and others.

Case material

In contrast to Doris's use of a psychic retreat to fend off both depressive and paranoid struggles, David was constantly feeling overwhelmed by both these internal threats without much respite or psychic shelter.

I have been treating David in psychoanalysis, with multiple weekly visits on the couch, for seven years. Very predictably, he came into his session yesterday and began in the way he begins every session. He said, "Kill me, please just kill me! I am so sick of this thing they call life. How useless. How pathetic. Kill me, please! I want to have it over with. Won't you just put me out of my misery? If only I had a gun. But, of course, I am too much of a failure to be able to pull that off. My only hope is to get run over by a bus or come down with some quick acting disease and die without too much pain. Don't they put people out of their misery if they are no longer able to care for themselves? I am so fucked! I am a pile of shit. I hate myself.

I am sorry. I am really sorry. How do you put up with me? You must be so sick of me by now. I must leave you so fucking bored and pissed. I am really sorry. Please forgive me and give me a chance. I am sure you will toss me out on my ass. I need to see you. I probably would kill myself if I wasn't able to see you. This is the only point of stability in my life. This is the only place I have to really be honest and get out what is inside my head. That way I can make it through another day. I need to come here and take a mental shit. I get all this crap out of me.

I hate myself. I should find a way to kill myself. I wish I could just disappear. If it were not for our sessions together, I would have left this town long time ago. There is absolutely nothing keeping me here except this. Maybe that is wrong. Maybe you are part of the problem. Maybe the answer is to quit everything one more time and get out of this shithole. I am such a loser. How do you stand it? I hope I don't make your life too unbearable. I look around and see how everyone else has money, a family, a nice job, plenty of vacation time, lots of love, kids, and time to do as they please. How do they pull that off? They have it made and my life is shit. Why can't I have that too? When is it my turn?

Fuck it. I don't want that phony crap anyway. It is just some shitty commitment to the corporate mindfuck. I am glad I don't have any commitments and no ties to anyone. It is not worth it. It is fake and plastic. I want to be as far away from that as I can get. Are you part of that? I wonder.

God, I hate myself. I just want to die. Kill me please! How long do I have to wait till I am relieved of this prison sentence. I have never had a chance. I guess I fucked it up early on and I am just paying for that now. I am out of control. I am so stupid. Just kill me. Please kill me. I hate myself."

I routinely interpret how he is making sure to keep us separate and distant by having such a monologue. And, I mention that he is very committed to convincing me that there is no love, hope, or joy in his life and in our session. Bit by bit, very slowly, this line of investigation has been fruitful.

During another session, David said, "How do you stand me? I am such a piece of shit. I know you barely tolerate me and all my bitching. I am very sorry. Thank you very much for allowing me to be here. I am sorry. I am very sorry. It is just that I hate myself so much and I am so sick of this pathetic thing called my life. I can't go on at my job much longer. I feel I am ripping everyone off and charging them too much. I am worth nothing and I feel so guilt if I charge them anything. I am sorry. I apologize. I know I had added that extra session last week and then called to cancel it and told you I couldn't afford it. I felt so bad that I disappointed you that when I was invited to go to a party on the weekend, I said no. I couldn't bear to have any fun after I hurt your feelings. It didn't seem fair. I am sorry. I am such a loser. I hate myself. I am a fucking loser! I don't feel like I fit in anywhere. Everyone else has something, is someone, and has found a way to live successfully. I have not been so lucky. I just want to die. I hate myself."

David will often lie on the floor instead of the couch. I have interpreted the obvious, he doesn't feel he deserves to use the couch. He feels he is only fit for the floor, literally putting me above him. And, he is avoiding being close to me by being several feet away on the floor. So, from his vantage on the floor, he could see that I moved my head back and forth a bit from a sore muscle condition I had that week. He took it as ammunition for his ongoing attacks on himself and on our relationship. He said, "Oh! I knew I would wear you out. I am sorry. I can see I have outstayed my welcome. I am sorry. You must have reached your limit of trying to tolerate my crap. I am sorry. Please forgive me. I take up your time and wear you down. Let me give you a break." He got up and started to leave the office. I said, "You are so quick to see blood where there is no wound. I just have a sore neck but you use my movement to quickly verify your case against yourself and against us. Why so mean? Why so cruel?" David thought for a moment and said, "I see what you mean. You are right. You catch me at that and that is good. I shouldn't be like that. But, maybe I should. I am a shit and if you don't think so maybe you are the one who is deluded." I point out, "you are ready to fight me for the title of loser." He says, "Yes, because I am the world's biggest loser!" I say, "You say that with pride. Maybe that is more comfortable than to feel pride about your life, your personality, and your talents." He says, "There you go again bringing up things you will just rub my nose in." This refers to his feeling of being humiliated whenever I point out he has had a success or if he seems proud of some achievement or even simply happy that day.

David's background is important to consider in understanding his dynamics. The internal world is always shaped by the external and vice versa. David's father was an angry alcoholic who ruled the house with shouting and chauvinistic control. David, his three brothers and his mother all lived in a state of tension and conformity, trying to not "light the fuse." David's mother was schizophrenic and was hospitalized several times before David was in his teens. She would "talk to the television, tell me about the messages that she was receiving from far off lands, and sing at the top of her lungs for no reason. But, she was a good mother who loved us. I feel so sorry for her. I should have been able to do something for her, to make her life better. I feel like I failed her. When he would yell at her or hit her, I felt so bad for her."

Here, David sadly feels more in need of being the parent to her than to be able to fully enjoy the care of a functioning parent. During the course of David's seven-year treatment, one brother who has been psychotic and unable to function finally killed himself. David's second brother, also psychotic, still lives at home and is completely unable to care for himself. Finally, David's mother died of a heart attack last year. These losses only confirmed David's vision of himself as completely broken and irreparable, possible at fault for these losses and worthless as a result.

In the transference, depressive and paranoid states of mind create rapidly shifting phantasies that often leave us both reeling. David wants to be cared for and have the comforts others have, but without working for it. He feels it should be given to him. This is a narcissistic phantasy in which he considers special and ideal states of wealth, power, and pleasure a natural right for all and if he can't have a piece of that perfection he is being cheated. This is also a defence against the fear he holds in thinking that if he went ahead and pursued any success, joy, or closeness himself he would get into trouble, offend others, and "someone would have to pay." This is partly depressive in that he imagines hurting others if he tries to earn money or if he searches out someone to love. He sees pursuing a job, a career, a date, or even a hobby as too presumptuous and arrogant. He remembers his father as arrogant and doesn't want to be like that or have someone look down on him as he did on his father's righteous tirades. David is furious he doesn't have money, love, or joy in his life but he feels very guilty and fearful to seek them out.

Some of David's communications are clearly more paranoid than depressive. One session was taken up by his angry attacks on society at large. David told me, "I am so screwed. I have nothing and I am nothing. But, that is no surprise. I have never gotten a break and I will never get one. That is not the way the world is set up. It is so obvious that the rich pull the strings and make everyone like me do there bidding. It is the captains of industry, the filthy rich players that are safe behind their curtains of power and money. Those are the bastards who call the shots and twist this country and this world into what it is. Life has become a hellhole of desperation. Everyone is under the same hammer, desperately trying to make it day to day and never feeling like they can get ahead. It is very much part of their plan, the military industrial complex. The more we fear the more they rise to power. They have us by the throats. It is nothing new. This is classic capitalism in action. The small select group of shits have it all to themselves and then they find a way to steal more from the rest of us. I can't make it much longer. I can't hold out against this type of system. The odds are stacked against me. It has been that way from day one."

I asked him if maybe he was talking about day one in his family. David said, "Well, that is no different. My mother was carted off to the hospital and given pills and electric shock. What kind of cruel treatment is that? She was just trying her best, crazy as she was. I guess I sound like my father. He would get drunk and scream and rant about the way the government had fucked him over. But, maybe he was right. I don't see any good coming out of this world and the way the cards are stacked. How am I supposed to ever get ahead? They come after you and fly down like a pack of hungry vultures, picking away at your bones. Fuck it. Go ahead. Take what you want. Have it all. I don't care. I just hope I can go out gracefully, without too much pain. I am so alone. And, that is how I will die. Alone. No one gives a shit. You don't, no one does. I am sorry. But, I pay you for this. If I didn't have money, you would not be in my life, so I appreciate what you do but I have to realize this is fake. It is a part of the bigger fake world where they say they care, but no one does. Why would they? They have their cars, their homes, their expense accounts. The only time they care is if someone is in their way to getting more."

During these types of sessions, it was difficult to establish analytic contact with David. My impression is that David is much more comfortable, in charge, and safe if he makes sure to only relate to me as the downtrodden loser with his latest tales of woe. This intense masochistic transference makes it impossible to explore anything beyond his misery and determined hopelessness. I have interpreted that by maintaining this masochistic relationship, he doesn't hurt me, disturb me, challenge me, or give me reason to question his opinion. If he has no identity, I can't attack it. If David is the ultimate servant, he can't offend or hurt and he can't indebt himself. When I make these interpretations, I also comment on how he uses this transference to avoid the risks of autonomy and closeness. In other words, his combined paranoid and depressive anxieties drive him to avoid any demonstration of need or desire and attachment while he also shies away from relating in a more separate, distinctive, or expressive manner.

A major problem in David's treatment is that to get better, to have needs, to feel joy, to be close to the object in a vulnerable and expressive way is to be arrogant, angry, and hurtful. In normal development, striving, wanting, and receiving can be in balance with giving, sacrificing, and negotiating. But, for David this give and take world is dangerous to himself and his objects. To have his own expressive identity where he can be successful, competitive, and proud is sinful and superior. In his phantasy world, this would immediately lead to injured or murdered objects, eternal abandonment and irresolvable loss, followed by vengeful ghosts bent on punishment and cruelty. This is all produced by a pathological reliance on splitting and projective identification that intensifies both paranoid and depressive phantasies, bringing them together in a vicious cycle from which there is no escape.

So, over the years, I have taken an interpretive direction in which I frequently interpret that David wants to make everything and everyone have zero value. This is in order to not risk harming the object and to prevent the attack of the object. By cancelling out all his needs and wants and any evidence of trying to connect with me, David feels in control and safe. I interpreted that this of course leaves him feeling he is surrounded by nothingness, so he becomes envious of others who are able to assign value to self and object and then he feels entitled to have that given to him, which is safer than having to work for it or ask for it. One moment in which I made such a comment was after he told me about how overwhelmed he felt and how "there hasn't been a minute that goes by that I don't think about suicide and that can't be good. I just can't move beyond it. The thoughts about it are so thick. Life is so hard and I don't see it ever getting any better." He paused, almost ready to cry and then said, "I know I am bothering you, draining you. How arrogant of me to take up the space like this. Please don't hit me." I interpreted, "you were really sharing yourself with me, depending on me and not censoring yourself. Then, you began to worry you have made me angry somehow and I will lash out. Your helper turned into a drained and burdened who will punish you and hurt you. You must feel like your needs for me are so intense, hurtful, and wrong." He was visibly relieved and seemed to spend a moment reflecting. The rest of the session felt calmer and he was not so bent on attacking himself or the world. It is this type of slow but steady movement that has characterized David's analytic progress. However, it is a fragile growth that sometimes withers and still needs frequent care.

This brittle growth is due to the nature of constantly feeling in the midst of both paranoid and depressive threats without much hope of resolution. If David admits to any need and desire or to any joy and pride, he feels at risk for hurting the object and being hurt by the object. Therefore, he must deny any skill, goal, or pleasure. An example of this is if he tells me about having fun over the weekend and I say anything about it David feels I am "rubbing his nose in it." I interpret that he makes sure I can never be proud of him or happy for him and he can never be pleased to convey his own goals and achievements, since this could lead to unforeseen consequences. Instead, he plays it safe by wanting me and others to tell him what to do and how to live. Thus, he feels safe in a sadomasochistic relationship, much like as a child being under the wing of a controlling parent, secure but suffocated. He can hope to be rescued by that object and given to, but it all comes with endless emotional debt to that object. So, while he has changed in significant ways over the course of his analytic treatment, the remnants of his life-long internal struggle remain. However, compared to the case of Doris in which

I had very little success in reaching her through the immovable psychic retreat, I was able to make significant analytic contact with David along the way. David is still living in a world of internal combat, in the middle of both depressive and paranoid threats, trying to find a way to not be brought down by either one, looking for a way to surrender, but convinced no side takes prisoners. However, he is gradually and reluctantly amenable to working with me to face these dual threats. There is constant fear of the object, doubts about the advantage of change, and an intense reluctance to give up the status quo. Therefore, we limp along. But, we limp forward.

CHAPTER THREE

When patients face the dual threat of depressive and paranoid phantasies

Most of our difficult patients have a hard time accepting themselves as lovable despite their flaws. Due to projective identification, they cannot envision an accepting, tolerant object that would love them regardless of their imperfections. Hinshelwood (1991) states that the depressive position enables the object to be loved despite its faults but in the paranoid position awareness of bad parts in the object cause the ego to abruptly shift the object into a persecutor. The patients presented in this Chapter fail to find the hope, restitution, or forgiveness that provide the stability to withstand the severe disappointment, loss, or pining involved in the depressive position and the pain of finding bad mixed in with their good objects.

The loss of the object is one thing but the finality of that loss is another. I see the importance of depressive integration to be the acquisition of a fundamental trust or hope that somehow, someday, maybe there will be reconciliation, a healing, and a reunion, regardless of prior conflicts and separations from the object. However, while the patients I am examining have found some whole object footing in their psychic relating, they are unable to establish a secure faith regarding what is broken being fixed. Hinshelwood (1991) speaks of the subject's anxiety over repairing something that is "irretrievably damaged or dead" (p. 144). Klein (1935) notes that the depressive position and its phantasies of a lost object are determined by the subject's sense of failure or success in reattaching to the object, by either reparation, negotiation, or other means of finding resolution to this internal chaos and conflict. If the ego finds no means to reach the dying or dead object and no way to revitalize it or make peace with it, persecutory fears take over and out of the gravesite of the good dead object rises up the horrifying, vengeful bad object bent on harm and rejection. Without the sense of finding the good object or repairing the broken object, the ego is left adrift and alone, afraid for its own survival.

Klein (1935; 1940) and many of her followers have investigated the depressive position and written about the various issues that arise. If depressive anxieties become too overwhelming, it is common for paranoid, manic, or obsessive defences to be utilized. These three internal reactions compromise most of what we witness clinically. However, there are a number of patients who are not simply defending against depressive phantasies, but actually exhibiting a psychic corruption of the depressive position. They are unable to establish a secure psychic foothold in the depressive mode to begin with and face the combined threat of depressive and paranoid phantasies. Unlike those patients who can find refuge in a psychic retreat (Steiner, 1993), these patients remain at the mercy of the worst of both paranoid and depressive phantasy states without any significant mental refuge.

Melanie Klein and others have drawn attention to this idea before, but this paper will draw sharper attention to how this psychological phenomenon is present in many of our more difficult patients and therefore needs to be better understood as to afford these patients a chance at change and growth.

Literature

Klein (1948) stated that paranoid anxiety deforms ego integration and cancels out depressive capacities. As a result, the "loved injured object may very swiftly change into a persecutor and the urge to repair or revive the loved object may turn into the need to pacify and propitiate a persecutor" (p. 121). This is the core phantasy state many patients live within, suffering both primitive loss and guilt as well as frightening persecutory attacks. This persecutory guilt (Bicudo, 1964; Rosenfeld, 1962) is more about a demanding, punitive object than an understanding, guiding parental figure.

Alvarez (1992) explored the idea of harmed, destroyed, or used-up objects that cannot be repaired. Alvaris suggests that this irreparable object is felt as such not just because of the intensity of the child's rage, but because of properties of the real object, which make it intractable to reparative efforts or to the infant's precursors of reparative capacity. Alvarez's idea raises the question of how such an object would be experienced internally. I propose that the ego becomes inconsolable, left without any goodness but now through projective identification and splitting is forced to face an unforgiving and vindictive object.

In 1946, Klein states, "The drive for reparation, which comes to the fore at this stage, can be regarded as a consequence of a greater insight into psychic reality and of growing synthesis, for it shows a more realistic response to the feelings of grief, guilt and fear of loss resulting from the aggression against the loved object. Since the drive to repair or protect the injured object paves the way for more satisfactory object relations and sublimations, it in turn increases synthesis and contributes to the integration of the ego" (p. 105).

After outlining this normal course of psychological development, Klein (1946) notes, "If, however, development during the schizoid phase has not proceeded normally and the infant cannot—for internal or external reasons—cope with the impact of depressive anxieties, a vicious circle arises. For if persecutory fear, and correspondingly schizoid mechanisms, are too strong, the ego is not capable of working through the depressive position. This in turn forces the ego to regress to the schizoid position and reinforces the earlier persecutory fears and schizoid phenomena. Thus the basis is established for various forms of schizophrenia in later life; for when such a regression occurs, not only are the fixation points in the schizoid position reinforced, but there is a danger of greater states of disintegration setting in. Another outcome may be the strengthening of depressive features" (p. 105).

Here, Klein is examining the "vicious cycle" of unresolved paranoid phantasies and intensified, overwhelming depressive phantasies. This is quite different than the healthy working through of the depressive position that she described occurring after the normal resolution of the paranoid-schizoid position (Klein, 1946).

In 1940, Klein was exploring the more fruitful and hopeful outcome when she stated, "In regards to the successful development of the depressive position, all the enjoyments which the baby lives through in relation to his mother are so many proofs to him that the loved object inside as well as outside is not injured, is not turned into a vengeful person. The increase of love and trust, and the diminishing of fears through happy experiences, help the baby step by step to overcome his depression and feeling of loss (mourning). They enable him to test his inner reality by means of outer reality. Through being loved and through the enjoyment and comfort he has in relation to people his confidence in his own as well as in other people's goodness becomes strengthened, his hope that his 'good' objects and his own ego can be saved and preserved increases, at the same time as his ambivalence and acute fears of internal destruction diminish" (p. 128).

In 1948, Klein wrote about the regression to paranoid-schizoid conflicts when depressive concerns are too difficult. She states, "In psycho-analytic practice it has been found by a number of workers that the differentiation between persecutory and depressive anxiety is helpful in the understanding and unraveling of emotional situations. To give one instance of a typical picture which may confront us in the analysis of depressive patients: during a particular session a patient may suffer from strong feelings of guilt and despair about his incapacity to restore the damage which he feels he has caused. Then a complete change occurs: the patient suddenly brings up material of a persecutory kind. The analyst and analysis are accused of doing nothing but harm, grievances which lead back to early frustrations are voiced. The processes which underlie this change can be summarized as follows: persecutory anxiety has become dominant, the feeling of guilt has receded, and with it the love for the object seems to have disappeared. In this altered emotional situation, the object has turned bad, cannot be loved, and therefore destructive impulses towards it seem justified. This means that persecutory anxiety and defenses have been reinforced in order to escape from the overwhelming burden of guilt and despair" (p. 37).

However, Klein goes on to then say, "In many cases, of course, the patient may show a good deal of persecutory anxiety together with guilt, and the change to a predominance of persecutory anxiety does not always appear as dramatically as I have here described it" (p. 37). Here, Klein is bringing up the less differentiated mix of paranoid and depressive issues that some patients exhibit. It is my contention that there are a number of patients in analytic treatment who suffer from not just a paranoid-schizoid dilemma or a depressive conflict, but who are mired in an overwhelming and unbearable combination of paranoid and depressive phantasies that occur simultaneously.

In order to better understand the complexity and the emotional trauma that occurs in this sudden psychic intersection of the paranoid and depressive modes, the writings of Joan Riviere are indispensable. While her writings in 1936 are of her understandings about the depressive position at that time and place in history, my belief is that she brilliantly articulates this crisscross between the two mental states, describing the primitive depressive state that often includes certain various and intense paranoid-schizoid phantasies.

Riviere (1936) explains, "The content of the depressive position (as Melanie Klein has shown) is the situation in which all one's loved ones within are dead and destroyed, all goodness is dispersed, lost, in fragments, wasted and scattered to the winds; nothing is left within but utter desolation. Love brings sorrow, and sorrow brings guilt; the intolerable tension mounts, there is no escape, one is utterly alone, there is no one to share or help. Love must die because love is dead. Besides, there would be no one to feed one, and no one whom one could feed, and no food in the world. And more, there would still be magic power in the undying persecutors who can never be exterminated—the ghosts. Death would instantaneously ensue—and one would choose to die by one's own hand before such a position could be realized" (p. 311). Here, she is describing a corrupt depressive experience in which there is no hope or forgiveness. All is lost and in the place of the dead good object comes the "ghosts" and "undying persecutors."

She continues, "To save his own life and avert the death of despair that confronts him, such energy as he has is all bent on averting the last fatalities within, and on restoring and reviving where and what he can, of any life and life-giving objects that remain. It is these efforts, the frantic or feeble struggles to revive the others within him and so to survive, that are manifested; the despair and hopelessness is never, of course, quite complete. The objects are never actually felt to be dead, for that would mean death to the ego; the anxiety is so great because life hangs by a hair and at any moment the situation of full horror may be realized.

But struggle as he may and does under his unconscious guilt and anxiety to repair and restore, the patient has only a slenderest belief unconsciously in achieving anything of the kind; the slightest failure in reality, the faintest breath of criticism and his belief sinks to zero again—death or madness, his own and others', is ever before the eyes of his unconscious mind. He cannot possibly regenerate and recreate all the losses and destruction he has caused and if he cannot pay this price his own death is the only alternative" (pp. 313–314).

Here, when Riviere points to the shred of hope that "hangs by a hair," she seems to be pointing to the moment of greater depressive health in which things can be put right, change is possible, and relief can be found even if in such tense and uncertain moments. But, then she also describes the crumbling of this hope and the return of more paranoid fears. In this regard, she adds, "All his efforts to put things right never succeeds enough; he can only pacify his internal persecutors for a time, fob them off, feed them with sops, 'keep them going'; and so he 'keeps things going', the status quo, keeps some belief that 'one day' he will have done it all, and postpones the crash, the day of reckoning and judgment" (p. 314).

So, I think Riviere, while writing about the depressive position, is in fact exploring the very core elements of patients who experience an ongoing pathological combination of both paranoid and depressive phantasies. In fact, she describes this in detail, "The patient's conscious aim in coming for analysis is to get well himself: unconsciously this point is relatively secondary, for other needs come first. Unconsciously his aim is: (1) on the paranoid basis, underlying his depressive position, his task is something far more urgent than getting well; it is simply to avert the impending death and disintegration which is constantly menacing him" (p. 315).

Here, I believe she describes the unending despair and the unending task of trying to repair a damaged object that can never be fully righted. This primitive depressive experience encompasses a fundamental paranoid base, creating an overwhelming dual conflict for the ego that is felt to be inescapable. This is the premise of the paper.

Case material will show how this dual phantasy state unfolds in the clinical situation.

Case 1

Patty came to seek help with her "life long trouble finding a decent relationship." We quickly found answers in her recollection of her past, her current way of relating to others, and in the transference. Patty grew up as an only child with parents who fought a great deal and divorced when Patty was eight years old. She looks back to realize this was due to her father's drinking problems and his infidelity. However, his "unpredictable temper" was also a factor. The way Patty remembers it, her father was fairly pleasant most of the time but if he decided you "had gone against him," he would "flip out and completely severe the relationship for good." This had happened once to a cousin and to several friends of the family. Patty said she "did her best to never put herself in that kind of position." To do that, she "simply avoids bringing up anything in which she might be going against what he thinks or anything in which she would be calling his actions into question."

As an adult in her early thirties, Patty has found herself "stuck in the career world." She accepted a job several years ago with the "hopes that if I worked hard they would notice my efforts and move me up the ladder." In each yearly review, she was reluctant to voice her desires for a raise and a promotion. Recently, she was "brave enough to tell them what I wanted" only to find out that they had no plans to ever move her up in the company. Patty was furious that "they strung her on that way" but could also see how being quiet and just hoping they would reward her efforts was a way she sabotaged herself. We explored the meaning behind this and found that she was reluctant to "make a fuss" and "didn't want to appear pushy." I added that she feared being punished or rejected if she was to be too fussy or pushy. Here, I noted her fears of burdening others and added that she seemed to add a more punitive vision of the world.

One way Patty felt hopeless and depressed was in terms of finding a boyfriend. While attractive and outgoing, once she felt there was a possibility of a closer connection with a man, she became worried about rejection. So, she withdrew, hoping he would not notice the things she felt could cause rejection such as her weight, her job, where she lived, her education, and so forth. But, since she was now maintaining a distant limbo way of relating, she wasn't offering much to the relationship and would not ask for much either. This led to her either being rejected by men who thought she was too cold and aloof or being stuck in relationships with men who didn't give her much and left her feeling unloved and disappointed. Either way, she felt the results confirmed her feelings that she was essentially unlovable.

In our analytic exploration, we discovered that she did not want to hope or risk being vulnerable only to be disappointed or rejected again, as she felt she had been with her father. In fact, Patty wanted a guarantee that she would be accepted and liked before she would share herself with the object.

One way this emerged in the transference was her avoidance and almost outright refusal to share anything but negative stories with me. I interpreted that she controlled me with her scheduled reports of what ailments she had, which then kept us in a restrictive but familiar relationship of power imbalance. So, it was a selective way she related to me, keeping her in an illusionary state of control, safe from rejection or judgement. I interpreted that if she were to share her whole self with me, the good, the bad, and all things in-between, she would feel vulnerable and uncertain of my reaction. Patty replied, "Why should I tell you about things that are going well? I am here to fix the things that are broken. I can tell my friends about happy stuff!" I replied, "In only telling me what is wrong, you are censoring our relationship, so I only see you in one way. That is probably safer than letting me in on everything, all of you." She said, "Oh. I see what you mean. Thinking about just talking to you about everything makes me feel nervous, like it's too intimate or weird. I guess I want to keep you at a distance, you are just my doctor."

I interpreted, "it sounds like by controlling me with what you share, you feel you can predict how I will see you. But, if you share all of yourself, you probably are not sure how I will react to what I see and hear." Patty said, "You might turn on me! I like keeping you on a shelf, so I can see you. I don't want you running around and having opinions about me. I might not like those opinions."

So, we explored the ways in which she wanted my help, my understanding, and my encouragement, but if she felt I knew her too well, I might withdraw my help, misunderstand her, and even reject her. When I made this interpretation, Patty said, "Well, I don't want to offend you or bore you or irritate you. I certainly censor what I say as far as only telling you the bad stuff. But, I also censor the bad stuff. If I think you will be irritated or offended by something I want to complain about, I keep it to myself."

We discussed this delicate, fragile image she had of me in which I was easily offended. The more we spoke about it, it seemed evident that on one hand, she was both worried about hurting me or draining me. This came out in her visions of "you being tired already and then having to take me on with all my stupid complaints. I figure you have had a hard week already and now I am going to bore you to tears or basically be a pain in your neck. I feel bad that I come here and make your day that much harder. It's like you don't deserve that. No one does. So, I often want to apologize ahead of time before I start unloading all my crap."

On the other hand, Patty also felt I could easily be tipped over into being angry or rejecting of her. This came out in her visions of "I worry that one day you will just tell me to shut up or get out. You probably have a limit to what you can endure before you blow your top." These two phantasies existed side by side. It did not seem like one stood as a defensive retreat for the other. Rather, they were simultaneous states of mind that left Patty anxious about hurting me and about being hurt by me.

Patty didn't want to risk being vulnerable and dependent with me or other men, but then wondered why no one liked her or knew her. She projected her uncertainty, mistrust, and fear of the object's stability and then felt like the object's love was fragile and easily lost. So, she used distance as a defence and then felt distant and alone or she tried to please the object and keep it afloat but then felt cheated, burdened, and always walking on thin ice. Patty told me, "I start with the premise that everyone hates me and I work from there." An example of this internal perspective was when she arrived for a session at the wrong time. The waiting room accommodates patients from several therapist's offices so when I came out to greet my next patient, there were five or six people in the room. I did not consciously notice her sitting there and she made no movement or did not say anything when I asked the other patient to come in. Later, when we discussed this, Patty told me she thought I deliberately ignored her since I was angry at her for some unknown reason and I wanted to punish her. She said I probably wouldn't want to ever see her again. So, here again she felt she had hurt me or offended me in a way that led to my retaliation. She wanted to please me but didn't know how to achieve that. Indeed, we discovered that this was an impossible task as she always felt the object had newer and harder to accomplish expectations. I emphasized in my interpretations that she decided there was no understanding or forgiveness to be had, no way of flexibility or security in the way she kept me as her object. This exploration led us to examining how she resisted letting go of this type of control and stance in her relationships because she "didn't want the risk of facing the unknown that would result."

I interpreted that this "unknown" included both what the object might be like as well as the unpredictable way she might express herself. In other words, I interpreted her fear of her own love, hate, needs, and desires as well as her fear of how the object might react. This was an analysis of her use of projective identification that opened up more of a vision of her in relation to her objects (including her analyst) instead of such a one-sided, masochistic phantasy that she usually maintained.

Patty told me she was "willing to do anything to please others" and she "knows how to have a face for whoever she is with." This left her "with fragmented groups of friends where I am different for each group." I asked her what "face" she puts on for me and this lead to more exploration of how she thinks she needs to bring me problems and "be the good patient who works hard to solve their problems." I interpreted that she only gives me one slice of the pie. This leaves her feeling safe and in control, but angry that I only have a small piece of her in my mind and ignore the rest of her. She said she "wants to give me the whole pie but it feels too dangerous and too intimate." She added, "I know its crazy, but I am angry that you don't like all of me but I don't want to give you all of me either." Another manifestation of this came out when she told me she "wants to be my favorite patient, the one I like to see the most and think most pleasantly about. But, if I think you don't see me that way, then I feel like either the worst one or just another faceless patient in a long line of your daily grind."

Finally, she also felt a combination of being let down and always letting down her objects. So, she dated a man several times who seemed to be unreliable and not prone to making any commitments.

When he said he would call her about getting together for the next date and didn't call for a week, Patty began to emotionally crumble. She said, "What have I done? Why don't they ever like me or love me?" This lament expressed a dual phantasy in which she failed and disappointed the object (depressive) and she felt deliberately punished (paranoid). In interpreting this overwhelming combination of anxieties, I traced this to her desire to control the object and secure love out of the object without having to give much or risk much in return. But, this meant she could never really reach the object of her desire because she kept herself out of reach. And, her own disappointment was projected and she found herself with a pining, sad object that felt neglected. What brought Patty into treatment was a fundamental lack of hope in the capacity for forgiveness, understanding, or reparation in these chronic phantasies.

Case 2

Carol came to me for help in "making up her mind about what to do with her boyfriend, who is never really able to make a commitment to the relationship." Carol told me she stopped seeing her last therapist because "she started acting like my friend and told me to break up with him. Even though I think she was right in what she said I should do, I didn't feel comfortable with her telling me her opinions. I felt she was biased after that." I took this as a positive sign of Carol's ego strength in separating from a bias object that ignored her own true feelings. I said, "I am sure it is more complicated than just breaking up with him." Carol said, "That is exactly it. I think I should learn to live my own life better, but I have a lot of feelings that keep me where I am at. So, I am hoping you will tell me how to fix that." I was surprised at this turn in her way of relating and interpreted, "Suddenly, you want me to be bias and tell you what to do. So, maybe it is uncomfortable relating to me from your own identity. Maybe it is easier to slip into having me call the shots." Carol replied, "Damn, you are good. I know I do that. I don't want people to push me around but I do easily fall into letting them." I added, "Letting them or even setting the stage for it as you just did with me." Carol nodded and gave me the thumbs up sign.

In volunteering information about her family and upbringing, Carol presented two different feelings. One was pity and compassion for both her mother and father. The other central feeling was dread and disappointment. While she shifted from focusing on one and then the other, I had the consistent impression that she lived within both states much of the time.

Carol was the only child and her mother was a chronic drug addict who suffered from depression that left her hospitalized every few years. When Carol was ready to move out of her home at age eighteen, feeling "she finally would be independent and not have to bend to whatever her parents' moods were," her mother committed suicide. Carol blamed herself in some ways even thought this was the result of her mother's lifelong depression and frustration with her marriage. Carol's father was a volatile man with a temper and an alcohol problem. He was a cross-dresser from the time Carol was an infant to the day he died. She said, "It was weird and strange. I always felt sorry for him and how he obviously didn't feel he had picked the right life for himself. We were a burden for him. He wanted a different life. I wish he had been able to find that for himself." In this way, Carol felt concern and sorrow for him and thought that she had been part of what caused him to be so unhappy. She was convinced she brought him pain and frustration but never felt she could do anything to make it better. At the same time, she felt "sad that I never had a normal father. My whole time growing up, all I would think about was why couldn't I have a normal father, not this angry, cross dressing freak that made the family a hell on earth." Here, she felt more persecutory, hopeless feelings about being neglected and abused.

Carol's parents divorced when she was six years old. She remembers going back and forth, "between my angry, unpredictable cross-dressing father who never seemed to pay much attention to me, and to my mother who was always depressed, getting high, and feeling attacked by my father. I know my father loved me and I could tell that in how he was, some of the time, but overall it was so far from what I wanted or needed." I interpreted that she was caught between two dreadful feelings. She had the pining and guilt for both her parents in which she felt she caused them both great grief, feeling sorry for them and wanting to somehow heal them. And, she felt the anxiety of living with mother's depression and suicide as the ultimate abandonment combined with the threat of father's rage. Also, I interpreted that she was caught in the guilt of being very angry about his cross-dressing and her anger at mother's depression but also feeling she shouldn't lash out at such weak and broken individuals. But, Carol also felt her anger brought about their punishment and abandonment. She responded, "Yes. You got it on target. All of it! And, I was always in a state of terror from his combined drinking, his crazy paranoia, his cross-dressing, and his angry rage. I never knew when or why he would turn on me." She went on to describe her combined depressive and paranoid experience of him, "I always felt sorry for him and wanted to help him. But, it was like feeding a starving wild animal and getting your arm torn off and eaten. He was that unpredictable. I never knew when this sad and troubled person would turn into this monster that pushed my mother to kill herself. I loved him and he loved me but it was in a way that was so twisted and insecure."

In the transference, some of these phantasies and memories took hold. When she was late to a session, she said nervously, "sorry I am late, but it is only five minutes." It was clear what she meant, so I interpreted, "you are trying to tell me or almost beg me, "it is only five minutes, please don't punish me too much." I interpreted her fear of my anger and my rejection and she went on to tell me how she is "always trying to please people and wanting to accommodate to their needs but she ends up scared of failing at that." The scared of failing part was the point when her phantasies shifted from very conflicted depressive concerns that were coloured by paranoid anxieties to a more base paranoid fear of reprisal and punishment.

This combined tangle of paranoid and depressive experiences surfaced in a rather profound way when she discussed her feelings about her father. We had been talking about her frustrations with her boyfriend and how she couldn't ever trust him to follow through or show her that he cared. Carol told me she can't ever get her hopes up for too long before they are dashed. I remarked that she had initially met with me in the hopes of finding a quick resolution to an "irritating boyfriend issue" but when I made some interpretations about her internal sense of chaos and despair, she associated to, "I am so disappointed. I thought I had dealt with my father. Oh no! Not that again." So, in response to me tying together her disappointment with me and her hopes being dashed currently, she said, "that makes me remember such sad and terrible times with my father. I remember when I was like ten or eleven years old and it was his birthday. I had helped my mother stock the refrigerator with all his favorite foods and I had spent all day making decorations and cards for him. I dedicated myself to him that day because I loved him and wanted to show him love. I recall him coming home and he was in a terrible mood and he started drinking and yelling. He ripped up all my decorations and he threw everything out of the refrigerator onto the floor. I think he hit me too, but all I remember is then running to my room and crying all night. I was terrified. No matter what I ever did, good or bad, he could turn into a monster." So, for Carol, even loving her father could make him upset and angry. Thus, love was always linked to pain, fear, and suffering.

In another sad recollection, Carol told me about her father's funeral. He had died as a result of complications from drinking. When she went to his home to pick out a suit for the burial services, she found a "handsome suit that he reserved for special events. When I saw him lying in the casket dressed in that, I broke down sobbing." In telling me this story, Carol was near hysterical with tears. She continued, "I realized that he finally looked like the father I always wanted. I finally had what I needed. He was a respectable looking man with a calm look on his face. There was no women's clothing and no makeup. He was a man. He was my father." Carol paused and began sobbing even more, "But, now he was dead!" She explained that the tragic irony continued in her walking away from this realized ideal to when she went back to his home to sort through a wardrobe of women's clothing, cans of makeup, and a dairy full of his angry ranting about how much he felt wronged by life and hated everyone around him. Carol said, "Reality hit and it hit hard. This was who my father was, not the person in the casket."

One way that Carol's phantasies of harming the object and being harmed by the object combined in the transference was how she was withholding in expressing her feelings to me. In relaying her stories about her upbringing, her troubled relationship with her boyfriend, or general matters about her day-to-day life, she tended to buffer, censor, or minimize the feelings aspect of each story. Most of the time, this was an emotional cauterization of offensive, angry, needy, or assertive feelings. So, she might be telling me about her frustrations with her boyfriend, some problems at work, or her memories of her family. But, these were muted and without the full emotional stamp of her feelings and experiences. I interpreted that she wanted me to stand in as her guiding, empathic father who would finally be there for her and understand her. But, I interpreted, this also meant she had to be dependent in a way on me that meant she was powerless and mute, relying on me to translate what she really meant and felt. This put her at a disadvantage and she could never feel she was an equal or ever feel she had the ability to find her own voice. I added that this way of relating to me was a repeat of how restricted and limited she felt with her father and a repeat of her current frustrating relationship with her boyfriend. In other words, she wanted me to tell her what to do and say which initially might feel comforting and safe, but soon would feel controlling and dominating.

In the transference, I also found Carol wanting me to reassure her that she was not harming me with her needs or making me angry by depending on me. At one point, she said, "you work so hard. You are always here when I come in." What she meant was that when she came in the office lobby every three months to see her psychiatrist for medications, she noticed my sign in the lobby said I was in my office. I replied, "You must worry that you drain me and you worry I need rest from your needs. You care for me and are anxious that I might be hurt or angry with the way you need me." Carol said, "I do feel like that. Am I too much?" I said, "Let's talk about those feelings of me either being drained and hurt or being angry and resentful."

So, at this point in her analysis, we have established a foundation of analytic contact and continue to work through her phantasies and transference vision of both persecutory and depressive objects.

CHAPTER FOUR

Unresolved depressive and paranoid phantasies: Certain clinical difficulties

A s Klein (1946) has written, "side by side with the destructive impulses in the unconscious mind both of the child and the adult, there exists a profound urge to make sacrifice, in order to help and to put right loved people who in phantasy have been harmed or destroyed" (p. 65). It seems Klein was also pointing to the faith a child and adult has in actually being able to help and put right their injured objects. There are certain patients encountered in analytic practice who have not ever found that deep relational confidence and therefore struggle with a sense of catastrophe regarding themselves and their beloved objects.

Klein (1946) continues, "in the depths of the mind, the urge to make people happy is linked with a strong feeling of responsibility and concern for them, which manifests itself in genuine sympathy with other people and in the ability to understand them, as they are and as they feel" (p. 65). Because of some patients over reliance on projective identification as well as unresolved paranoid issues, a more corrupted depressive position exists in which this genuine sympathy for others and this ability to understand other's feelings and motives is fragile and distorted.

Gabbard (1994) points out how Klein discovered that when patients believe they have harmed or destroyed their good objects with greed, aggression, and envy, they feel persecuted by the bad objects that remain. Gabbard states, "this feeling of being persecuted by bad objects while pining for the lost good objects is what constitutes the essence of the depressive position" (p. 224). In this Chapter, I will expand upon Gabbard's and Klein's clinical discoveries and examine the group of patients who are essentially fixed at that place where both paranoid-schizoid (Klein, 1946) and depressive (Klein, 1935; 1940) anxieties combine. While they are overcome by endless guilt and a feeling of having lost their beloved objects forever, they also feel attacked and hunted down by the bad objects. The combination of both phantasy states leaves them without much psychological respite or resource, other than to rely on projective identification and splitting for temporary protection and shelter. The brittle nature of this immature depressive/paranoid condition involves many factors including the lack of strong and resilient internalized good objects. The degree of aggressive need, oral demand and rage, and persecutory fears also influence this condition.

The ego's ability to tolerate the grief, loss, and mourning that occurs when faced with a past that was not ideal and a present that is less than desired is decisive in determining how the depressive foundation is maintained or broken. When difficult depressive conflicts combine with unresolved paranoid issues, psychological stability is difficult to maintain.

If the depressive position brings with it a meagre object easily hurt or damaged, the ego is flooded with too much grief and loss. If forgiveness and reparation are not in ample supple from either the ego (as a result of anger, envy, greed, etc.) or from the object (as a result of both actual past experiences with the external object or projective identification situations in which the object is stripped of goodness), then the ego may be more influenced by its still unresolved paranoid phantasies. In the transference, this leads to a search for ideal objects that can provide safety and reassurance from the bad objects that come with this breakdown of depressive functions (Klein, 1952).

Spillius (1994) notes that the anxiety felt in the depressive position is a mix of fear that the object is beyond repair, concern, and guilt for the wellbeing of the object, and responsibility for the damage one has inflicted. Spillius (1994) states, "the actual state of the external object is extremely important" (p. 337). If the object seems to be damaged or unable to be empathic with the subject about their concerns, reparatory efforts and trust in the restoration of peace, safety, and love are dangerously unbalanced.

Even in the best of either internal or external situations, integration and working through of the depressive position brings on considerable emotional pain and internal tension, often leading to various defensive reactions. Acceptance of the reality of the whole object with its associated mourning is traumatic and difficult even with a history of good object experiences. Unfortunately, the patients I am examining in this paper have usually had very troubled childhoods punctuated by various forms of abuse, neglect, or chaotic uncertainty on the part of their primary objects. This seems to combine with as well as create vicious cycles of phantasies that are then maintained and increased by a pathological reliance on projective identification for defensive purposes and sometimes for communications. This creates a very fragile setting for the already delicate task of mourning that is necessary in the depressive position. Mourning is partly the psychic acceptance of what is, separate from what we wish for or deny. Patients who are suffering from both the conflicts of persecutory phantasies as well as depressive problems find this grief for the object and acceptance of the object very difficult. In this struggle, they encounter unbearable levels of sorrow, anger, and disillusionment. When they step away from their idealism, rage, and denial and rely less on projection and splitting, they are left with a broken and meagre object hard to rely on and one that is hard to mend, resurrect, or reconstruct. This state of primitive loss (Waska, 2002) is frequently the core issue in our more difficult patients.

If the original object was fundamentally frustrating and lacking in soothing and if the infantile ego's primary link was of a persecutory nature without adequate containment, this sense of loss will be overwhelming. This prompts even more reliance on projective identification and splitting. The broken object cannot be properly mourned and to accept that one's needed object is inadequate, unavailable, or even unwilling to be available is to accept unbearable aloneness without resolution or rescue. This is the extreme psychological pain Reveire (1936) spoke to and also is similar to the precocious mourning that Bicudo (1964) wrote about.

Part of the issue that these dually conflicted patients have is that they experienced a lack of protection, refuge, or solace with their early objects, creating strong phantasies of loss, attack, grief, and fragmentation. This anxiety-laden mix of fear, anger, and inconsolable need is not fully resolved when they enter the depressive position and creates an unstable depressive experience. Stein (1991) reminds us that Melanie Klein found both hate and love to create phantasies of an object that has been eaten up and destroyed, leaving the child to feel, "what have I done?" This desperate panic state brings out the desire to restore and repair the relationship and the object.

The patients I am investigating are left with a terrible doubt of "what if I can't restore or reconstruct the object?" Because of their dual phantasies involving both depressive and paranoid anxieties, these patients then feel their good object is not only lost and destroyed permanently, but it also returns as a bad, persecutory object without understanding or acceptance. As Stein (1991) notes, the lack of a good object is experienced as an attack of a bad object. This switch is partly an aspect of paranoid-schizoid functioning but is also part of a primitive or fragmented depressive experience these patients live with. One clinical distinction they have is that their depressive concerns for the object quickly shift to a concern for themselves. Keeping the object happy because of empathy and love shifts to keeping the object happy to avoid attack. It is more of a keeping the peace than a loving worry for the other's wellbeing.

Frequently in the transference, the patient will feel ignored or judged, having phantasies that they have done something to hurt or burden the analyst. But, very soon this concern for the object shifts and they worry they are all alone and forever abandoned, so the focus is more on self-survival. Is this merely a regression from depressive tension to paranoid worry? That would imply a patient with a healthy foothold in the depressive position, utilizing a paranoid defence temporarily. These more complicated patients are better described as high-functioning paranoid or borderline individuals who have found a meagre and slippery foothold in the depressive position, chaotically existing in both worlds without truly mastering either one.

When Spillius (1994) discusses the phase of mourning in the depressive position, she states, "mourning that is successfully worked through leads to a deeper and stronger establishment of the good internal object" (p. 338). But, she also states that mourning "leads for a time to a feeling of losing all internal goodness" (p. 338). The patients I am examining cannot tolerate the "for a time" because of their unresolved paranoid-schizoid phantasies as well as intense depressive conflicts, both distorted and warped by excessive projective identifications. In fact, they shift to feeling that all internal goodness is lost for all time, with no hope of return. Abandonment never stops and feeling lost never changes to feeling found. The loss is so great that it brings out the shift to a persecutory vision of returning demons, set on revenge and rejection.

Segal (1977) has pointed out that a critical issue in the working through of the depressive position is a gradual withdrawal of projective mechanisms. The patients I am discussing rely heavily on projective identification for defence, communication, and basic security so that it is very difficult for them to move away from this mode of relating and face the painful pining, mourning, and lack of control that is so necessary in the gradual integration of whole object↔whole self-functioning.

Bicudo (1964) has outlined many of the same elements I do, in which paranoid patients obtain a significant foothold in the depressive world only to face an overwhelming combination of guilt and persecution. However, Bicudo's focus is more on patients who adopt a defence of apportion to escape both depressive and paranoid fears. They turn their power over to the object in a masochistic compromise.

The patients I am investigating in these and previous Chapters are mostly relying on projective identification to face the combinations of primitive loss, guilt, and cruel retaliation. This over reliance on projective mechanisms for communication and defence tends to escalate those very phantasies of irresolvable loss, abandonment, betrayal, and guilt that the patient is trying to escape. This internal state of dread is comparable to Joseph's (1981) notion of psychic pain in that the emergence into relation with the object is felt as so fused with loss, persecution, dread, guilt, and fragmentation that it is often very difficult for the patient or the analyst to clearly understand the particular details of the moment-to-moment internal states that unfold clinically, often very erratically and intensely. Depressive and paranoid states combine to produce irresolvable loss and grief linked with objects that shift loyalties and betray instead of soothe or forgive. They become vengeful ghosts rather than helpful memories. This unbearable dread is found in narcissistic and borderline patients who cannot effectively grieve (Searles, 1982).

Case material

George was a bank vice-president who wanted help with his anxiety and his temper outbursts. It very quickly became apparent George was angry that his objects were not helping him, loving him, or recognizing him enough. In the transference, George wanted me to "give him the answers" immediately and was frustrated that "I was holding back what he needed." This strong sense of oral deprivation extended throughout his life. At his job, he was always incensed that his superiors didn't see him as their "special and prime worker" and couldn't figure out why "they always passed him over for the top positions and leadership roles." This constant state of wanting more and never feeling filled up was so engrained and forceful that it pushed his actual success to the side. He actually was already someone in a high position of power and prestige. George had been given a new position only a year earlier, but now he felt "ripped off and ignored" because they hadn't asked him to head up the entire department. Rather quickly, this same impatient hunger to be given to or to be acknowledged surfaced in the transference. George wanted me to "tell him how to change" and wanted to "hurry up and turn this around." I interpreted that he couldn't tell what success he was having at work or in the analysis because he was wanting so much more at every moment that he saw what he had as insignificant. Over the course of several years, we explored these frustrated, desperate feelings of not ever having enough, which left him feeling he had nothing. He wanted my constant reassurance and felt he deserved the best out of everyone and everything. When that wasn't forthcoming, George felt lost, rejected, and unfairly passed over. We came to understand this as his search for the ideal self and the ideal object, creating an eternal reassurance that everything and everyone was perfect and permanent.

At the same time, through projective identification, he frequently sided with the underdog, championing the ignored, the downtrodden, and the helpless victim. So, he was on the board of directors of several charities and felt strongly that others should be willing to donate to a cause that "obviously makes sense." During the course of a meeting in which various ideas for how to channel funds were discussed, George broke down in tears "over the plight of those poor souls who have no one. They are alone and without anything. We have to do something to save them." I interpreted that he felt utterly lost and without aid and desperately longed for someone to save him. I interpreted that he felt I was there for him in his hour of darkness but that he wanted so much rescuing from me that I was bound to fail and disappoint him. I added that I thought he might feel the same pressure of having to save the object and thus felt destined to fail them as well.

George replied, "I agree with you in all directions. You have helped me in a special and meaningful way, different than my other therapists. But, you are right. I feel like I want you to fix me and fix me right now! You never do that, you hold out on me and leave me suffering. I know I have to be patient and figure out the answers, but I don't feel like I have the time and in some ways it feels like it is too late. I have been out on a limb my whole life, waiting to be found and helped and reassured. I can't picture it ever getting better. And, like you said, I do feel like I am never doing enough for others. I feel like I am never being the husband I should be or the worker I could be. And, those charities I work with, the people we try and help seem beyond help. I feel I have failed them." I interpreted, "So, you are caught between feeling abandoned by everyone and feeling like you never are there for anyone either." George replied, "I am trapped, confused, and alone!"

In the transference, George would bring me into this combination of paranoid and depressive anxieties. One day, he started thinking about the number of patients I must see each week and "all the paperwork and miscellaneous crap that you have to attend to when you are running your own business." He said, "Your job is so hard. You are my hero. It must be tough, but you obviously pull it off and are the master of your domain. Still, it has to be rough to answer to all those insurance companies, listen to everyone's problems all day long, and find a way to help each person like you do. How do you do it?"

From my strong and immediate counter-transference feelings, I was quickly aware that this was a projective identification-based transference dynamic. In the counter-transference, I felt pulled to quickly share all of my burdens, to the tune of "Oh, you have no idea! The paperwork is staggering, the insurance companies are brutal, and the patient's are overwhelming." Noticing these phantasies, I became aware that George had put me in a double bind. If I shared these feelings with George, with genuine emotion, I would essentially be asking him to reassure and rescue me, letting him be the empathic charity like he enjoys doing in a perverse game of underdog and loving master. I interpreted this but also commented on the second layer in which he was trying to shape me into being a new hero in his collection of rescuing parental heroes. This part of my interpretation had to do with his tendency to look up to and seek out the reassurance of authority figures. I pointed out that to find this pleasure George had to become a helpless little boy.

George said he "understood what I was saying and felt it on some level as he was doing it, but it wasn't quite deliberate, more like something that just pulls me in that direction." He added that he "realizes he was also trying to get me to like him. If you think of George as my nice good patient who is concerned about me, maybe that puts me on your favorites list." When I explored these wishes and desires for my love and for me to be his hero, as well as exploring the reversal in which he would be my hero and rescue me from all my burdens, some of his more base conflicts emerged. The more we discussed it, it gradually became clear that George worried that without "the extra amount of concern or good behavior on my part, you might feel tired, angry, or drained by seeing me and then you would want to fire me as a patient. Then what would I do, I would be all alone!" This depressive fear of draining and hurting me seemed to easily shift into a more paranoid phantasy in which I would not recover. And, I wouldn't give him a second chance. I would simply fire him, get rid of him. Here, there was the persecutory phantasy of being rejected and being alone, without hope of redemption.

Another example of this mixture of depressive and paranoid concerns came out around his request for a receipt for the cheques he wrote me each week. I asked George for details. He said, "Well, if somehow you forgot that I had given you a check and then you asked for it and told me I didn't already pay you, there would be a conflict. We would have a disagreement." I said, "it sounds like the idea of us having a conflict is very scary, something to avoid. It sounds like you don't think we could get through it, no patience, no understanding, and no forgiveness." George said, "That is exactly it. Also, to be more honest, I don't want to get ripped off either." I said, "So, it becomes confusing who is the bad guy, you causing a terrible conflict or me ripping you off. Someone gets hurt and there doesn't seem to be a way to make it right."

Here, I was noting the lack of faith in reparation and the confusion that occurs in the combination of paranoid and depressive states. He added, "I just want you to reassure me that we are going to be ok. I want to hear that everything is smooth and peaceful."

This desperate and demanding need for reassurance was a core element in the transference as well as every other aspect of George's life. I am emphasizing the combination of desperate and demanding because that was the consistent theme. He was demanding in a way that through projective identification he created the scary world he feared and it made for a place where hurt and offended objects were rejecting him and leaving him all alone to perish. I interpreted this type of circular dynamic in how he always wanted to be the centre of attention and the object of everyone's love and respect, but then felt that since this level of perfect love was missing, he was completely unloved and forgotten.

One way this aggressive hunger for the object's blessing took over his life was in George's phantasies about cancer. About once a month, he would become convinced that he had developed cancer somewhere on his body. A pimple on his face was skin cancer, a bruise on his leg was a malignant tumour, and a sore muscle was probably bone cancer. These feelings and ideas left George in a panic, completely helpless and doomed. He would rush to his internist and ask for tests and reassurances. Each time, the doctor would tell him to not worry and that every thing was ok. This felt soothing and "wonderfully reassuring." I interpreted that this was almost an addiction to seeking out a parent who would make it all better. He agreed but said he truly felt he was going to die and he didn't want "to have to suffer on his own." Of course, I brought up the parallel process in which he sought out my perfect parenting and constant soothing. Also, we looked at how these episodes of cancer scares usually occurred after he felt ignored or denied.

So, I interpreted that it was a physical focus of his feelings of being terminally abandoned, left to wither away without love. Over the course of two years of analytic treatment, he slowly had less of these moments and reduced his search for the physicians' immediate attention and comfort. During this time, we focused on the pull he exerted in the transference for me to be concerned, worried, and reassuring. At the same time, I interpreted the double bind he put us in because if I didn't dote over him and his cancer fears, I would be callous and rejecting, ignoring him in his darkest moment. Here, I was interpreting the demand for a loving, soothing object that could easily shift into an abandoning, cruel object.

During these times in the analysis, George's transference stance would follow a particular pattern. When I pointed out how he was trying to control me by putting me into the reassure me or reject me bind, he thought about it deeply and was able to engage with me about it for a period. Then, he began to feel guilty for controlling me and manipulating me. He would apologize and talk about "his regret" in many different ways. This seemed at first to be a genuine depressive worry and a real attempt at mending bridges he felt he had burned. But, this feeling then shifted from a "what have I done" concern about the damage to his object to a feeling of deprivation and abandonment. George said, "now that I have pissed you off and left you burnt out from all my complaining, I feel like you won't want to help me anymore. So, now I am left alone to suffer and I don't have a map to know how to get out of this mess. I feel like you have the map but you don't want to give it to me because I blew it. Please give it to me! Don't take it away. I feel like I hurt your feelings so now I have to pay. But, I feel like the sentence exceeds the crime. Life without parole for a petty crime." I commented on how it was now "a petty crime," meaning he was looking down on his actions and on me perhaps with a sense of "I am above all that." He agreed and said, "I still get sent to jail, whether I feel superior or not." So, his depressive fears shifted to depressive phantasies combined with narcissistic and persecutory feelings.

Another instance of a similar transference situation came about when George came into his session with a computer and said he was ready to discuss our schedule changes that were coming up. He seemed to be proudly showing off his computer and ready to excite me with his technical prowess. But, he had difficulty turning it on and then it was incredibly slow to begin functioning. Once he accessed the calendar portion of the unit, he had a hard time making it accept the dates he was putting in. His childlike desire to please me and show off turned into panic and anxiety. His wish to look big and important turned into a fear of "being stupid and infantile" and "a terrible way to waste your precious time and make you bored and irritated."

I said he felt his failure was pushing us apart. He said, "Absolutely. I am so sorry I came in here behaving like a child, trying to show off and act like I am master of my computer. You must be so over me by now." So, George seemed to feel concern for his impact on his object and lament how he had possibly hurt me or offended me. This left him feeling overcome with grief, anxiety, and guilt.

At the same time, George started to collapse, feeling there was no forgiveness, working through, or understanding available. So, his multiple apologies turned into being scared that I was now angry with him. I interpreted that in his mind I start off hurt and drained and end up resentful and unforgiving. He feels unable to imagine I could tolerate or understand him and he can't imagine making any meaningful restitution. It is all very final. The object is dead and the ego has been permanently banished without hope of pardon.

George was crying and felt hopeless about our relationship during this session. In the counter-transference, I noticed the pull to be the reassuring parent and tell him to not worry, it was ok. I interpreted, "you feel you have hurt me or offended me and that there is no way to make it better. So, when you feel we can't find a way to stay friends, you are convinced we are now enemies. Let's look at how you picture it so impossible to get along." Here, I was interpreting that George was the one who had control over us getting along, not a mysterious outside force or me as a rejecting parent. Bit by bit, we worked on building up the fragile hope of reparation and worked through the intense conviction of his needed, good object turning into an unavailable attacking object. We continue to focus on the delicate mix of concern for the object and keeping the peace with an uncertain other with whom "what have I done to you" turns to "what have I done and what will you now do to me in retaliation?" In other words, the concern about the other's wellbeing shifts to a desperate attempt to "keep the peace" and control the relational environment to make sure the object is happy, because an unhappy object means a bad, mean object.

These clinical approaches are based on Melanie Klein's belief that the infant and child is capable of both depressive and paranoid experiences at a very early stage and if these states are disturbed by difficult external or internal situations, or a combination of both, there will be deformities, distortions, and exaggerations of each psychological experience. The patients I am investigating have had this traumatic chaotic background in a manner that leaves them with an undeveloped, unsuccessfully resolved paranoid-schizoid experience and an immature grasp of the depressive position that is prone to fragmentation.

With George, and many of the patients who are caught within the complex net of both depressive and paranoid experiences, their traumatic and chaotic backgrounds have left them with a narcissistic view of relationships. The depressive component of their psychic lives is a need to please and sustain the object, but often this shifts very quickly from an altruistic concern to more of a self-centred anxiety. Specifically, patients who are viewing life from this brittle dualistic state of conflict are often encased in a view of either the self or the object as elevated and superior or failing and inferior. This idealizing and splitting creates a state of narcissism that when projected with depressive colouring creates a hurt or damaged object that is too inflated to forgive or forget. In fact, this narcissistic object seeks revenge to bring itself back to superior status. So, once again, the phantasy of what have I done to my poor object combines with what have I done to make you so angry and unwilling to pardon.

George's narcissism came out in vivid detail during one session. I had commented that when he felt so hungry for my soothing and the object's love, he only wanted, he never thought of giving. I suggested that perhaps by giving to the object, he might find he receives something back in return, thereby soothing himself. George said, "I never honestly considered what I could give to another person. I am always so focused on what I can get from them or what they are not giving me." Here, there was an important moment of analytic contact that provided insight, reflection, and an opportunity for change.

CHAPTER FIVE

Longing for the disappointing object and dreading its return

Klein (1952) states her view that "the young infant experiences love as well as hatred towards his mother, and when he misses her and his needs are not satisfied, her absence is felt to be the result of his destructive impulses; hence persecutory anxiety results (lest the good mother may have turned into the angry persecutory mother) and mourning, guilt and anxiety (lest the loved mother be destroyed by his aggression)" (p. 121). These states of persecutory and depressive anxiety are usually thought of as occurring in an either/or mode, rarely in combination. This Chapter concludes this section of the book by further illuminating the struggle of our more disturbed patients who have psychic experience of both.

In other words, I think many of our most difficult patients are so difficult because they are suffering with a combination of paranoid and depressive phantasies that together create much more complicated and intense psychological struggles for them then for patients who are struggling with either paranoid issues or depressive matters. In this vein, Segal (2001) reflects on the impact family has on the child and states, "in opposition to some people who say Klein is not sympathetic or empathetic with the child, I say on the contrary, other people imagine the poor child suffering from the badness of the adult. Klein thinks that the poor bugger not only suffers from the badness of the adult but also guilt from having produced it! Because it comes from an omnipotent part of the child's mind" (p. 3). Grinberg (1964) echoes Klein as well as the theme of my paper when he states, "there is still another kind of guilt which appears at an earlier period with a weak and immature ego. This guilt increases in intensity parallel with the anxieties of the paranoid-schizoid phase, or in case of frustrations or failures during the evolution towards the depressive phase" (p. 366).

So, there has been some mention in the literature about patients dealing with both states of mind and being overwhelmed by the combined phantasy state but overall there is little mention of both positions being equally in sway with a patient's phantasies and transference state. Usually the literature makes mention of an oscillation between the positions in the course of normal development that can become either pathological or hopefully progressive (Britton, 2001).

Steiner (1987) has made excellent clinical and theoretical contributions in describing pathological organizations as defensive stances against the unbearable experience of both mental states, but usually occurring as one in reaction to another. He states that the pathological organization "acts as a borderline area between the other two positions, where the patient believes he can retreat if either paranoid or depressive anxieties become unbearable. It is common to observe that a patient will make contact with depressive position experiences and then retreat again to the paranoid-schizoid position as if he could not tolerate the mental pain he encountered. He then meets the disintegration, fragmentation, confusion, and persecutory anxiety of the paranoid-schizoid position and if these too become unbearable the patient has nowhere where he feels safe unless he can find or construct a defense against both positions" (p. 71).

So, while Steiner explored the retreat from one or both positions, this paper will focus on patients who are unable to successfully defend from the dual psychological impact of pathological phantasy states from both psychic positions. In doing so, the paper will illustrate Klein's discovery of how the ego can experience both the phantasy of an injured, destroyed, or murdered object and the resurrection of an enraged, persecutory object seeking revenge. These patients may find temporary respite in some form of a pathological organization, but are mostly lost in a sort of eternal limbo, constantly floating with paranoid-schizoid (Klein, 1946) experiences and primitive states of depressive (Klein, 1935) anxiety. So, these patients are unique in that they are facing phantasies of an object that is unavailable because the ego has somehow caused pain and disappointment to the object, but at the same time this injured or burdened object is transformed into a violent attacker that cannot forgive, only judge and punish or a withholding, cruel, unavailable object that never pleases. It is this sudden and violent transformation that creates such ongoing despair and sense of hopelessness. With a pathological organization in place, the ego has at least a sense of temporary safety. The patients I will explore have not been so lucky and instead feel a constant state of raw exposure to this alluring object they need, a sense of guilt regarding what they may have done to not deserve the object's love, and a shattering anxiety over the mutation of an almost love to a certain hate or constant lack. Thus, primitive loss, persecutory guilt, and conflict without recourse are elements of a frightening internal world these patients struggle with.

The case material in this Chapter will show how particular patients struggle with rudimentary footholds in the depressive position that are fragile and brittle and easily crumble under this more primitive paranoid vision of the self and object. The loss, guilt, separation, and dependence of the depressive state are corrupted by paranoid phantasies and experienced in a violent and traumatic way. This idea concerning the depressive position has been explored by Grinberg (1964). However, this paper contends that it is not just pre-neurotic guilt that is problematic but rather the combination of paranoid and depressive experiences that lead to a primitive view of self and object, which is uniquely tragic and difficult to emerge from. It is a situation of being both in-between the transition from one position to another and being overwhelmed by both at the same time. When patients are under the sway of both, the resistance to growth and change is intense and transference work is difficult. Regret and remorse are hard to find from either self or object and in their place, self-hate and object retaliation occur. Both depressive and paranoid states exist together, overwhelming the ego and producing a state of both fight and flight. The positive aspects of this problem is that these patients have a small foothold in the depressive position so they keep trying to developmentally advance towards a whole object rather than fully retreat, but the anxiety of both positions handicaps them in this advance and in fact pulls them down into more primitive defensive functioning and at times into pathological organizations that create therapeutic stalemates. As Klein (1952) has stated, the ego is overcome by both an absent object that has been destroyed by the ego's craving and anger as well as an object that is seeking out revenge and believes in an eye-for-an-eye method of relating.

Attachment tainted by neglect, rejection, or abuse is often a major factor in our patient's early childhood. Klein emphasized the importance of the environment's influence on the child's ego as well as how the ego translates the external world. Whether it be excessive neglect/abuse, an overly demanding/aggressive ego, or both, the phantasy of a persecutory loss that is irreversible becomes the core ego experience. This type of paranoia and guilt involves not just the experience of a terribly injured object but also an object that will not understand regret or remorse. So, rather than a state of mind in which the patient feels "I have done a terrible thing but I can try to reverse it," which allows the ego to feel active and hopeful, it is more a state of mind in which the patient feels, "what have I done? This is unforgivable and they will surely leave me and I can't do anything about it." This is a much more passive and hopeless place that quickly shifts to an even more traumatic state of persecutory anxiety, in which the patient feel, "now I will be abandoned forever or hunted down and made to pay."

Another way to view this same psychological collapse is that the ego has attacked the object in search of love, praise, or soothing and since the demand is so great, the object is seen as unwilling to give, generating more anger and attack. Guilt sets in when the ego realizes how destructive it has been. Sadness and remorse become overwhelming and persecutory because the object is seen as both too fragile to survive this destructiveness as well as too intolerant to forgive it. Through projective identification, the object now seems enraged and seeking retaliation. The ego is now on the run, feeling alone and close to annihilation.

Case material

David was in his late forties when he came to see me in a state of despair and hopelessness. He had just gone through his second divorce and was "finally ready to take a long, hard look at himself, so he could finally figure out what made him end up in such bad situations." He also "wanted help with the relentless feeling of emptiness and futility in his life." David was a self-employed carpenter who had many satisfied customers. But, he was struggling financially since he was paying off years of back taxes. This history of denial and dismissal of what he owed the government was a pattern of avoiding issues with giving and taking that permeated most of his life. For example, it had been central to his addiction to gambling. For more than thirty years, David had frequented casinos, back-room poker games, internet betting, horse tracks, and local betting pools. He felt convinced that "his system" was full proof "except when he got too excited and went overboard." By this, David explained that he loved to gamble for the "excitement and high" it provided. The way he talked about this excitement that "he craved" and felt "flat and bored without," left him with the sense he was talking about a primitive experience of being united with an idealized or longed for object that provided him with a sense of soothing, aliveness, and bliss. When David was separated from that sense of excitement or couldn't find it, he felt "aimless and down, flat and bored." Later in the analysis, this description would turn out to be an identification with a depressed, lifeless father who would not get out of bed for days.

Interestingly, his description of his two marriages and several close friendships fit these same patterns of emotional fluctuation. His first wife was "initially very exciting, pretty, and made me feel really good just being together. But, in the end she really turned on me and accused me of being physically abusive and got a restraining order on me. Then she took me to the cleaners financially." His second wife, from his description, was a narcissistic woman who was "a sexual dynamo and the life of the party. She made everyone around her feel great even though she only talked about herself." During the marriage, his wife manipulated David to undertake extensive remodel projects on the house she legally kept in her name. David paid for expensive projects that extended over several years and when they divorced, he "never was repaid a dime."

David was hurt and angry at how he had been treated, but he also felt "guilty that he hadn't found a way to make her happy." Now that she refused to see him or return his calls, he felt "put down and broken." David said "how could she do this to me, what have I done to deserve this," a feeling that left him depressed and suicidal at times. In this state, he felt he was been abandoned and banished unfairly but also that he must have done something to warrant it.

So, this was a simultaneous combination of guilt and persecution. He had done something horrible to his object that had caused this catastrophe and he felt guilty for taking away her happiness. But, David also felt he had been attacked and abandoned for retaliation or perhaps for no reason at all. He felt somehow to blame for the badness of the object and the death of the relationship.

At the same time, David remembered her as an ideal, exciting object that "brought him to life and made the world go around." Created by splitting, the ideal object was something for him to pin for and worship with memories of joy and excitement. The rejecting, abusive object was one that blamed him for never being enough or never giving enough. This splitting process, characteristic of the paranoid-schizoid position, stood side by side with David's primitive depressive position phantasy of guilt, loss, and separation.

In the analytic treatment, David resisted my interpretations of this splitting process because it meant he would have to give it up and face the guilt and fear and loss. This line of interpretation would cause him great anxiety as he saw me wanting him to go to the source and origin of his anxieties. I would make interpretations along the lines of "you feel like you haven't been enough for her so she has cast you aside. You feel guilty that you failed her and scared that you did something wrong. Now, she is angry with you and is out to make you hurt as punishment." This sort of dual interpretation of his paranoid and depressive phantasies would initially create panic. Without any direction from me, David said, "I don't want to talk about my childhood." It is striking that I never once brought up the subject of his childhood or his family. But, my interpretations brought him in touch with feelings and memories that were being relived repeated in the present. He continued, "It is all in the past and I don't see why you want me to dwell on that, it only makes me feel depressed. I can't afford to break down, I have to maintain my business and live my life." The way he said this made me feel he was suddenly terrified about completely collapsing internally and breaking down in a way that was permanent. And, he was suddenly feeling pushed and forced by me to enter this dark and dangerous place. It seemed he pictured I was angry with him or was making him do this thing as a punishment. In other words, in the transference, he now felt he had hurt or offended me in some way and that I was now forcing him to endure this extreme sense of loss and collapse as punishment. I made that interpretation and he told me he "couldn't do it right now, maybe a bit at a time later on. But, why is it necessary? Why do I have to do that?" In the counter-transference, I felt David was partly bargaining with me and partly begging me to not force him to face this paranoid↔depressive pain.

I told David he was in touch with very old feelings of fear and persecutory guilt (Grinberg, 1963). Over the course of several months, this exchange slowly expanded. He told me, "My past is overwhelming. It doesn't seem productive to talk about it. I have tried to forget about my childhood. I can't get down like that. I feel like I will not recover." This transference experience made more sense when David explained that his parents divorced when he was eight years old and he was raised by his father. He described his father as "extremely strict, demanding everything be perfect and his way. He was always super-pissed if you didn't agree with him or do things his way." David added that his father was "prone to bouts of depression. He wouldn't get out of bed for days and just starred off into space. Then, when he felt better, there was usually hell to pay for something." Within this early environment, David came to see his time at home as "boring and shitty, with lots of crazy anger in-between" and his time spent outside of the home as "wonderful and exciting." Thus, splitting was a primary way he dealt with his depressive and persecutory feelings. Anytime he could be outside with friends or just by himself was a "wonderful fun time, like magic," before he had to "return to the doom and gloom" of home and his father. I also interpreted that David's "boring and shitty" feelings were probably guilt, fear, and confusion over his helpless, depressed father. David said, "I felt I couldn't make him better. I couldn't save him." Here, we see the collapse of reparation as the object dies and the ego is left lost and without hope.

So, the more we explored this traumatic time and the way he has internalized it, we came to see how he at times felt sorry for his father and guilty because he thought there should be some way he could make his father happier. David thought he might have been the cause of his father's depression. He said, "Maybe it was the burden of having to raise a kid by himself. I couldn't have been that easy to be with. I was hyper and rebellious." This moment sounded more like normal depressive concerns that might eventually lead to mourning, forgiveness, and integration of self↔object conflict. However, for David this more neurotic guilt quickly shifted to include something more sinister and primitive. Burch (1989) describes this as the turn from concern for the object because of what was done to the object to concern for the self because of what the object will do to the ego in retaliation. With David, his guilt involved feelings that he may have caused his father's pain and sorrow so he tried to be a good boy and do his choirs and homework to atone for his faults in the hopes of making his father feel better.

But, at the same time, David felt his father's condition was so much his fault that he would be punished or rejected if he didn't find a way to make it up to his father. This sense of guilt also included the feeling that his father's anger and being demanding was somehow his fault. This was more a fear for himself and an attempt at self-preservation. He said, "I tried to figure out how to avoid him at all costs, because he seemed to hate me for what I couldn't ever figure out. But, I had to keep out of his way or he would lock horns with me. So, I tried to escape his moods by always being gone. I was ok and happy out of the house. I was under his thumb in the house."

I interpreted that David felt that way in the transference as well, that with me he had to face this fear and guilt, both at the same time, or he could pretend to be free of it by focusing on being away from me. Indeed, he looked forward to "not being subjected to this downer stuff and getting to the weekend for some gambling and good times." We investigated his gambling and his view of women as an internal combination of his longed for idealized mother and a vengeful, depressed father. Gambling and the search for an ideal woman served as a temporary, fragile escape into a magical excitement and a sense of belonging and soothing.

Specifically with the gambling, David saw it as union with an ideal, exciting state of mind, an object to be sought after and cherished. When he gambled, he felt, "good, whole, and right." But, sooner or later, he would start losing money and go into debt. Then, the depression intensified until he went back to even more gambling or went into hiding and contemplated suicide. I interpreted this as his search for a loving, exciting parent that he never had who would provide perfect attention and make him feel loved and important. But, then because he demanded this state of perfection, he soon felt the good object was destroyed and taken away and he was left with a depressed, broken object that he felt trapped by, responsible for, and persecuted by.

I interpreted that this cycle of feelings regarding gambling was the same cycle he felt with his father and his mother whom he tried to keep elevated in his memory. In addition, I interpreted that this cycle lives on in how he related to women currently and how he related to me in the transference. Technically, I found it helpful with David to start on this more genetic focus and its tie to current phantasy states, and then include his current relationships and his transference stance. Most of the time in treating patients, I find it best to focus first on the immediate transference, which I also did with David. However, he was initially unresponsive to any transference interpretations and treated them as confusing detours to overcome.

As O'Shaughnessy (1983) noted, instead of focusing on the patient's intra-psychic dynamics, interpretation should be more about the interaction of the patient and analyst at the intra-psychic level. However, some patients such as David cling to fears and guilt so rigidly and the acting out of those paranoid/depressive phantasies that the transference is very difficult to access. I have found it helpful to give equal value to genetic and general interpretations of phantasy in these situations. When doing so, it is common to find multiple phantasies regarding guilt and persecutory fears of object attachment. This then provides an opportunity to introduce the transference and to investigate how those feelings and phantasies permeate the transference relationship. So, with these sorts of patients, genetic interpretations and interpretations of external situations or general phantasy states provide a helpful backdoor entrance into the more central transference issues.

As previously noted, counter-transference was useful with David. I noticed at times I would feel left out and ignored, as he focused on his ex-wives, his current girlfriend, his customers, his family, and his friends, but never me. The more I felt this way the more I wanted to attack him with intrusive interpretations about the transference and his withdrawal from me. I also felt guilty that I must be failing David somehow since the best way a psychoanalyst helps a patient is to work within the transference. Therefore, I felt I must be neglecting my job and letting him down by having periods where virtually no transference work was occurring. When I noticed myself caught in these moments of guilt, confusion, sorrow, anger, and fear, I was gradually able to understand this to be part of a projective identification process in which David was communicating and discharging his core phantasies onto me. It was he who was struggling with feelings like, "what have I done to deserve him not paying any attention to me. Why is he being so mean to me?" Then, I was able to start making interpretations to David about how I thought he might feel I was ignoring certain aspects of his internal world and ignoring how deeply guilty and scared he was, leaving him depressed, anxious, lost, and empty. This brought about a period of more fruitful work on the transference until he again withdrew into a more distant, standoffish place and looked for respite in gambling and exciting women.

When we were able to more openly explore the transference, I noticed several levels of phantasy regarding his connection to me. David felt he could come to me with tales of how exciting his gambling trips were and how he was sure to always win money. Also, he could bring me tales of how wonderful his ex-wife was or how fantastic his current girlfriend was, or how perfect his time outside of his father's home used to be. But, he felt that I, by confronting and interpreting this splitting as part of his depressive and paranoid state, I was taking away his cherished object, his magical excitement, and his peace of mind and replacing it with pain, guilt, and suffering. In fact, during his now two-year analytic treatment, there has been several times in which he has suddenly stopped attending. When I contact him, David tells me he is "too down, too depressed to face anyone." He said, "I can't be seen that way and need to re-group on my own for awhile." The way he says it contains the guilt and shame that sent him into hiding, a withdrawal from my interpretive attacks that made him "so down." Sometimes, when I made interpretations regarding these phantasies of not wanting to let me down by sharing how depressed he was, he felt less anxious and returned to treatment. Other times, he was "missing in action" until some time went by and he called me "begging forgiveness" and "hoping I would take him back because he knows he needs it and feels so depressed that he was scaring himself with his thoughts." Again, this was more of a depressive cry for help, but combined with anxiety over whether I would find it in my heart to forgive him or would I become angry and abandon or attack him.

Steiner (1979) has identified this projective pattern as part of a common borderline cycle in which the patient feels cruelly banished from the maternal space and tries through various means to regain his position inside the idealized womb object. I think the patient may also feel he must be on his best behaviour to win the hoped for status with his object and can in turn feel guilty of committing some infraction that results in his object's depletion or collapse. Also, the same patient may feel abandoned as an attack or revenge for that infraction. I believe some of our more difficult patients experience both of these internal tragedies at the same time. As I have mentioned, echoing Steiner (1979) and others, patients can as the result of projective identification processes feel that once they have found their way into the sacred womb object they are now owned and mistreated by the object so they seek some form of escape. I think this is also the result of a corrupted container↔contained relationship in the patient's mind in which they project the guilt, anger, and anxiety but then feel the object is unable, due to being overwhelmed (guilt phantasies) and unwilling, due to rage and resentment (paranoid phantasies). Therefore, the object/container is now toxic and must be avoided or escaped. Again, these internal patterns emerged in David's transference reactions and in the way he related to his childhood memories, to women, and to gambling.

At this point in David's treatment, he is making progress in all these areas, but the progress is slow and fraught with periodic setbacks based on intense guilt and persecutory phantasies regarding the safety of bonding with his objects. It is unclear if he will be able to make it through these difficult psychological conflicts. But, he is willing to show up most of the time and engage himself and his analyst in trying to understand and change these complex mental experiences.

This Chapter has examined and expanded Klein's ideas concerning the parallel experience of paranoid and depressive pathology. While some patients struggle with psychological hardships of one position or the other, some other patients are actually suffering the internal anxieties of both psychic situations simultaneously.

O'Shaughnessy (1981) states,

> Some patients seek an analysis at a moment when they hope not to extend their contact with themselves or their objects, but,

on the contrary, because they desperately need a refuge from these. Once they are in analysis their first aim is to establish, really to re-establish, a defensive organization against objects internal and external which are causing them nearly overwhelming anxiety. The current lives of the patients I have in mind are permeated by infantile anxieties that have not been much modified. They are patients with a weak ego who, with more persecution than normal, arrive in infancy at the borders of the depressive position as defined by Klein (1935), but are then unable to negotiate it, and instead form a defensive organization. The defensive organization, however, proves precarious, since the combination of a weak ego and acute assailing anxieties that makes a negotiation of the depressive position impossible also makes it impossible for them to sustain a defensive organization. Their lives oscillate between periods of exposure and periods of restriction; they are exposed to intense anxiety from their objects when the defensive organization fails, and suffer restricted, though tolerable, object relations when it is again established" (p. 359).

The patients I am exploring in this and the previous Chapters are certainly more in the realm of what O'Shaughnessy calls exposure, where they cannot sustain any type of significant defensive organization because of the intensity of both depressive and paranoid phantasies. They live lives of overwhelming, unbearable anxiety and grief.

In psychoanalytic practice, many patients present with multiple defensive postures, defensive organizations, or psychic retreats that serve to prevent feelings of loss and persecution. But, when the internal experiences of mourning and loss are of the more severe variety described in this paper, the defences can be more global and fixed, such as borderline or narcissistic personality disorders (Gorkin, 1984) and manic methods of dealing with the internal world (Ury, 1997). These strategies are meant to overcome or avoid the more pre-oedipal experiences of guilt and the persecutory visions of object loss with retribution by complete abandonment and betrayal.

Patients similar to David in their intra-psychic makeup tend to not be able to organize such complex methods of dealing with these anxieties because the intense combination of both paranoid and depressive phantasies renders their egos weak and more liable to psychological collapse than to be able to erect sufficient defences. Instead, the self and object interplay of both the depressive and paranoid positions remain in place in a continuous projective identification cycle that leaves the patient anxious and depressed most of the time.

The case of David illuminates the dual some patients live with. On one hand, the patient is filled with the anxiety of self-survival, feeling one has caused the loss of the ideal and nourishing object that then leads to a crippling, emotional starvation and an eternal aloneness. This is followed by the image of an enraged object rising from the dead to exact revenge, bent on destruction without the possibility of understanding or forgiveness. In addition, for David and other patients in his dilemma, the guilt of having harmed or hurt the ideal object is not balanced with the sense of possible healing or repair. The damage is done and is permanent. Even if atonement is attempted, there is no way to fix or undo the break in attachment. So, the fear of what one is capable of and the fears of what has happened to one's object combines with the fear of the object and what the object can inflict on the self. This produces an unbearable phantasy state that leads to not so much a rigid pattern of defences, but more of a chaotic and drastic sense of internal collapse and hopelessness, fuelled by an ongoing projective identification cycle of anger, despair, guilt, fear, and emptiness. The guilt that David was victim to was not that of an injured whole object but of a weak and disabled part-object that had been trespassed upon, hurt, insulted, and made furious.

Espasa (2002) has understood the depressive side of this problem as a "para-psychotic depressive conflict" in which there is identification with aggressive aspects of the object resulting in a feeling of powerful, destructive aggression aimed at the object. Through projective identification, the object is now felt to be enraged and in search of a destructive revenge.

Grotstein (2000) has brought up the idea of paranoid-schizoid anger at the object to be a primitive prototype of reparation aimed at getting rid of the bad object and retaining the good object. But, in patients like David, the ego can feel its anger has not only killed off the bad object but also damaged or killed the good object, in a collateral damage scenario. Then, unbearable guilt and fear of a fatal revenge arise. Or, if the good object is felt to be weak, frail, or fragile because of the burden the ego has put upon it, the restorative effects of banishing the bad object with anger and rage, a sense of "I am angry that I can't have you all to myself and I don't like the interference with our union so I am going to throw a tantrum," can end up feeling like the good object was too weak to take the surrounding anger and conflict and succumbed to the ego's aggression. So, what was meant to be an effort at making things better for self and object are now felt to be a horrible bloody failure, leading to dark remorse and paranoid fears of deadly consequences and dreadful revenge. Payback is imminent and unavoidable.

With David, both depressive and paranoid fears left him vulnerable and exposed to his dark vision of self and object. The paranoid and depressive conflicts are not so much created as defences against each other as opposed to existing as parallel elements in a projective identification cycle that actually intensifies both sides. Charles (2006) points out that in Kleinian theory, early loss and conflict shape the infantile ego towards a fragmented view of the world. When attempts to find, own, and be unified with the good or idealized object coexist with efforts to expel, banish, or attack the bad object, integration and resolution of self↔object conflict becomes impossible. In this phantasy world, paranoid and depressive issues commingle and cross-contaminate each other, rather than act as a healthy cross pollination that creates growth and change.

For patients with such dual pathology, they are constantly subjected to the self-destructive combination of attempts at reparation with the wish of reunion with the idealized object and the desperate need to placate the bad object in order to avoid being destroyed, abandoned, or betrayed. As stated, each of these intra-psychic states actually intensifies the other, leading to a pathological projective identification process. Steiner (1979) describes this when he notes that for some more primitive patients, the absence of the good object is experienced as persecution and punishment rather than loss and guilt.

I have shown how in fact these patients experience absence as an intense loss that brings about the combination of crippling guilt and persecution. To mourn and let go of a particular way of being with the object, the ego fears it will be unable to survive. From a technical perspective, the analyst, at least initially, has to provide an interpretive bridge out of this dual anxiety into the realm of hope and integration. To do this, the analyst may need to provide the containment and symbolic function for the patient until the patient can trust that he will not be overcome by the paranoid and depressive threats that loom large in his moment-to-moment psychic terrain. Similar to what Searles (1973) has studied, the analyst may have to accept the role of emotional spokesperson (Waska, 2006) for the patient's internal conflicts until the patient can feel safe to emerge from the more concrete, defended state of denial and withdrawal typical of the collapse and confusion in patients like David.

By providing this type of ongoing interpretive bridge to a more hopeful stable view of the world and of the transference environment, the analyst assists the patient through their dark and difficult cycles of depression, guilt, paranoia, and abandonment. Ongoing interpretations of past and present, transference and extra-transference situations are part of a line of analytic contact (Waska, 2007) that provides links to the internal and external environment, a method championed by Klein (Segal, 2001). These types of interpretations also help the patient gradually bear the guilt, fear, loss, and anxiety so they can begin the transition into healthy mourning, change, and separation from their ancient objects of love and hate (Safa-Gerard, 1998).

Instead of longing for the disappointing and hurt object and then dreading its revengeful return and therefore trying to avoid or escape its arrival, the patient can begin to see themselves and their objects as flawed but available, vulnerable yet forgiving, separate and different but understanding, safe, and supportive.

Discussion

Chapters One through Five have examined patients with complicated object relational conflicts in which dual states paranoid and depressive dread predominate. This clinical situation brings about a transference profile of wanting to possess the object for its love and life but then feeling trapped inside a dead and vengeful object unwilling to provide the ego with its desired soothing and satisfaction. This is quite similar to Rey's (1994) concept of claustro/agoraphobic anxiety.

In trying to avoid these crippling anxieties and phantasies, the patient fears the change and growth psychoanalytic therapy can provide. While they want to find relief from internal terror and primitive guilt, they envision change as having to face irresolvable loss and unbearable guilt. Also, they would have to give up the quest for a guilt-free, pain-free world in which there is a conflict-free union with an ideal parental object. This utopian world is one in which the patient can be more of a passive infant who is taken care of and parented, rather than having to be more independent and creative in their own right.

In working out the developmental tasks and hurdles of the life and death instincts, the ego confronts the death instinct's impact upon the object. To counterbalance the vision of a damaged, lifeless object, reparation is vital. When patients are captured within a combination of more primitive aspects of both paranoid and depressive states, reparation is unavailable or unreliable. Therefore, the object seems to quickly vanish, die, and return as a vengeful or rejecting monster.

While Steiner (1987) notes the normal relation to the two developmental positions as P↔D, with the psychic retreat as a third area of refuge, the patients I am exploring have little or no ability to build or sustain a psychic retreat. So, they are constantly experiencing the worst of both positions, much as an innocent victim in a crossfire. Their internal state is more characterized as P→Subjective Self←D.

Steiner (1987) describes some of what I am talking about when he comments on the depressive anxieties the patient faces and the creation of psychic retreats,

> His psychic reality includes the realization of the internal disaster created by his sadism and the awareness that his love and reparative wishes are insufficient to preserve his object which must be allowed to die with the consequent desolation, despair, and guilt. These processes involve intense conflict which we associate with the work of mourning and which seem to result in anxiety and mental pain. A central theme in my paper will be that this is another critical point for the patient and if these experiences cannot be faced a pathological organization may again be called into play to deal with the conflict (p. 70).

Regarding the patient facing paranoid anxieties, Steiner (1987) goes on to say,

> in the paranoid-schizoid position the type of splitting described above can be considered as normal and distinguished from states of fragmentation which result from disintegrative splitting.

Projective identification of a violent kind may then lead to both the object and the projected part of the ego being splintered into minute fragments creating persecutory states often with depersonalization and extreme anxiety. Such states may result when hostility predominates and especially if envy stimulates attacks on good objects. When this happens the normal split between good and bad is likely to break down, leading to a confusional state (Rosenfeld, 1950); (Klein, 1957) and these states seem to be particularly difficult to bear and may lead to disintegrative splitting (p. 70).

Steiner's notion of psychic retreats is that they offer respite to the ego from both these difficult inner states. The patients I am examining are for the most part surrounded by these two states of mental breakdown all the time, without any psychic shelter. Therefore, their defensive reactions and transference states tend to be even more chaotic and intense, as they try to stave off the ultimate dreads of both internal pathological experiences.

Analytic contact is difficult to establish with these types of stormy projective identification-based transferences. However, with patience and diligent focus on the interpersonal, interactional, and intrapsychic dimensions of the patient's phantasy world, slow progress and change are possible. Interpretation and working through of the ongoing breakdown of paranoid and depressive functioning are vital in the journey towards integration.

Hinshelwood (1991) states, "persecutory anxiety is a fear for the ego and depressive anxiety is a fear for the survival of the loved object. The movement between the two is not a sudden once-and-for-all change from persecution to guilt but a gradual one with much to-and-fro, from persecution, to a persecutory form of guilt, to a form of guilt that allows reparation" (p. 273). The patients presented in this book find reparation difficult to access. They imagine objects that fail in their own reparative functions. These patients have come into touch with a fragile level of object integration, easily slipping back into persecutory guilt and outright paranoia. However, they still have this meagre foothold in depressive anxieties, so there is often a complicated mixture of phantasies that actually make them feel more helpless than if they were merely struggling with one or the other positions.

Klein (1957) thought that excessive envy at an early age brought on precocious guilt experiences. Furthering her thoughts, Feldman and Paola (1994) have noted that ineffective mourning for the lost idealized object foreshadows the development of an envious adult who feels cheated and bitter. The experience of never being able to attain the qualities of the idealized object feels unbearable to the ego. Feldman and Paola (1994) point out that the crucial aspects of envy are loss, lack, and unavailability of needed object supplies. In the infantile ego, this results in a chronic searching for what will never be found, a painful and overwhelming precocious mourning in which there is no resolution, no relief.

Clinically, I have noted that in addition to envy, excessive greed, oral aggression, and primitive states of loss can create this same type of guilt and precocious mourning that fails any healthy completion or resolution. Klein (1957) states, "if premature guilt is experienced by an ego not yet capable of bearing it, guilt is felt as persecution and the object that arouses guilt is turned into a persecutor. The infant then cannot work through either depressive or persecutory anxiety because they become confused with each other" (p. 194).

Here, Klein is examining the type of internal struggle many of my patients are living with. I believe this is the core conflict for many of our most perplexing patients. They are caught in the middle of both depressive and paranoid phantasies and often are not sure about where one begins and the other starts. Resurrection and restoration of the hurt or lost object can be a relief at times and other times results in the emergence of a punishing, evil object seeking revenge or wanting to abandon and reject without hope of negotiation or acceptance.

Hinshelwood reminds us that "the interplay of persecutory anxiety and guilt (now termed 'depressive anxiety') is extremely complex—. The preceding paranoid anxieties do not disappear but remain as a prominent background coloring for the depressive position" (p. 146). He goes on to note that guilt is a term Klein reserved for the combination of persecutory and depressive anxieties. With a reasonably consistent and supportive external object, the ego gains faith in reparation and forgiveness. The more severe, persecutory form of guilt recedes and gives way to a more integrative, compassionate form.

This is the analytic goal for patients suffering the dual agonies of paranoid and depressive conflicts. To find resolution, interpretation of the fierce and frightening combination of persecutory and guilty phantasies must be patiently pursued and worked through.

Klein (1964) states, "normally, the drive to make reparation can keep at bay the despair arising out of feelings of guilt, and then hope will prevail, in which case the baby's love and his desire to make reparation are unconsciously carried over to the new objects of love and interest" (p. 115). Later in the same paper, she states, "A good relation to ourselves is a condition for love, tolerance, and wisdom towards others. This good relation to ourselves has, as I have endeavored to show, developed in part from a friendly, loving and understanding attitude toward other people, namely those who meant much to us in the past, and our relationship to whom has become part of our minds and personalities. If we have become able, deep in our unconscious minds, to clear our feelings and to some extent towards our parents of grievances and have forgiven them for the frustration we had to bear, then we can be at peace with ourselves and are able to love others in the true sense of the word" (p. 119).

Here, Klein not only outlines the results of optimal growth and development, but the general goals of psychoanalytic treatment. Patients who exist in a world of both depressive and paranoid anxieties live without the sense of hope or faith in reparation, forgiveness, or love. The good is breakable and not easily repaired and the bad replaces the good at a moment's notice. By gradually containing and interpreting this dual phantasies and conflicts, we can help this type of patient find a new trust in their objects and in their own abilities to care for themselves and their objects. In addition, when things go wrong, they can gradually find the confidence and vision of making amends, reverse mistakes, and find what was lost. Thus, love can temporarily be lost, but it can then be found again. Love can turn to hate at times, but resolution, understanding, and peace can be brought to bear. The world may feel like it is collapsing but the object can come to the rescue and the ego can put things right again. War is not forever. Peace is possible.

PART II

ANALYTIC CONTACT
IN UNTRADITIONAL
CLINICAL SITUATIONS

Low-frequency Kleinian psychoanalysis: Establishing analytic contact with a new case

From the first time I meet with a patient, I am searching for a window into their unconscious world of object and self-experience. Since my psychoanalytic perspective is based on the vital importance of phantasy, defence, and transference, my mind is constantly listening for any evidence of these essentials. In fact, I make a point of telling each patient very early in the first visit that I will need them to be on the lookout for any sign of deeper feelings about themselves, about me, or about our work together that they may usually ignore, downplay, or hide.

If I notice a foothold into some manifestation of transference, defence, or phantasy, I usually make some form of interpretation. Then, I wait for the reaction or response to my comment. Hopefully, these interpretations of transference, defence, and phantasy lead to a slow pattern of change and the experience of choice instead of psychic scarcity. If the patient is able and willing to interact to some degree in these ways, a therapeutic process of analytic contact (Waska, 2007) has been established. If this contact can be sustained over a period of time there is hope of learning, change, and integration, and mastery. This is my working definition of clinical psychoanalysis.

Research (Vaughan & Roose, 1995) has shown that only forty per cent of all psychoanalytic treatments evolve into a genuine analytic process. Much more important than frequency or use of couch, this research highlights the crucial variables as free association, resistances, defences, interpretation, containment, and working through of various self↔object transference and phantasy states.

This Chapter demonstrates the effectiveness of low-frequency Kleinian psychoanalysis in building a therapeutic process with a borderline patient. In working towards analytic contact, psychic phantasy is regarded as the core element of the transference (Segal, 2007; Joseph, 2007) and insight as the ongoing and evolving achievement of its working through (Segal, 2007).

Session 1

Nancy came to see me for her first visit looking rushed and anxious. She had never been in any type of therapy before and told me she had been thinking about seeking help for many years and "now it was time." Nancy told me she was feeling more and more depressed and "found herself sleeping a lot and crying a lot." She said her drinking was "out of control" and that she had known that for a long time but now she was "taking a hard look at it." I asked for details. Nancy had been drinking four to eight drinks almost ever day for "the past ten years or maybe more." She described blackouts and a high tolerance. Nancy said she was "really ready to try and get the drinking under control and wanted help so she could finally lick that problem." She said, "I am willing to do anything to get your help. I am ready to change. Just tell me what to do!" She said all this with a tone of demand and desperation.

Nancy was an attractive woman, so besides the demand for immediate and instant change, which I took as a transference stance and a diagnostic clue, I felt she was setting up an erotic transference in which she was "willing to do anything" and I could "just tell her what to do." I said, "The way you said that shows you are really motivated to make some important changes in your life. The way you say it also seems to be a way of giving yourself over to me, putting me in charge. Is that familiar in any way?" Nancy replied, "Wow. That is exactly how I would describe most of my relationships with guys. I throw myself on them and let them call the shots. I see them as kings who are the perfect fit with me and I am sure we will live happily ever after. And, this is after meeting them for five minutes at a party. It usually doesn't work out too well, but I keep trying and run after them until they sort of dump me and then I am depressed for a long time." Here, I was analysing the transference and gathering more diagnostic information. She responded by associating to deeper material.

The striking aspect of her drinking problem was how she told me that "without it I don't think I will be a part of my friends. Without drinking, who am I and why would they care?" I took this as a transference remark as well and said, "You probably worry that if you stop drinking, we will not have that to focus on anymore and then maybe more difficult matters will surface."

At that point, Nancy looked anxious and became silent. She gathered herself and said, "There are other things I need to talk about. I know they have affected me and I have known for years I should do something to understand it, but I have put it off." After some more silence, she said, "I was raised by two very nice parents. They were good to me and my older brother. They did their best and I don't really have any bad memories of them in my childhood. But, when I was nine years old, my brother told me it would be fun to 'fool around'. So, we started to have sex whenever we could. I would sneak into his room after my parents went to bed. Or, if we were visiting someone and had to share a bed, we would have sex. It wasn't every night or even every week, but it was pretty consistent from when I was about nine till I was twelve. He is four years older. After about a year or so, I didn't want to do it anymore. But, I never said anything. So, I would just lay there pretending I was asleep. He would go ahead and do it anyway." I said, "It sounds like you were uncomfortable asking him to stop. So, you hoped he would notice your being passive and acting asleep and understand that you didn't want to anymore." She agreed. Nancy said, "I think that has impacted my life in ways I don't know. It probably affects my relationships with men. I think its time to find out about it."

Finally, Nancy repeated some of what she had said earlier about wanting to stop drinking and start "a new life," with the same frantic wish for immediate results and gratification. She also repeated her fear about what life could be like without drinking and "how empty and alone she could feel if no one wanted to be with her anymore."

So, from a psychiatric perspective, Nancy presented as a patient with a depressive disorder, alcohol dependence, a possible anxiety disorder, and a borderline personality disorder with dependent and hysterical features. From a psychoanalytic perspective, she displayed a transference that combined a borderline pathology with an erotic, manic way of relating. I saw her as having to rely on drinking to prevent an inner collapse, abandonment anxiety, and primitive loss (Waska, 2002). She had high hopes for the object that rapidly caved in to disappointment, which she internalized as rejection. The history of sexual relations with her brother seemed to have a great impact on her psychological wellbeing and shaped her current view of self and object, leading to a passive yearning and a helpless fear.

Finally, I told her that I thought she didn't see herself as having much value or identity unless it was defined by me or others. I said that if she gave herself over to me and did whatever I wanted her to, she might end up different but it would be a change I choose instead of a change she chose. I added that we would have to see if being herself with me presented a danger and if so we would need to learn about that.

Session 2

Nancy began using the analytic couch this session, on my recommendation. I explained to her that it would help both of us to focus on her feelings and thoughts rather than be taken up with face-to-face social interaction. I had provisionally assessed that the issues around her brother would probably be raised by the use of the couch but not in any negative way that would derail the treatment. Also, I thought she was not narcissistic, paranoid, psychotic, or obsessively concrete, which are all conditions that can preclude the early use of the couch.

She lay down and started to tell me about "how hard she was trying to stop drinking" and that she was "doing everything I said for her to do." She reported that she had not drunk for several days and had "gotten drunk two days because I went to a party both nights and felt out of place and alone without drinking." My counter-transference to her comments about "doing everything I said" was that she was expressing her devotion to me and her loyalty to whatever I recommended. Therefore, I interpreted, "the way you say that makes it sound like you want to please me and do it for me. Maybe you are not used to doing things for yourself, that it feels safer to try and do what will make me or others happy." Nancy replied, "Well, I definitely want to stop drinking, but you couldn't be more on target. I usually try and figure out what everyone wants and then I make that happen. I usually don't give much thought to what I want." I said, "Could that be because you think I will not care about what is important to you?" "I never really think of other people being interested in me," Nancy replied. Then, she associated to different situations with friends and former boyfriends where she tried her best to please them and "make everyone happy, so they would accept me."

After awhile, I interpreted, "there seems to be a parallel between how you want to please me and others, because we only care for our own needs, and your history with your brother." She was quiet and then said, "I did want to make him like me. It seemed like our special time together, even though I didn't really like it." I said, "So, maybe you are still searching for 'that special time together' but you think I don't really want to be with you unless you find a way to please me and cater to my needs. Just being loved for who you are seems foreign." She replied, "I have never thought anyone would want me just for me. I always feel like I have to do something extra to keep in everyone's good graces."

So, in this session, there was a behavioural change, the reduction in drinking, that we came to understand as part of her transference to me. From a psychoanalytic perspective, we made progress in several directions. As a result of my awareness of counter-transference feelings, we investigated her need to please me and find some way to be accepted. We noted how she aborts her own worth and identity in order to focus on me and find some way to gain my care and love. As a result of that exploration, we also focused on her general phantasies, which included her need to please her objects as a way to fend off abandonment, neglect, and intense emptiness. This need to please and be accepted led to a discussion of the parallels in her current psychological life to the emotional fallout of her sexual relationship with her brother. I told her, "you must feel you have only one thing to give me or please me with, that being whatever it is you think I want. The idea of having all of your self, your identity, as something that would interest me is uncomfortable."

"Completely!" she said. I added, "In feeling so desperate to find a way for you to matter to me, there is never room to figure out what you want from me. So, the relationship is a one-way street." Nancy said, "I never ever thought of it that way. For me to want something from you is really strange. Except if you can help me to make someone love me." She broke down sobbing at this point.

Session 3

During this session, Nancy reported success in drinking less and feeling "less nervousness and chaos." However, she told me that at first she was able "to spend more time with myself, just doing all the things I want to do or think of doing. I started cooking more, I did some art, I watched movies, and I finally got around to reading some books I have wanted to read. This is very different for me. I never think the things I like or want to do are worth it, unless someone else tells me to do them." I commented that she wanted to stop drinking but also turned it into something I wanted her to do, as if that was easier to comply with this. She agreed and said, "If I do what want I want to and spend time on myself, I feel really good at first but then I start to get really anxious and confused. I get scared. Then, I start thinking of how my friends are probably out drinking and having a good time and I want to go join them. Actually, I ended up doing that a couple of times but I didn't get drunk." I said, "I think you are telling me that you don't feel important or valuable unless it's defined by someone else." Nancy said I was right and she "never felt she had the right to her own life. I feel if I take the time to be with myself, I will get left behind or end up all alone. I really want to spend time cooking, reading, and relaxing but I get worried that something will happen." I interpreted, "if you honor yourself, I will reject you or punish you?" "Something like that. I feel like there is a thin line there and if I don't do what someone else wants, there will be consequences," she replied.

With Nancy, there is a delicate balance between interpreting the patient's material and enacting her projective identification process. At this point in the session, I was certainly thinking that she was describing a vivid parallel to her sexual relationship with her brother. So, I wanted to interpret that she most likely felt she had to please him or suffer rejection and abandonment. In that sense, she wanted to have her alone time but felt compelled to be with him out of fear of being forgotten. I think this was a correct interpretation, just as my transference interpretation seemed accurate. However, I also thought she was drawing me into making rather fast links to the brother in a slightly erotic, invasive, or authoritarian manner. This was true of the previous two sessions, but seemed more outstand-ing in this one. Therefore, I chose a contain-and-interpret approach (LaFarge, 2000; Rosenfeld, 1987) in which I waited to gather and understand the various counter-transference reactions I experienced before formulating an interpretation that put together the different aspects of her object relational conflict.

In this particular case, I waited a bit and said, "I think you are trying to pull us along very quickly, so we don't have to linger on anything that might be too painful. It would be easy to come up with a 1-2-3 formula to solve everything, but I think that would be a reac-tion to anxiety instead of something we could actually use to make changes." Nancy replied, "I tend to jump around and want things to happen right away. I want it simple and fast." I said, "It sounds like that can lead to results you actually don't want." She said, "Well, that is a big part of how I screw it up with boyfriends. I always speed it up and try to create a perfect instant relationship with them. I get so excited and happy in the beginning. Then, I think things are going great but the guy doesn't like me or doesn't call or something. Then, I feel completely rejected and depressed."

I interpreted, "so, you begin to hope and wish for a perfect match with a man but you start to try and control it, demanding it go a certain way. When it doesn't go your way, you feel betrayed and abandoned. You seem to want to control the relationship and have it go your way but then it backfires on you and you feel like they have control over you."

She answered, "Absolutely. But, I never really thought of how I am trying to control it." She went on, "another thing that happens around guys is really weird. There is this thing I do and have done for as long as I can remember. I guess you would call it a daydream or something. After a guy dumps me or doesn't call me back or something, or even when I am not going out with anyone, I will be sitting around and suddenly start thinking about what it would be like if they came up to me and apologized. Basically, I have this story about what if a guy comes up to me and says he is sorry for what he did to me. He says it in a way that I can tell he is being honest and really means it. I hear him out and it feels really good to have him say he is really sorry. I feel like I am getting my revenge in a way, but it also just seems like such a relief. He is finally admitting to what he did to me. I feel good but I also cry."

Several things came to my mind. Certainly, once again, I could make the direct link to wanting her brother's apology. Instead, I choose to weave this in with the rest of her material as a more balanced interpretation. Also, what she said made me think of a classic paper by Kubie (1955) on needing the object to provide atonement. This helped to inform my interpretation. Finally, I was struck by how in Nancy's phantasy, she was passive, the lucky recipient of the man's apology.

So, I interpreted her phantasy state and her internal conflicts as well as the genetic material I believed to be within. I said, "I think you are referring to a conflict you have in which you want your brother and all men after him to realize how they hurt you and to make amends. But, in wanting them to come to you to show remorse, you have to remain passive and without much say, which is part of what hurts so much. To get your apology you have to be hurt. I think that will continue here as well depending on if you struggle to be passive and let me do the talking or take the lead and make your own discoveries." Nancy said, "I see what you mean. I am more comfortable being in the shadows. I never thought about how it might make me more upset. I thought it was a way to avoid trouble." I added, "I think you desperately want to be included, understood, and accepted. But, maybe you have been excluding yourself by rejecting yourself as having no worth. Then, you are only good if you can serve others."

Session 4

Nancy told me "it has been a crazy week with her parents visiting." For awhile, she told me about how "she felt so embarrassed to be with them, they just end up acting weird. I feel ashamed to be seen with them and feel like walking ahead of them when we go out somewhere." There were no real details except the description of embarrassment and frustration about having to be with her parents. The more she talked about these feelings, I had the impression she was describing the typical feelings of humiliation a teenager feels when wanting their freedom and independence but feeling like they are still a little kid. So, I made that interpretation.

Nancy replied, "Well, it is like that but it is more about how they act. They just get stranger and stranger as the day goes by. By the time we are hanging out in the evening, I feel really embarrassed." I asked her "what happens as the day goes by? How do they change?" She said, "They end up drinking so much it gets weird." I asked for details about her parents drinking and without thinking it was out of the ordinary, she described her parent's obviously alcoholic pattern of drinking first thing in the day and continuing way into the night until they were obviously drunk by nightfall of everyday. I was struck by how Nancy seemed to not notice the problem with alcohol but was simply left feeling embarrassed. I said this to her and she said she had "never really put it together like that, but that they had gotten drunk on a regular basis from as far back as she could remember." I thought to myself that when Nancy had told me that she "had a good upbringing" and that she "was a little surprised that her parents never realized what was going on with her brother" that perhaps they had been too drunk to notice.

The more we discussed her parent's drinking and her "embarrassment about it," Nancy began to partly notice something. She told me that she never thinks about their drinking when it is happening and usually doesn't feel much about it except the embarrassment." "But," she said, "I always wake up the next day in a really bad mood and I never can figure out why. I spend the morning or the day feeling angry or upset and it is kind of mysterious." I felt I was in the middle of three interpretive modes: a transference moment, a current extra-transference state, and a genetic situation.

As a contemporary Kleinian, I combine the classical Freudian and early Kleinian approach of genetic, extra-transference, real-world situations, and the transference proper with the more modern Kleinian approach of here-and-now, moment-to-moment interpretation of interaction and transference. Therefore, over a period of ten minutes, I made several interpretations. First, I said, "I think you want me to be the one who tells you what is going on, while you lie passively. Perhaps you are more comfortable giving me the lead because you think that is the way we will get along best, without any conflict. I think you have more insight into things than you let yourself have because you are not sure if it would break us apart. To let me be in charge is to keep us safe and together." Nancy said, "I think I know what you mean. I tend to do that with most of my friends. Come to think of it, I do that with everyone."

Next, I said, "I think you are aware of your parent's alcoholic drinking but you put it out of your mind to avoid any conflict or rejection. You tolerate their behaviour and suffer the embarrassment to keep the bond safe. But, you can't keep it out of your mind too long because you are angry and hurt. So, the next morning, like an emotional hangover, you are upset and angry but you don't let yourself really know why. It looks like you are sick and tired of seeing your parents drunk but that may be the only bond you have with them so it is also frightening to look at it too close. You said you don't have much in common with them. It looks like you are angry and hurt that drinking is the one thing you have in common."

Nancy replied, "Jesus Christ! I never saw it like that before. You are right. That does seem to be the only think we ever do together. That is so weird that in the morning I am angry but I never put two and two together and realize it is about the night before."

So, then I also interpreted, "I think that may be the same pattern of defense you use with your feelings about your brother. Perhaps you tried to ignore your feelings about having sex with him but the next day those feelings were still there and you did your best to keep them separate in your mind from everything else. By keeping your feelings about your brother or your parents separate from everything else you don't have to face the perverted relationship you have with them and the pain that goes with that. That way you don't have to tell me about your feelings either and then you don't have to feel ashamed or embarrassed with me." Nancy said, "No wonder I drink so much!" I replied, "up to now, that has been your best way of coping. Maybe we can come up with a better approach." She said, "I am all for that!"

Nancy then told me how she "fears being forgotten." She told me, "I feel like I only last for a day or a night in people's minds, so I have to find the one thing they want or that we have in common to please them and win them over so they might keep me in their mind and not forget me." Here, I noticed her pull to again bring up her brother's sexual acts and her feeling she had to please him to keep herself in his mind. But, I decided that this was again part of a projective identification dynamic that was constantly occurring in which I was invited to invasively bring up her brother again and again, right after very obvious references to him in her material. Rather than waiting for her to elaborate into that material, I was being invited to quickly pounce on the genetic link and almost re-molest her over and over again with it.

So, instead, I interpreted, "I think you are sometimes scared to think for yourself. You want me and others to think for you and then if you let us be the leaders in the relationship, we won't forget you. But, that also means you have to feel surrounded by people who just want to dominate you and you are only loved for what you can sac-rifice. You end up feeling like an empty vessel needing to be filled up by others." Nancy said, "I have done that my whole life. And, you are right. I end up feeling empty and worthless, just waiting around to see what others want and hoping they will like me."

Session 5

Nancy entered my office looking rushed and energetic. She lay down on the couch and began telling me "how far she had advanced" and how "she was ready for the next level and wanted to find out more since she had been able to figure out everything so far." She told me she was "so happy to find the truth out about herself and to be shown the way to change. I haven't drunk and my life is changing. Things are so good. I am really glad we have figured these things out. I want to thank you for all the help you have given me. I feel very positive."

At this point, I noticed that I felt taken away on a cloud of opti-mism and progress. We had fought the demons and won the victory together. We were the invincible team! So, I interpreted, "I am inter-ested in how positive and hopeful you feel. I am glad to hear you are hopeful and interested to find out more about yourself. But, you seem to want us to be a perfect team that has already figured every-thing out. It is like you want us to have an instant, perfect relation-ship but we have only known each other for four visits." Nancy said, "Oh no. That is exactly what I do with all my boyfriends and then it turns sour pretty quite." I replied, "That is probably because there is no foundation yet but you go ahead and trust it as if it is solid. Maybe you feel more in control if you imagine us in a perfect relationship with no problems then to have to be yourself and have me get to know you." She said, "Yes. That sounds much scarier. I don't have any guarantees that you will like me." I interpreted, "So, it is important for us to understand why you avoid our growing relationship and want to force us into this perfect success story instead."

Using my counter-transference, I added, "Maybe you get excited to think we can have an instant union where you get instant acceptance and it's scary to suddenly realize you don't even know the other person. You are ready for this instant intimacy with me but you don't really know me yet so you must feel very empty and distant when you see the reality of it." She replied, "You are describing my history with all men." I asked, "Including your brother?" Nancy said, "I think so. The times we had together, especially the first year before I starting feeling weird about it, were very special. I felt he was really interested in me and we had this wonderful, exciting secret. It was something we had in common and it was our bond. But, it turned into something I didn't like and ended up feeling alone." At this point, I also interpreted, "The way you are looking for something so special with me makes me think you don't think I would be interested in you just as is. So, you are always looking for something extra, something behind the regular. But, that means you are always working hard to please me since you are convinced I won't be pleased with the real you, the regular you." Nancy added, "I don't think much of myself as-is either."

Session 6

Nancy came in looking upset and anxious. She told me she had gone out of town on a business trip and "got drunk everyday. I just wanted to be seen and included. I saw it as a giant opportunity to be seen and accepted. It was like the love was right there in front of me and all I had to do was to perform and I would be included. So, I really slipped up. I thought it was going to be so easy to not drink. I did not factor in something like this. I felt I had a new audience to win over and be loved by." I asked, "We talked about how you want to be remembered in my mind and other's. Did you keep us in your mind or did we vanish?" Nancy said, "Well, I did feel guilt that I was messing up and I would have to tell you. But, mostly I kind of woke up from how giddy I felt last time we talked and started to realize how finding the cure isn't going to be that easy. I realized this is going to take a while."

I brought up the transference by asking, "You mentioned you were excited to encounter a whole new audience to throw yourself at and to win over. In a way, you have seen me as an audience to become fast and perfect friends with too. I wonder how that worked as far as turning from us to them. Did you think about us as you dove into them or did we just go up in smoke?" Nancy replied, "That is a very interesting part. After a couple of days of drinking and trying to make all these new friends, I started to think about moving there. It seemed like the best of all worlds. I started to get really worked up about it but then I realized I would miss you. I immediately realized this is important and I don't want to mess it up. I don't want to lose you." I was very clear in her telling that this was a genuine, heartfelt feeling that was both erotic but also a very real and committed sense of trust and sincerity. I said, "You have developed a real bond to me and what we are doing together. Instead of the fast and crazy instant relationship we spoke of last time, this seems to be more of a sensitive, genuine feeling of closeness to me." She said, "It is. And, I don't want to screw it up. This is important."

Session 7

Nancy started out this session telling me how she received a call from a former boyfriend who "had used her and never really paid much attention to her." He asked her to find a particular book that he wanted to give a friend as a gift. He knew Nancy had a keen interest in a variety of subjects and was very knowledgeable about certain books. Nancy told me, "I immediately said I would because I thought it meant he was interested in me again. For a moment, I even thought he might want to get back together and maybe if I find him the book and please him that way we would get back together and, who knows, maybe we will get married some day. So, I really went out of my way to search this book out and I finally located it. I called him and I was hoping he would ask me out to dinner or something. Instead, he seemed like he didn't even care and barely even thanked me. He said to put it in the mail. And that was it! I was so disappointed. I felt put down, used, and really sad. Normally, I would have gotten really drunk. Pretty soon afterwards, it occurred to me that this was the same pattern we had talked about, where I think I will have an instant relationship but there is no real foundation to it so then I leave myself feeling ripped off and alone."

I interpreted, "That is the same excitement for a special perfect relationship you wanted with me and perhaps the same hope of being special in your brother's eyes. But, in all three situations, you feel you must sacrifice and suffer to win our love." Nancy replied, "I don't see any other way to it. I can't find it. I don't really believe there is another way." I said, "For right now, that is your conviction." Here, I was pointing to the side of her that stands for and defends this internal bargain of passive suffering in exchange for love.

Session 8

Nancy started off this session very frustrated. She said she had been drunk several days in a row and she "was really angry about it. I see all my problems right in front of me but then I go ahead and do them anyway. This is not working out too good. I feel like a real failure. I went out with some friends and I thought about not drinking but then I was sure I would be the oddball and I didn't want to be left behind. I am so angry with myself." She went on for awhile about how "pathetic" and "stupid" she was to have "caved in again just after she had learned so much about everything."

I made two interrelated interpretations. I said, "You are saying you want to change but I think you are not giving yourself any credit for also not wanting to give up the prize of having an instant and constant connection with everyone. You are not very compassionate about the side of you that sees sobriety as a lonely terrible rejection and the loss of anyone to be close to. You want an instant cure and a new you without any work and now you're angry and disappointed that you can't have it right away. In other words, just like you want an immediate connection and love from me and other men, you demand immediate and perfect change from yourself. When it doesn't magically happen, you feel abandoned and like a loser." Nancy replied, "I never considered that I was being demanding of myself. I see what you mean. It's funny. The idea of being compassionate or giving myself a break, that is not something I ever thought about."

Next, I made the interpretation, "you are like a demanding cruel parent who gives no wiggle room for the child to make mistakes and learn. Maybe that confuses you to think I might be demanding that you change right away or I will be disappointed too." Nancy replied, "I do worry about that. Between the anger I have towards myself and the disappointment or frustration I think you might feel, I think I better get it together or else!" I said, "So, it becomes about a horrible panic to please-or-else instead of us helping you to change and learn." Here, I was interpreting her projective identification process in which she saw her own demanding cruelty in me.

Nancy began telling me how she had talked with her mother and how "wonderfully different it was." She told me how "instead of my mother being self absorbed and only talking about herself or her being drunk one more time, we actually had a good talk. She actually asked me how I was doing and acted like a real mother who was concerned about her child. It was a real surprise but a welcome one too!"

I thought Nancy was making note of the transference and her own projective identification system of phantasy so I said, "you want me to be compassionate and you need yourself to be understanding and patient. But, you are worried I am selfish, demanding, and angry with you just like you are with yourself. This is a struggle and conflict for you. You want to have a tolerant guide and compassionate parent who is on your side but then you get demanding and judgmental so you feel like an unwanted failure of a child."

Pointing out these specific self↔object phantasy relations is a Kleinian technique that helps stabilize the patient's internal conflicts and assist in self-mastery (Clarkin, Yeomans & Kernberg, 2006). Nancy responded, "My parents were never like that, so I guess that is me doing that. It helps to picture it that way. It is almost like I could try and be a better parent to myself."

Session 9

Nancy came in and told me, "I was thinking of quitting therapy and not coming back. But, since you warned me I might feel like that and that it was important to talk to you about it, I thought I would give it a try. This is exactly what I do with most of my boyfriends and recently with my French teacher too. I didn't get what

I wanted so I stopped going. It didn't seem to work out between us so I disconnected." I asked how that has happened with us. She replied, "I don't feel I have learned much at all here and nothing has really changed for me. This isn't going anywhere." I interpreted her attack on us and pointed out how when she hasn't obtained an immediate sense of love, fulfilment, and success in the total of eight short visits, she is angry and rejecting. I pointed out she is doing to us what she is most afraid of others doing to her. In fact, I said, this fear of rejection from not being enough for others is the main reason for her drinking.

Nancy responded by telling me how after a "couple of days of being sober, I fucked up and got really drunk. I feel really embarrassed and ashamed of myself. I was out with a friend for dinner and we had some wine and then some cocktails. Next, we went to a bar and kept drinking. By the end of the night, I met some guy and went home with him. I am so pissed. That is exactly what I usually do. I thought he seemed so nice. Now I regret it." I interpreted, "So you wanted someone to like you right away and have a perfect match up but it backfired. I think what happens is that you get very demanding of that immediate reassurance and then if you don't get it you become very angry with yourself for failing that demand. If you assume I am going to have the same reaction to you, I see why you would think of quitting. We need to see what gets in the way of seeing yourself in a more compassionate light. Everyone makes mistakes. We are trying to find out why you keep making the same one and why you are so punitive about it."

Nancy responded, "I am so upset that I continue to do the same stupid thing over and over again. I do something that I feel is wrong and it hurts me, but I won't stop it." I interpreted, "when you use the word 'won't stop it', I think that is important. There is a part of you that sees drinking and going home with men as essential and therefore it feels scary to give up even though you logically know its hurting you. I think you are scared that if you stop that behavior you will lose out on the attention, love, and reassurance that you crave so much. That might be the same kind of anxiety you felt with your brother, wanting it to end but worried about his reaction if you stopped."

Nancy responded, "I think you are right. What you are saying feels totally right and I feel like I am learning something. But, I also feel this weird guilt about my brother sometimes. I don't know why but I feel like I somehow caused everything to happen. It is like a wave of guilt about him. I hear he is having a lot of problems with drugs and I think I caused them maybe." After Nancy talked about this for awhile, I said, "It is interesting that you are able to be understanding, forgiving, and accepting of him but not of yourself. You see yourself as the criminal and him as the victim. I think that is more comfortable than to feel the opposite feelings and then to have to put all of your feelings together as a whole. Keeping it all black and white is easier but it keeps you trapped feeling unlovable and desperate to please others."

Here, I was again interpreting her projective identification process in which she switched her feelings towards her brother around and tried to take care of him instead of hoping to be cared for in a better way by him than the sexual relationship they had. Nancy replied, "You are making sense. This is the first time in my life that I have felt like aborting the entire thing and then didn't. I wanted to bail ship but I stayed. This is really different."

Session 10

Nancy was feeling better and spoke of "giving herself a break" as I had suggested she might actually want from me to counteract her own no-break angry demand onto me. She said that one reason she thought of stopping treatment was that "it felt like a confessional instead of learning." I interpreted her projective identification of a harsh demanding object onto me that she then had to confess her sins to and hope for my forgiveness instead of my rejection. I commented that this angry parent/confessing child prevented learning that might leave her more independent and strong but becoming independent and strong also left her feeling alone and aware of scary feelings she usually deflected. In other words, fear and guilt were a defence against anger and separation. I said, "You won't give us much of a chance as long as you see it that way."

Nancy then "confessed" to getting drunk again and making out with a coworker at a bar. She went on for awhile about her guilt and disgust with herself. I interpreted that here she was again confessing instead of learning. Then, she told me that he had called her the next day and asked her out to dinner. Nancy told him she would like to go to dinner but advised him that "she normally doesn't act like that and hoped he didn't think he could expect more of that after dinner." He said he understood and would simply like to get to know her. Nancy told me she was "really afraid of how to interact with him." I asked her if she meant without drinking. She said, "Yes. I am scared because this will be a real test of how to relate to a man as just myself without being drunk."

I said, "You are struggling with that here, with so success already. You want to be yourself but your default is to be the confessing child that is going to be rejected by me unless you find a way to please me and make me proud. By telling me the story about going out to dinner, I think you are trying to show me you can be a competent woman who respects herself and believes she is lovable. You want to love yourself and find love from men just for being who you are." She answered, "That is my goal. I am excited but really nervous about getting there."

With Nancy I tried to be aware of how she was using me (Joseph, 1983) to both fulfil and fend off various phantasy states. She seemed to use projective identification in both communicative and defensive manners (Bion, 1963; Rosenfeld, 1971). In her projective efforts, I sometimes found myself pulled into her phantasies and conflicts. One example with Nancy was how she excited me and drew me into her manic cure phantasy where we had an instant and trouble-free relationship.

As Steiner (1984) has noted, it is common for us to become part of the patient's phantasies and projective identification efforts, succumbing to various enactments. These enactments are essential to recognize, monitor, and understand so as to regain therapeutic balance and build a better interpretive footing.

So, the case of Nancy, only in its beginning stages, is illustrative of how to establish analytic contact using a Kleinian approach. While this case, twice a week on the couch, is a low-frequency treatment in terms of classical norms of external criteria, it is defined as psychoanalysis based on how it successfully established a therapeutic analytic process. This treatment was a combination of exploring, interpreting, and working through the transference, phantasies, internal conflicts, and defences. Counter-transference was also essential in better understanding the patient. Containment and interpretation were utilized hand in hand.

In the case of Nancy, successful analytic contact was reached. The intensity of her paranoid (Klein, 1946) anxiety and the lack of significant depressive (1935) integration eliminated her ability to find healthy mourning with which to foster reliance on a consistently supportive good internal object. This makes for a difficult and rocky treatment. However, with continued efforts by both Nancy and her analyst, to understand, contain, interpret, and work through her core relational conflicts, a slow and successful integration is possible.

CHAPTER SEVEN

A Kleinian view of psychoanalytic couples therapy

Many couples and families struggling to improve their relationships are in treatment with psychoanalysts. In this complex and often quite challenging clinical arena, the central goal remains true to Freud's and Melanie Klein's original vision, the cultivation of a therapeutic process aimed at modifying core unconscious conflicts and object relational dynamics.

In the previous Chapters, I have described a clinically based approach to defining psychoanalysis-termed Analytic Contact that emphasizes the understanding and modification of internal states rather than relying on external criteria such as frequency, diagnosis, or duration as the primary focus. As such, analytic contact involves the consistent exploration and interpretation of the patient's core phantasy states, which include self-object wishes, conflicts, fears, defences, and compromise solutions. In addition, the transference, counter-transference, extra-transference, interpersonal interactions, dreams, and the total intra-psychic landscape are given constant interpretive priority.

In conducting psychoanalytic couple's therapy, I also strive to build analytic contact. In establishing analytic contact with couples, I invite both parties to learn about their individual as well as mutually interlocking projections. In understanding, accepting, and working through their individual and jointly acted out conflicts regarding love and hate, the couple can begin to create a new ability to manage and modify their interpersonal, interactional, and intra-psychic experiences with themselves and their objects.

Literature

When it comes to the topic of couple's therapy, the analytic literature is relatively barren. While there are a far number of books with the words "couples therapy" in the title, there are very few with the words "psychoanalytic couples therapy" in the title. Usher (2007), Lachkar (1992), Grier (2005), and Ruszczynski (1993) are some of the books that do advocate a more Kleinian psychoanalytic approach to the work. Overall, there are many guides on how to work in a cognitive, behavioural, or psychodynamically informed manner with couples. However, there are far fewer books looking exclusively at a psychoanalytic approach to treating couples.

Even more interesting is the total of less than fifty articles that appear when searching the bulk of all psychoanalytic journals published internationally over the last hundred years. Many of these articles see couples therapy as something therapists do but not something usually practiced by psychoanalysts.

In this Chapter and the proceeding Chapter, couples treatment will be discussed as a psychoanalytic procedure equal to that of individual psychoanalytic therapy in therapeutic value but having some unique points of emphasis. In particular, the analyst works with two patients at the same time individually and later as a unified psychological matrix. Another element that stands out as unique in couples work is the concept of one party bearing witness to the other party's working through process and what that can mean for the each party's view of self and object. In addition, there are issues in thinking, phantasy, containment, and projective identification (Klein, 1946). Case material will be provided to illustrate these points.

Clinical strategy

Most couples enter treatment with the psychoanalyst suffering with various unconscious phantasies within the paranoid-schizoid position (Klein, 1946). It is often not until later in the treatment that either party can begin to find more of a psychological balance within depressive (Klein, 1935) functioning. Many authors describing their approach to couples therapy advocate the ongoing focus on the couple as a unified matrix instead of trying to simply analyse two individuals at the same time. This is certainly the right way to go if both parties are operating in the depressive mode and able to see past themselves and conceptualize the joint dynamic involved in the relationship. However, as mentioned, this is almost never the case until later in the treatment.

Therefore, I find it clinically necessary and therapeutically beneficial to begin by treating each party more as an individual until they can consider and work with the dynamics of the couple. At the same time, I am constantly advocating what I call "witnessing" as a supplemental method to slowly bring about more depressive perspectives in which each party can find empathy and understanding for the other and thereby take a closer look at themselves as a result. The ongoing attempt to establish analytic contact with each party first and then eventually with the couple along with the cultivation of "witnessing" are the two bedrock elements of psychoanalytic couples therapy as I see it. This therapeutic approach is held within the clinical context of container-contained, thinking, projective identification, and interpretation.

Container-contained

The container-contained model developed by Bion (1962a; 1962b) has become a cornerstone of theory and technique within the Kleinian community and is now regarded as clinically vital in many other camps. Many papers have examined the importance of the container function for normal mental development and many papers have explored the various perversions (Lamanno-Adamo, 2007) and corruptions that can take place within the container-contained experience. Spillius (1983) has summarized the links Bion made between the container-contained function, the components of thinking, and the dynamics of projective identification. I believe she is also identifying the core elements of psychoanalytic couple's therapy.

One important aspect of the container-contained principal comes into play with couples where in one party is far too disturbed or anxious to tolerate individual psychoanalytic treatment. The triangular, oedipal envelope of both parties being together with the analyst allows the disturbed individual to feel soothed, contained, and less prone to persecutory phantasies and transference anxieties. Of course, many of these more difficult patients will also feel ganged up on by the analyst and their partner, distorting the oedipal experience into a pair of critical, attacking parents. However, the containing environment of both analyst and the other partner can sometimes serve to better counterbalance this persecutory view of the world and provide space for analytic contact to take place. Exploration of transference states that would normally trigger severe acting out or complete flight from treatment can be cushioned by the combined presence of analyst and the other party.

Witnessing

A unique benefit of psychoanalytic couple's therapy involves the interpersonal, interactional, and intra-psychic witnessing of each party to the therapeutic relationship between the analyst and the other partner. Each party is witness to the exploration and working through of the other party's transference and phantasy state. Here, the container-contained situation, the analysis of problems with thinking, and the understanding of projective identification dynamics converge for the couple as they are individual observers as well as participants in a parallel process.

A significant curative function of psychoanalytic couple's therapy involves the witnessing of the self-object struggle in which each party must slowly take ownership of their conflicts rather than blame, deny, or split them off into their partner. It is typical for a couple to begin psychoanalytic treatment in a state where they are constantly blaming each other, only finding fault in each other due to projections of hostility, guilt, and conflict. In this more primitive, paranoid state, each party typically does not view the object as willing to consider their own flaws and thus each patient feels, "why should I take ownership of my faults if he/she never does." This is often experienced in an early parent/child manner in which there is a phantasy of a parental object refusing to be a container and always wanting to be superior to the child, never offering the model of reflection, regret, amends, and resolve. So, each patient is often locked into a projective identification cycle with objects that never admit fault and never want to make it better. These objects only seek narcissistic superiority and sadistic revenge. Other times, in an equally dysfunctional projective cycle, the object is a resentful victim, overburdened and wanting masochistic attention, unable to admit to any contribution to current problems.

If the analyst can engage each party in a therapeutic exploration of their inner world and establish analytic contact with them, the other party is witness to their externalized object's slow transformation. This can provide hope, trust, and increased willingness to do the same themselves. Over time and as a result of working through each parties individual issues in front of the other party, more understanding and compassion can emerge, engendering self-reflection, and a desire to help the other and change the self for the good of the relationship.

Certainly, with patients who are gravely disturbed, caught within strong internal conflicts and phantasies, there will be great resistance to internalizing this new view of the object. Envy, guilt, paranoid hostility, and narcissistic independence all preclude these positive witnessing experiences. However, as the analyst notes the negative reactions to being an observer to their object's honest struggle to change and learn, the analyst can interpret these pathological reactions. In doing so, it can provide a window of understanding for the other party about their resistant partner.

Each partner is distorted in the other party's mind by massive projections of other archaic phantasies. One of the central aims of psychoanalytic couples therapy, similar to the goals of individual psychoanalysis, is to help separate the reality of the external world from the patient's personal unconscious vision of the world. By observing their external love object working with the analyst, this psychic separation is easier to allow and to accept. In watching their partner differentiate between what they really feel about the relationship and what feelings and thoughts belong elsewhere, they can begin to do the same.

Often, one partner is more integrated than the other. Or, over the course of the treatment, one party is able to begin functioning in more of a depressive state than the other. The partner who has made more progress can often serve as a protective presence or container to the other when they feel persecuted by the analyst or by being in treatment. So, when the first party clings to their projected phantasy states, having the second party present often makes it easier to investigate the resistance to giving up their inner world of wishes and fears because the second partner can act as an encouraging, compassionate, curious, and trusted bystander.

Again, this can also go the other way when some patients are so paranoid or narcissistic that they feel overcome with shame or anxiety at the idea of having their partner view them in distress. Or, the distressed partner may feel the analyst and their partner are ganging up on them. This creates difficult moments but overall, the presence of another encouraging, containing object can elevate the escalating anxieties and bring about more windows of opportunity in the moment-to-moment work.

Certainly, it is possible to begin a couple's treatment where in neither party has any compassion or empathy for the other due to excessive paranoid (Klein, 1946) states of mind. In fact, many cases begin in this stormy manner. However, as each party is witness to the one-to-one exploration of their partner's issues with the help of the analyst and are given a window into understanding what sort of internal experiences fuel their partner's view of self and object, each partner can move towards a less defensive posture as they understand "where their partner is coming from" instead of seeing the partner as a faceless foe. This less conflicted view of the external and internal object can lead to a new openness and desire to change.

This process of bearing witness and the resulting internalization of new object relations brings about a new ability of negotiation, and tolerance. In addition, it provides a new oedipal experience in which one is able and willing to learn from others, internalize others, and feel supported by the image of a relationship (analyst and the other party) in which tension may arise but things can be worked out. Conflict is ok and resolution of conflict is possible. To be part of such a triangle provides the patient with a level of parental, oedipal containment that might be very different than the oedipal experiences they had with their family of origin.

At the same time, prior oedipal experiences of trauma, loss, and aggression may be triggered by the couple's therapy and acted out in the treatment. In these cases, one patient may try and side with the analyst against the other party, creating unworkable depressive or paranoid conflict between the analyst and the other party or they may feel fearful, envious, or rejected by the oedipal situation in a manner that causes them to retreat or react aggressively. These competitive, withdrawing, or aggressive responses need to be carefully interpreted and followed through to avoid collapse of the treatment setting.

By bonding with the exploratory, curious stance of the analyst, the patient can observe and understand their partner in a new way, from a safe distance. In this way, they begin to establish a sense of seeing and knowing the other, rather than feeling consumed, burdened, or attacked. Part of the new oedipal experience is feeling the analyst/parent offers some buffer or safe envelope from the other party/parent if there is any danger or dispute. The child must trust that each parent will act as a container/buffer if the other parent temporarily fails at being a container/protector. In this sense, the analyst acts as an emotional referee in both an external reality-based manner but also in a very important unconscious, internal manner for the patient who has lived life devoid of that security, safety, and trust.

Klein (1928; 1931) wrote about the child's instinctual need to learn as part of normal growth and object relationship. When development is hindered in some manner, this need can become more defensive and become a need to know all so as to control and master the object. Bion (1962b) elaborated on these ideas and explored the mutual dependency necessary for healthy learning and knowledge to unfold. Bion emphasized that learning comes from the container object being willing and able to be flexible and open to new experiences. The contained self internalizes this flexible, open, yet psychologically defined and separate container object and thus learns how to learn. If the object is defensive and rigid to these new experiences, instead of being receptive, knowledge is blunted or blocked.

In psychoanalytic couple's therapy, this process takes place within the interpersonal, interactional, and intra-psychic sphere of each party, as well as the combined couple, as they relate with the analyst. Hopefully, over time, one party can become part of the flexible, growth-directed relating. And, as this occurs, the second party is witness to this healthy expansion of container-contained and therefore can be more forgiving to their previously rigid, cruel, or threatening image of their object. As they reduce their hostile or frightening phantasies of their object by reducing their attacking projections, there is opportunity to take in their partner as a more welcoming, helpful container. In a positive cycle, they can then develop the desire to be a warm, healing container towards their object as well.

However, Bion and others (Joseph, 1982; Segal, 1981; Waska, 2005) have noted how envy can play a destructive role in the development of knowledge, the acceptance of growth and change in the container, and the acknowledgement of mutual dependence.

Bion (1962b) points out that envy can create a hatred of any new development in the self or object and phantasies emerge of a hatred rival that must be punished, eliminated, or destroyed. The healing process of psychoanalytic couples treatment that involves "getting to know each other and getting to know oneself better" can only occur when each party can tolerate the pain, fear, guilt, and confusion of not knowing, not immediately changing, or not immediately seeing change in the other. Giving and receiving are part of this, as change in each other involves a natural give and take process. If these dynamics trigger too much guilt or feel too persecutory, the patient may employ massive projective identification attacks on the other party, the analyst, or both. Through these attacks, the patient may try to both deny separateness and create the phantasy of fusion or they may try to create great emotional distance, producing a sense of isolation and alienation in the other. Of course, these pathological processes inevitably boomerang back to haunt the patient with feelings of claustrophobia or loss and abandonment.

As Waddel (2002) notes, healthy learning and knowledge require the ego ability to tolerate never knowing everything, not being able to immediately know, and the uncertain imperfection of sometimes doubting what one knows and being willing to upgrade, disregard, or question what one has relied on up to now.

Projective identification, thinking, and interpretation

Thinking is a natural process that becomes hindered or corrupted by defences against conflicts and traumatic phantasy states. In many of our more disturbed patients, the experience of independent thought creates great anxiety regarding separation and loss (Quinodoz, 1993). In psychoanalytic couple's therapy, the analyst commonly finds one or both partners to have trouble with reflective, emotionally focused thinking and to suffer with phantasies regarding the threat that thinking poses to either self or object. Tuch (2007) believes our interpretations are not as helpful with this problem as our ability to tolerate the patient's view of us in the transference, until they can see we have survived their distorted view. I would agree that this container function is critical with difficult patients but I believe we must tolerate and accept the patient's transference and phantasy state while we make careful and thoughtful interpretations. Letting the patient see that we are thinking independently while we interdependently relate with and to their projections provides them with the view of an object that has not only survived, but is not retaliating. It is offering them a non-collapsed, none-offended object that can be separate as well as connected.

Even if the patient cannot assimilate interpretations in the moment, he is being shown that the analyst can think about him in a thoughtful and interested manner. Both parties of the couple are therefore shown a model of concern and interest that may be internalized at some point as a counterbalance to their more warlike view of self and object. This is important because so many couples come to treatment in a state of mutual blame, acting out, and massive projective identification that erodes the capacity to think and to allow the object permission to think.

Another element of psychoanalytic couple's treatment has to do with patients who are afraid to think for themselves as a result of a variety of depressive or paranoid phantasy conflicts. Their partner may try over and over to communicate with them, but this is felt by the patient to be a challenge to think, which triggers various counter-measures to avoid mental catastrophe. The more the analyst or partner tries to encourage the patient to think, the more the patient will shut down any efforts at thinking, creating frustration and counter-transference reactions in their object, who may either distance or bully in turn. I find it common for one patient to pull me to do the thinking for him or for the couple and the other partner in turn to feel threatened by my thinking, especially if it is a counter-transference reaction to the first party's phantasy agenda. Steiner (2007) has noted the pull for the analyst to become not just the thinker for the patient but the critical superego, thinking judgementally.

Many couples enter psychoanalytic couples treatment removed from their paranoid and depressive problems by hiding the emotional pain and conflict of their relationship within a psychic retreat (Steiner, 1993). When the analyst invites the couple to think and feel about their individual and couples dynamics, this is experienced as a threat to the psychic retreat. Britton (2001) has written about the analytic goal of helping patients establish a progressive oscillation between the paranoid and depressive positions. Again, the desire to avoid thinking and having to face certain anxiety-producing phantasies will not only prevent such positive cycles of oscillation and psychological growth in individuals or couples, but also engenders a reliance on pathological projective identification systems that block thinking and create corruptive and negative oscillations between paranoid and depressive states. Thus, the worse aspects of both psychic experiences flood the couple's relationship, eliminating thinking and creating more chaotic levels of anxiety, acting out, and defence.

Without thinking, without trust in a container, and caught within intense cycles of projective identification, the couple often is reduced to basic concrete functioning and stubborn patterns of acting out. The analyst may have to spend a great deal of time investigating the deeper meaning of the couple's focus on concrete objects (Selon, 2006). Gradual interpretive translation can bring the couple back to the realm of thinking and more into a focus on their hopes, wishes, fears, grief, and anger towards themselves and each other, in a manner that is accessible and workable. Analytic contact is difficult with couples like this but essential to continuously strive for.

One important aspect of this continued effort at analytic contact is the dual interpretation of not only the current pain, grief, guilt, and fear the couple is eluding, but the unknown future of their relationship if they give up the current struggles and begin to change. Indeed, some couples come into treatment wanting to change but when change actually becomes a viable possibility, they construct a mutual defensive stance against it.

Psychoanalytic couple's therapy is quite taxing on the analyst as there are essentially three entities to work with at all times. There is each individual's internal state as well as the matrix of the couple's psychology. The couple's defensive and repetitive stance is hard to change because the letting go, loss, grief, unknown future, differences that change brings, and the ongoing active emotional expression that must take place all bring out intense paranoid and depressive reactions. Each party in the couple initially feels threatened or traumatized by the destabilization of the prior psychic system. However, establishing new and healthy compromises and changing old internal object relational bargains can gradually be experienced as a friendly and helpful move forward that actually becomes reinforced by new paranoid or depressive phantasies that are growth orientated. In other words, the depressive patient can begin to feel, "oh, so you are not threatened or hurt by my confidence and opinions. It is ok for me to express myself and you actually like me better that way. My desire to please you and not hurt you used to mean I needed to crush my own desires. Now, I realize it not only pleases you but it benefits me to be myself. Now, I feel encouraged to express myself. I respect myself more and I know I am helping you too."

Similarly, the paranoid patient might begin to feel; "now I see that you probably won't attack me for my new confidence so I feel safe to be myself. I don't feel like I am bad and am about to be hurt or abandoned anymore." The core issues of being caught up within a rigid system of either paranoid or depressive phantasies may still need to be worked through for a better integration and balance, but couples therapy can help to mitigate the more severe aspects of these pathological states for both the individual and mutual mindsets.

Another curative element of psychoanalytic couple's treatment is the focus on each patient to take ownership of their contributions to the couple's mutual problems and projective identification matrix. Several helpful situations occur in this realm. First, the patient is encouraged to examine their own contribution to both their partner's anxieties as well as the overall dysfunction of the couple. Usually, both partners enter treatment either denying any ownership of contribution or one party will feel so guilty that they claim all ownership while the other partner denies any culpability. So, the analyst is in effect encouraging integrative depressive position experiences by asking the patient to look at how they are affecting others. This helps create both a new sense of active participation in the relationship, of personal agency and an ability to master and succeed, along with a desire to repair, resolve, forgive, and restore. Give and take is no longer experienced in pathological excess, but more as healthy components to a loving relationship. Instead of "they did a bad thing first so I justifiably reacted in revenge," there can be an empathic curiosity about "why did they say that, what could be going on for them right now that made them act that way" along with "I want to not just react to his/her stuff, I want to be able to communicate how I am honestly feeling so we can make it over this impasse and see each others point of view."

For all these changes and transformations to take place in the course of psychoanalytic couple's therapy, each party must be willing to work on their own psychological issues. It can be very helpful if each party is also in individual treatment, but either way, I believe there needs to be a partial individual analysis that takes place in the presence of the other. Obviously, this analysis is different than what occurs in an individual psychoanalysis, but it still can contain the basic elements of such exploration. As already outlined, the benefits of doing this in front of the other party (witnessing) are invaluable. Both parties get to see that the analyst is not destroyed by the partner's projections and the analyst doesn't retaliate in aggressive ways. As a result, the patient begins to feel it might be ok for them to test the same waters with their partner. Also, by working out some of their over reliance on projective identification with the analyst, they can begin to sort out their unhealthy relationship with their partner without relying so much on their usual defences. When the patient sees conflict with the analyst can be worked out and healthy compromises and resolution occur, the patient gets the idea that they could do that with their partner as well. Meanwhile, their partner is witness to this same reassuring process and can approach the couple's issues without so much fear and anger. Conducting this partial analysis of each patient while the other partner is present also shows each party that while they are both different and unique, separation is safe and workable, rather than being so threatening that there is a defensive demand for unity and singularity.

Now, difference and even each party's separate relationship with the analyst can be experienced as positive, restorative, and forgiving. This leads to the formation of empathic curiosity rather than fear of difference. The right to personal privacy and breathing room is no longer experienced as exclusion or forced banishment. Wanting to know more about each other as a way towards healing replaces the experience of emotional suffocation. The instinctual desire for knowledge and truth can flourish in a healthy relational manner rather than a competitive or intrusive manner. The more each party can think about and tolerate their own conflicts, the more they can think about and tolerate the object. This reduces the need for reliance on the aggressive aspects of projective identification.

Ideally, interpretation should be aimed at the couple's mutual transference to each other, at the couple's transference to the analyst, and at each individual's transference and phantasy state to the analyst (Nathans, 2007). In addition, I believe it is clinically important to establish a line of investigation and interpretation into the couple's mutual projective identification match in which certain desired, yet threatening and guilt-ridden aspects of the self are projected into the partner for safe keeping, for escape from incrimination, and for communication.

However, as I have explained, most couples enter treatment in more of a primitive paranoid state and benefit from more of a focus on their individual pathology in the presence of their partner. Over time, the working through of their own projections and phantasies combined with the benefits of "witnessing" can bring them to a more receptive and depressive stance in which they can expand their awareness to the union of the couple and its duality.

At that point, they can work on their own need to project into their partner without it being an automatic process that rules the relationship. They can start to appreciate each other's need to use the other as a container for certain projections and start to have an understanding, appreciation, and a choice in that psychological relational dynamic. At that point, the analytic focus would be on the couple as a joint dynamic entity, constantly influencing each other in mutually beneficial ways.

In other words, it is common for people to seek out a partner who can act as a vehicle for the wishes, hopes, and opinions they feel frightened, guilty, or threatened by. They are able to use this partner in a healthy symbiosis where in they find vicarious satisfaction by having the partner contain and live out these overwhelming, forbidden, or unorganized pieces of their personality. Thus, the person finds understanding and acceptance by being in the shadow of their own projections. This idea of the healthy aspects of projective identification has been explored by Bion (1959) and Rosenfeld (1987). The interpretation of the positive, loving, or communicative aspects of projective identification is an approach favoured by some analysts and not by others (Waska, 2004). Personally, I find it to be a helpful aspect of psychoanalytic couple's treatment.

When projective identification is being used as a vehicle for forbidden, frightening, or toxic aspects of the self, the patient's strong projections end up experienced as overwhelming, damaging, unwanted, and foreign to the object. This brings about phantasies in which the object is a withholding, rejecting, broken, or angry container. There is a shift to pathological envy or pathological avoidance of the projected elements, leaving the ego feeling starved, attacked, or betrayed. It is in this state of dread and rage that many couples enter treatment. Therefore, their mutual defensive avoidance of thinking, usually aimed at blocking the analyst's interpretations, needs to be analysed and worked through so the couple's intense reliance on pathological projective identification can be addressed.

Psychoanalytic couple's therapy should minimally aim to rebalance the mutual projective identification system so that the couple is at least restored to its prior state of projective identification, if indeed a healthy cycle actually existed prior to their need for treatment. However, the primary and more ideal goal of treatment is to find the hidden potential of better psychological health and integration. If an individual or couple leaves treatment reset to a prior level of functioning that was and now is once again balanced and developmentally vibrant, we have done a fine job. But, if we can show the couple how their individual and mutual mindset works, how and why their defences emerge, and how their core conflicts manifest within their transference, projective identification and phantasy states, then they have more emotional choices in their lives than ever before. This can hopefully lead to a path of new growth and change not only within the treatment setting but long after termination. In this way, we help the couple realize their full psychic potential as a unit and as separate persons, opening their eyes to better acceptance of each other and providing a lasting capacity for psychological transformation as individuals and as a couple.

Case material

C and D came into treatment when their three-year marriage was at a critical impasse. After having their first child, "as agreed upon,"

D now wanted to have a second child. At the first session, D said she "loved being a mother and wanted her child to have a brother or sister to go through life with, enjoying the companionship and sharing the joy of being a family." C said he felt very uncomfortable with the idea of another child because he "already felt enormous pressure and a great deal of stress keeping up with their one child along with everything else going on in life." C described being overwhelmed by "the feeding, the changing, the scheduling, the disruption of our life, the giving up of what we used to have, the responsibility, and the financial challenge." I said, "If you are so convinced your child is a burden, it must be hard to notice the fun, the positive changes he brings to your life, and the love he has for you." C said, "Don't get me wrong. I love the little guy, but it is not what I really wanted to start with. I understood that D really wanted a child and we talked about it for a long time. I saw how it was a real deal-breaker for her so I agreed to one child. But, the idea of having this amount of stress doubled is too much to think about. Also, in the last two years, I started a new job, we moved in together, we got married, we had a child, —wow!"

I noticed D was mostly listening to C and didn't seem very much in touch with herself in the moment. So, I asked her what she was feeling or thinking. She explained that "for her this was not a question of stress or burden. It was a decision to better our lives and to enjoy the growth of our family. It isn't about finances, responsibilities, or stress. It is about the love we feel for each other and our family. This is very important to me. This is part of my dream in life and I feel like C is taking that away." She began to cry and added "I won't let him do that. If that is where he is at, I have started to think that maybe I need to protect myself and stay true to myself."

C said, "I know you have told me that if I can't be on board with this you may have to seek out someone else who would want what you want." D nodded yes. At that point, I interpreted, "it seems like one way you are both at a crossroads is that C feels he is being made to take in something that feels threatening. He feels forced to give into something that feels overwhelming. On the other hand, D seems to feel like her dream is being taken away and her core needs are being ignored and invalidated. With those kinds of strong feelings, you both are ready to either retreat or to fight for your safety and needs."

Here, I was interpreting what I thought to be a mutual projective identification cycle. I explained that I thought C felt a basic paranoid threat of having to give into D's demand. He felt like she would be invading and overwhelming him. D felt like C was about to steal her core dream and that would leave her without love and happiness, in a state of loss. Indeed, she seemed to be driven to always avoid loss, trying to be positive and upbeat at all times. Everything had such a silver lining I was suspicious about where all the clouds might be. So, they both were reacting to these primitive threats. It was a frightening give and take system in which C felt forced to give and D was convinced something dear to her would be taken.

It was interesting how they responded to my interpretations. C told me he was from a family in which, "when he was ten years old, his parents announced their divorce out of the blue. There was no warning and I never saw it coming. It was devastating." C went on to say he "thought his childhood experiences left him with a basic mistrust in relationships, especially in marriage. And, the idea of having a child and putting them at risk for the same kind of devastation was something he would make sure to prevent." C explained that "it was a big deal to agree to live together, an incredible leap to trust that we could weather marriage, and an even bigger risk to agree to have a child. But, to do that again would be to double the risk to myself and the child." I interpreted, "you say the risk to yourself and your child. So, maybe you feel like both an unwilling parent and a scared child." He stopped and thought. C said, "I never picture it quite like that but I think that is exactly right. I can't see the difference though; I feel both things all the time." Here, he was relaying the internal burden of being overly identified with his burdened father and feeling trapped in his memory of being an unwanted, scared child.

Since C seemed to feel so very alone in all of his phantasies and anxieties, I commented, "You talk like you have to shoulder the majority of the burden of the childcare, the finances, the responsibilities. Is that true?" D answered, "That is part of why I am so frustrated. In fact, I do the bulk of our bills, I stayed at home for the first seven months after our baby was born, and I still do most of the housework. And, I don't see it as work, I see taking care of our child as fun and fulfilling. Sure there is lots of hard work, but it is our child! I love him!"

At that point, C said, "I can't guarantee that in four or five weeks of coming to this therapy I will be able to turn my feelings around and agree to what you want. I just can't guarantee that." I saw this as a reaction to D's overly positive attitude in which there was a denial of any difficulties. I thought that this created a lack of container-contained for C and instead fuelled an overly negative↔overly positive projective identification process between them. So, first I interpreted that by saying, "it looks like you both get into a standoff with each other where D is always positive and optimistic and C is always negative and pessimistic. Then, you both react to each other being that way." Then, I choose to interpret the transference phantasy that C had shown in his remark.

I interpreted, "Since D never put that demand on you, it is you who is suddenly putting a deadline on us and then feeling the pressure that something could collapse if you don't manage to meet that deadline. So, out of the blue, you are creating a feeling of fear and you are all alone to make it happen or else. You are making our relationship here today something that could suddenly collapse in a few weeks, out of the blue, much like you described your experiences as a child when your parents divorced."

This was a transference comment about his lack of trust in the treatment container after he projected such demand and uncertainty into it. As a result, C felt overwhelmed in trying to manage his anxiety on his own without a reliable container to help. In fact, he converted the container into an unpredictable pressure cooker that made him feel more and more anxious. He replied, "I think I see what you mean. I can try and slow it down, but I do feel D has a timetable." D said, "I do have a timetable, but the more important thing to me is to know you are willing to look at this with me. I don't want to feel like I am over here waiting by myself to see how my future will turn out." Noticing the in-the-moment nature of their anxieties, I said, "We have to stop for today, but you both just indicated how alone you feel in this issue. It shows us how you both have ended up feeling like the other person is against you instead of being a team trying to sort it out." Here I was commenting on the isolating experience of being within the phantasies of a mutual projective identification system that left each party separate, angry, lost, and frightened.

For the first session of a psychoanalytic couple's treatment, there was a great deal of material covered and some core patterns revealed. The act of witnessing each other's struggle with private internal conflicts was important but too early in treatment for it to make much impact on either party. I think it was too early for this process to really have much counterbalance to the already entrenched sense of wrong and blame each had for the other. Indeed, the more depressive position responses that this witnessing can engender were prevented by the more paranoid outlook each had for the other. Given this, it was an optimistic sign that both parties were willing to explore their conflicts without too much initial defensive reaction or acting out. Therefore, the prognosis for gradual analytic contact and a working through of mutual projective identification, phantasy, and transference states was positive.

In the second session, C and D made more inroads to understanding themselves and their relationship to each other. When talking about recent family activities, it was striking how polarized C and D were. In describing a trip to the beach over the weekend, D remembered it as idyllic, with "the family functioning as a unit and everyone enjoying themselves." When relaying the problem of a flat tire and waiting for hours for the tow truck, she said it "was a great time. We just made up games to play and enjoyed the good weather." For C, it was a "grueling hell, stuck in the hot sun, waiting forever with a cranky kid." I pointed out that they both maintained this polarized way of relating, possibility providing some balance for each others extreme views of the world. I said that this way of relating may have been soothing and seductive in the beginning but now has become a source of trouble. At that point, C said, "I don't know if I will ever be able to see things differently. This is just me and I have always been like this. I can't see myself changing anytime soon." He said this to me in a way that was full of anxiety, pressure, and obligation.

This was a moment of transference anxiety and I interpreted, "you seem to feel under the thumb of this therapy to hurry up and please me and D. You are anxious that you have to change for us and you are not sure you can pull it off." C said, "You are right. I don't know if I can pull it off." I replied, "We need to understand why you put yourself under such pressure to please us, since we aren't demanding that from you."

This interpretation seemed to allow C to open up and be less withholding. He began to talk about his experience of being a parent and how hard it has been. He went on to describe the many ways he felt burdened and overwhelmed by all the obligations of parenting. I remarked, "Your view of having to do it right which makes it all so difficult and miserable seems to mask the pleasures you might also be having. I get the impression you do love your child." C said, "Oh yes, I really do. And, I do enjoy time with her and watching her grow up. It is incredible. But, I am always waiting for it to get harder and I am worried another child would just put me over the edge."

At that point, I had the counter-transference impression that he was now talking about a feeling from his past, not actually connected to the reality of his current life, but more of an internal experience with a historical object. So, I said, "I wonder if you are talking about a feeling from your past that is coloring the way you see the world now." C said, "It is the way my father felt all the time, completely overwhelmed and unable to provide any emotional stability. My mother was a heavy drinker and I had no relationship with her to speak of. I got along with my father and saw him as the one stable force in the house. But, he was completely squashed by the experience of being married and having kids and didn't really want to be a part of it. I think it must have been such a relief for him to divorce my mother." I said, "But that left you with nothing, all alone." C said, "Yes, that was the hardest period in my life. I was so lonely. It is a time that is like a block of ice, cold and dark. All I wanted was for my father to play ball with me, go to one of my games, or just talk to me. But, he didn't want to." C fell silent, visibly depressed, and shaken by his recollection.

D broke down sobbing. She took several minutes to collect herself and then was able to share that she "was overcome with how terrible it was for C and she never realized he had suffered so much. I feel so bad for him!" She continued sobbing and threw her arms around C. This was an important moment in the treatment for several reasons. For D, she was suddenly able to step out of her overly optimistic love conquers all attitude and realize the pain and suffering C still lived with. She could share his grief and sorrow. This witnessing of his own working through process in psychoanalytic therapy enabled her to find a new way of seeing him and a new way of considering the world. In that moment, the usual ways they related to each other and the pathological projective identification system they relied on shifted.

For a few minutes afterwards, C was able to elaborate on his memories and feelings. I interpreted that he was possibly caught between identifications with his father, seeing his own children as he pictured his father felt about him, and his own resentment at his father for being unavailable. Some of this seemed to make a great deal of sense to C as well as to D. However, it was a multilayered idea regarding his deep phantasies that would need to be explored over the course of many future sessions to really bear fruit.

So, this session demonstrates a successful psychoanalytic treatment with a couple. It is typical of an outpatient treatment performed by a psychoanalyst using the classic technical elements of psychoanalysis. Specifically, I was attempting to establish analytic contact with both individuals and we initially worked on their more paranoid phantasies. I interpreted their individual and joint fears and conflicts and they "witnessed" the other working on their own projections and slowly moving into more depressive functioning. Then, they started to deal with the relationship as a mutual matrix that had a life of its own to which each contributed particular elements to form a unique combined couple's profile.

This treatment of C and D, even at this early stage, can be considered a psychoanalytic procedure because of the establishment of analytic contact (Waska, 2006; 2007). Rather than needing to be tethered to external criteria such as frequency, diagnosis, duration, or use of couch, analytic contact focuses on the exploration of transference, phantasy, defences, and internal conflicts.

With psychoanalytic couples work, much of the successful analytic contact comes out of the exploration of transference, mutual projective identification cycles, the ability to freely think, and the act of witnessing one's partner involved in deep psychological reflection. In only two visits, the case of C and D illustrates the importance of analytic contact and the utility of psychoanalytic couple's treatment. Obviously, this is only the beginning of a much longer therapeutic process but it provides a window into the clinical benefits of treating couples within a psychoanalytic framework.

CHAPTER EIGHT

Clinical issues in couples treatment

Case 1

E and F came to me for couple's treatment because of a seemingly concrete external problem. E had wanted to move to another part of the state "to get away from the crazy, over inflated lifestyle of money, cars, and commutes." She wanted a slower paced, easier lifestyle in which she could "get back to what is important, a sense of ourselves and nature." F was in agreement but E felt he had been "dragging his heels and never really making an effort to make it happen." F said, "I have been making the effort. I have been researching the move every month almost, for a long time. She is just too moody and critical." In fact, they both had been talking for years about moving out of the city to the country somewhere where the cost of living was less. They read magazines, did internet research, and talked with people who had made such a move. But, even thought it seemed like they were on the same page with this idea, E said that every time they were close to actually acting on their dream, "F finds something wrong with the plan and shoots it down. I am so frustrated at this point, I feel at a crossroads. I am getting too old to just be on hold.

I can't go on living like this. I need to see some kind of proof that F really means what he says or I think we are in serious trouble."

In response, F would say, "There you go again. You make threats and get so hysterical. I am making efforts all the time but you seem to just want to ignore them and get worked up instead. Obviously, this therapy thing is bullshit. If we want to have this kind of useless discussion, we can do it in private and not have to pay a stranger to listen." It came out over the next six months that F was coming to treatment to "stop her from hassling me all the time about something that isn't really a problem in the first place."

Also, F told me he was "a private person who has no respect for the field of psychology and sees marital problems as a private matter to be settled at home. But, in our case, I don't think we have any problems. The things E brings up are normal topics of conversation every husband and wife has, not something to take to a psychotherapist! We are doing fine as a couple. E just makes a big deal out of everything and blows it all out of proportion."

To this, E reacted and said, "You have no clue what is going on in this marriage. You are so unmotivated and lazy. I am not happy anymore and am serious about having to weigh all my options!" I asked if she really meant her threat of divorcing or was she just trying to find a way to have communication with F. E said "Divorce comes up in my thinking more and more when F doesn't want to engage me in any of these issues!" F shot back, "Any of these issues? What fucking issues? See! You are just making up crap now and creating problems. If you need to exit this marriage, go ahead. If you are done, then you are done. But, I am not going to listen to this crap anymore. I don't think I need to be here." At that point, he walked out of the office.

E and F continued to come to psychoanalytic couple's therapy for the next nine months. Much of their dynamic was a repeat of the material just presented. I was struck by how within their mutual projective identification cycle, E was prone to volatile, shifting ideas, opinions, and moods. She would go from feeling like the marriage was "over, hopeless, and useless" to "feeling like we are in a good place, really on the same page" in the same week and sometimes in the same session.

The more I investigated these psychological shifts, I noticed that much of it was a reaction to her feelings to her object. There was no real thought, only reaction. Indeed, it was a form of non-thinking.

In other words, in place of thinking, she had a desperate, angry, wild reaction to what she felt to be F's lack of caring, lack of motivation, and lack of love. She would blurt out whatever reactionary feeling she was having to anger, guilt, hopelessness, or fear, leaving herself and those around her either confused or reacting back. I gradually and tentatively interpreted that she felt such a combination of guilt, anger, fear, and desperation that she was like an emotional Ping-Pong whenever she thought about her relationship. Over time, I added that she related to me that way as well. The one very significant moment in which E was emotionally centred and able to not confuse herself was when she shared her great sorrow over never being close to her father. Now that he was dead, she "felt that chance was gone forever." I interpreted that this unresolved relationship seemed to be alive in the marriage and at times in the transference.

With F, he seemed stubbornly encased in his defensive shell, not wanting to share any part of himself. He said he was fine with life as is and resented any move to change it. The more he felt pushed by his wife or analyst to reveal his feelings or to make changes in his way of being, the more he resisted and took an independent, angry stance. I interpreted this projective cycle he had with E and with myself. This line of interpretation and exploration reduced their level of conflict for awhile, providing room to explore their needs and the emotional obstacles they put in the way.

However, along with this progress, I would also become a part of their more dysfunctional projective cycle. For periods of time, when they would become embroiled in a debate about moving or not moving, I would find myself slipping into that defensive posture as well. I found myself suggesting places to move to or reasons to not move. Fortunately, I could quickly see the ridiculous position I was in when I was becoming passionate about why they should consider coastal locations over mountain regions. I would then point out how we had all become very focused on something that kept us from exploring the feelings and difficult conflicts that were in the air. In other words, we were defensively moving away from deeper problems, moving was a symbolic defence against facing their fears and conflicts.

In fits and starts, E and F were able to explore their confusion about what they really wanted out of life and how they viewed their marriage. We would get closer to understanding some of this when E would lash out in her hysterical manner and ping-pong between saying everything was fine and everything was terrible. Then, F would lash out against me and therapy in general and tell E that "all she needed to do was calm down and stop complaining." At one point, E seemed to be able to focus more on her feelings and needs and she began to bring up topics that were more organized about her specific wants and how she felt unsatisfied in the relationship. When E brought up her unhappiness with their sex life, F said she "was totally out of line opening up something so personal in front of a stranger and if she didn't like the marriage, she would have to make some decisions!" He stopped attending at that point, but E continued seeing me. Unfortunately, this is not uncommon when working with more disturbed couples where either one or both parties have destructive patterns of acting and reacting to the object.

Over the next twelve months, there was both a continuation of E's patterns along with a significant shift in her dynamics. In the transference, there was a continuation of her scattered thinking when she tried to express herself to me. I interpreted that most of the time this amounted to her relating her feelings first in an exaggerated black and white way followed by a massive retraction, negation, and dismissal. Over time, I was less and less prone to being swept up into these mood storms and erratic declarations. Instead of getting lost in the content of what she was saying, a part of the mutual projective identification process she had with F and now with me, I was slowly able to interpret the thoughts and emotion she had which were causing so much defensive reaction. So, after she told me she "was completely over it! I think I am ready to look at life beyond F and this constant stagnation," I would say, "right now with me you are feeling something very strong. You are talking about leaving the marriage but I am not sure what exactly you are feeling right now." This type of interpretation would lead to her telling me she "felt scared, tired, frustrated, and alone." Then, I could ask her how she felt alone, as that seemed to be the leading edge of her anxiety. E would respond, "I don't feel like I can talk to E, we are not able to see eye to eye." I interpreted that perhaps she was speaking to him like she spoke to me, with an emotional shotgun blast that was difficult to understand at first and easy to be detoured by.

These sorts of interpretations led to a change at home. E reported that when she "got all worked up" at home, she "tried to focus on my feelings like you point out and I was able to calmly tell F that I was unhappy with x, y, and z. He actually listened and told me he is worried that I am unhappy and he wants to work together to try and make things better." So, E's ability to think and feel was slowly enhanced as she reduced her emotional shotgun approach.

Working on the transference aspects of this gradually opened up our understanding to the genetic source of this behaviour. After about six months of seeing me individually, E told me she remembered her father as someone "who was never available emotionally. I wanted to be the girl on television who could run to daddy and get help and love and attention. But, he wasn't like that. He was a strict disciplinarian who had rules for everything. We couldn't do this and we had to do that. It was all about rules. I never felt I could approach him to talk about anything. When I did, I felt frozen and would just ramble on about whatever and he would say, 'get to the point' and I didn't know what my point was."

I commented how important this memory was in that it was a direct parallel to our relationship. She had a hard time "getting to the point" and I sensed that she saw me as an authority whom she was so anxious to respect and please that she didn't know how to really relate to me. I said she was confused with how to think or feel around the authority figures of her father, her husband, and her analyst. She either retreated into not saying anything or she verbalized her conflicted, confused feelings in a way that brought out the authoritarian stance in the object. This was a real turning point in the analytic work and E began to experiment with allowing herself room to think and feel, sharing her deeper feelings with me and her husband more often.

Over the following months, she reported their sex life "was alive again" due to her "talking about it in a different way, realizing how I felt and dealing with the anger, hurt, and hopelessness before I opened my mouth." She reported that they were working together on a plan about when and where to move to and "it was suddenly fun and exciting, a project we are doing together."

Certainly, it would have been better if F could have remained in treatment and worked on himself just as E did. However, there are many times in psychoanalytic practice when the combination of external factors and psychological issues bring about a less than ideal therapeutic situation. However, if the analyst can remain steadfast in their goal of establishing and maintaining analytic contact, the work can be extremely beneficial and lasting.

Case 2

A and B came to see me on the request of B's psychiatrist who had been seeing her for many years to prescribe multiple anti-psychotics and mood stabilizers. A and B were married and B was now pregnant. A worked in a clothing store as an assistant manager and had always been a devoted husband and provider. He was "the stable one" according to B, which lead me to think of how their projective identification system was setup with him as the stable one and her as the unstable one.

B had been raised in a chaotic family and lived in a poor, crime-ridden area of town with her mother, after her parents divorced when B was ten. Starting at age twenty and up to now at age thirty-six, she had periodic psychotic breakdowns, major depressive episodes, and manic outbursts. After several hospitalizations, she was maintained on high doses of five different medications. While she worked at a small job in her twenties, she has not been able to hold down a job for the last ten years. B brought in a small amount of money from psychiatric disability checks, but relied on A to pay the rent and bills.

Even though she was against it but "went along with it to please him and to stop him from nagging her," they had decided to have a baby. This decision brought on a new level of fighting between them and a deeper level of fragmentation in B. Her psychiatrist had advised against having a baby, telling her she was sure to be hospitalized when she reduced her medications during pregnancy. So, her psychiatrist suggested she begin couples therapy to "have a psychological safety net" during her pregnancy.

A and B began seeing me once or twice a week, depending on what they could afford that month, their schedule, and their motivation that week. They initially told me they wanted help with B's psychological state as she reduced her medications, "help with the relationship," and direction on how to co-parent effectively. Very quickly, I was aware that B related in borderline, narcissistic, and psychotic ways during most of each session. Sometimes, it was very difficult to talk with her because she was so manic or delusional.

She was hospitalized several times in the first two years of treatment and often said she was scared to see me or be near my office unless she was with A.

Other times, she saw me as a peer and talked wildly about going to medical school and becoming an analyst. She said, "I think the state would give me a job coach and I could easily get through the school in a couple of years and start curing people right away!"

This delusion came up enough times that I took several approaches with it. Initially, I was swept up in a counter-transference role in which I took a more stern authority role, echoing her superego problems. I would remind her that she was about to have a child and that she was ignoring her role as mother. When I realized I was doing this, I interpreted she might be anxious with a feeling of obligation or responsibility to become a mother. She was able to say, "This is not what I wanted out of life, I think this is a mistake." She would then reverse her statement by saying, "I am looking forward to having a family and taking care of my babies." When I pointed out her conflict and reversal, she was unable to think about it at all.

Also, I interpreted that B wanted to be close to me but didn't know how to be herself while being close without having to become a clone of me and then we could both be doctors saving others. I said it might be scary to realize she needed to depend on me and be helped by me so she had to change our doctor-patient relationship into a doctor-doctor relationship. She acknowledged she was "uneasy depending on me" and in the same breath said she "felt nothing was wrong with her so she just wanted to find a job and start school."

I asked B if she might be anxious about becoming a mother and wanted to run away to medical school instead. She told me she could "easily do both and didn't think the baby would be a big bother." I interpreted that B was seeing herself as separate from the anxiety and hardship most mothers feel so she also didn't have any sense of excitement or joy about it either. She had sealed herself off from the object (her pregnancy) in a state of disconnection. I said that left her empty so she felt depressed some times and had to manically fill herself up other times. This interested A because B had continuously put them into debt with spending sprees at the mail and late night calls to purchase various television offers. B responded, "I feel like I don't have anything when I lay in bed. I don't feel anything.

There is nothing." A seemed to find some new compassion and understanding for what usually felt like a deliberate betrayal. He was witness to her gradually sharing the underlying feelings and phantasies that led her to some of her more psychotic behaviours. In addition, I felt her remarks were a small breakthrough to her transference of either fear or nothingness with me and a confirmation of what I thought to be a projective identification system of omnipotence and alienation.

Reflecting on my own feelings was helpful in that when she was so disorganized in the session, I felt like I was failing her as a container. Instead of an inviting, safe container, I pictured that she must view me as some sort of persecutory cage to always avoid, leaving her uncontained and scattered. As we proceeded, this transference phantasy was mixed with a genuine trust and desire for comfort, but it was a very fragile, tentative trust.

A was remarkably in denial about B's condition when we began psychoanalytic couple's therapy. He treated her like an immature child who had to be helped along and given great leeway when it came to responsibilities. B seemed to enjoy this role of the immature child who could not be expected to do much. Initially, I interpreted that they both assumed I was there to keep this projective identification system in place and functioning well.

One line of interpretation I began was to explore this system by looking at his need to care for her and be the soothing, tolerant one who never got angry, trying to just go along with whatever she wanted or said. He was very passive and compliant with B and never seemed upset or outraged by her inconsistent, strange, or alarming behaviour. The more I examined A's transference to B and now to me as well, it slowly came out that he saw his objects as both broken and stunted as well as in need of unquestioning respect and reverence. He saw B mostly in the first regard and me mostly in the second. But, viewing his objects in both ways left him in need of complying, tolerating, and sacrificing. He never questioned his objects. He put his life on hold for others and somehow tried to not be resentful.

Also, I interpreted that he might be conducting himself in that manner out of fear of causing pain or unrest in his object and that he may fear losing of the object if he were to allow himself to be more expressive and separate. In other words, I was interpreting his depressive conflicts that were evident in his couple's transference and in his way of relating to me. Over the course of two years, A was able to accept and acknowledge his split-off feelings of frustration, anger, and disappointment in his objects. This came out in his gradual speaking out about how inconvenient the appointments were to his busy work schedule, how upset he was to "not have a healthy wife who could be a loving mother to his child" and how angry he was at the many vicious insults B would hurl at him when she was in the middle of her psychotic states.

After they had a baby girl, A was also able to express his pleasure at being the parental figure to B, "taking care of business, doing what is right," along side of feeling "sad to essentially be a single parent." At the two-year mark, A told B he "didn't need to be at the sessions and had things he wanted to do for himself instead" and that she "needed to see the doctor alone and work harder at growing up, being a good mom, and being a partner in the marriage."

B's termination was positive in that he was honouring himself and expressing himself and his needs without feeling guilty, selfish, or concerned about hurting the object. At the same time, he certainly could have continued to work on his own tendencies to ignore his identity for the sake of the other, but on the whole, he seemed to feel more independent and be more willing to show me and B his needs and separate self. Also, I think it was important that he could separate from me without feeling he let me down or that he was "being a bad patient." Also, in his denial of B's psychotic state, there was often an element of supportive understanding that I interpreted and which remained apart from the more pathological denial. In other words, he would take B's non-thinking state and her psychotic statements and find the kernel of truth in them or merely accept them without reacting too strongly.

So, when B said, "I never wanted to marry you and now I am stuck with your baby. I could be a doctor or a lawyer making the big money and having a good life instead!" A was able to say, "I can't believe you are saying that. Your illness is taking over. You need to spend more time talking to your doctor or get more medication, this is crazy!" While he was expressing some of his hurt, outrage, and despair, he managed to muffle much of it and try to contain and cushion B's outburst. Even his irritated comeback of "you need to talk more with the doctor and get more medications" was an expression of a modest version of his hurt and anger as well as a genuine effort to help B in her psychotic confusion.

The same can be said for "this is crazy." A probably felt more of an angry "you are crazy" but was able to focus it into more of a comment on the situation and their relationship. Thus, it was a bit of his old denial and a bit of him acting as an understanding container instead of acting out from hurt feelings. Therefore, A was engaged in a compromise solution in which some of his depressive position feelings and phantasies remained and some were worked out in a healthy manner. I interpreted it as such and we worked on him finding more ways of directly expressing his feelings while still affording him the opportunity to care for B.

I interpreted that prior to treatment, A had a longtime projective pattern of trying to establish separation and differentiation (Torras de Bea, 1989) while still maintaining a close connection and link to B, but this had not been successful. A's projective identification efforts at finding a balance for his depressive conflicts were part of the emotional distancing B often complained about. She said, "He never wants to communicate with me and always looks away from me, like he is a million miles away. Why doesn't he like me or want to be close to me?" This projective identification stance in which he provided a false impression of conflict-free love but really was emotionally distant created benefits and problems for him and the relationship. He had to live in a state of denial to find the strength to care for a very disturbed person and to cope with overwhelming feelings of disappointment, hurt, anger, guilt, and loss. We worked on finding a way to still have some of these brave capacities but with the added ability to be himself and not sacrifice his identity as much. Therefore, there could be a more healthy process of differentiation and separation along side with close relating.

B's transference was a bit more complicated. One of the first transference reactions B had to me was a very quick erasing of anything I said that was related to her core feelings or about her unconscious motivations. B could easily track anything about her fee, the dates of our appointments, what medications she was on or what dosage, or upcoming sales at the local clothing stores. But, if I would make an interpretation about how and why she was so depressed, not getting out of bed for days at a time and then only to scream at her husband to demand new furniture, she had no idea what I was talking about.

Or, so it seemed. I also routinely interpreted that she was ignoring me and finding my words to painful to bear. When I said, "maybe being pregnant reminds you of all the misery you had as a child and what you wanted but didn't get. You resent the idea of a child being around getting what you never had." B would nod and say, "Yes, I think so." But, when I added, do you know what I just said?" She would say, "No, not all at."

All my remarks about her childhood experiences, her current mental anguish and unconscious conflicts, her feelings about becoming a mother, or anything about her feelings towards me were all met with the same void. B would not allow herself to think in the treatment for a long time. Instead, she focused on concrete matters and various delusions. Overtime, I interpreted that this was partly out of fear of allowing me into her mind and out of fear of what might happen if she trusted me. Gradually, she responded more emotionally to me and said, "You are my doctor. Why do you want to know these things about my feelings? I thought you were here to help me with my baby." I said, "You are focusing on me being a doctor and focusing on your baby. Maybe it is scary to focus on yourself your feelings and on our relationship." B responded, "I have always been afraid of people. They make me very anxious, like they are thinking something about me. I never feel like I belong."

This was the start of a successful exploration into how B felt judged by others as inadequate and inferior, somehow not ever good enough. We looked at this as a projection of her harsh superego demands to be someone who always fit in and knew what to say at all times. She shared her lifelong sense of isolation and exclusion that began in her childhood. For the first two years, B would only see me if accompanied by her husband. I interpreted that she was scared of me judging her and finding out who she really was and not liking it. She told me, "I am scared to be with you all alone. I don't know what I would say." I replied, "Maybe you are afraid I want something from you and if you can't think of how to give it to me, I will be upset and think badly of you." B said, "That is how I feel if I have to go to a party or a dinner! I don't want to be judged." I said, "It must feel good to not have that feeling with A." B said, "Yes, I am so lucky" and began sobbing.

For about six months before the birth of her child and until about nine months afterwards, B alternated between periods of mania and depression, while psychotic most of the time. When depressed, she slept till two in the afternoon, didn't bath, and never did chores around the house. Her husband and a team of social workers helped her with daily functions, especially once she had her child. Part of her psychotic state was a projective identification process in which she felt entitled to do as she pleased and wanted credit for everything even when she did nothing.

So, when I asked B how she was doing, she would often say, "Oh great. I am getting up earlier and taking care of the baby most of the day. Yes. Things are going well and A and I are enjoying being a family." At that point, A would break in to say, "Actually, B doesn't get out of bed until after lunch time unless I or one of the social workers drags her out and nags her to take a shower. The house is a pigsty and she won't touch the baby until I get home from work and ask her to. Sometimes she will tend to the baby and other times B starts screaming at me to leave her alone."

When B told me her idealistic version of things, I never felt she was consciously lying to me. Instead, it was clear she was absorbed in her narcissistic phantasy of accomplishing all that her superego demanded. When I confronted her on the discrepancy of this and began exploring it with B, she was able to be more in touch with the consequences of trying to serve this harsh superego. She said, "It is so hard to get up and take on all these chores and responsibilities. My baby has so many needs and I can't really tell what she wants. I don't understand her signals. A says I just need to pay attention to her and I will be able to tell, but I can never figure it out. Then, I just feel overwhelmed by it." I interpreted, "I think that when you demand so much of yourself you feel overwhelmed and want to retreat. Also, you start to see everyone else, your baby, A, and me as demanding. But, I think it is you who wants everything so perfect that it is too much to handle."

B was able to take in this interpretation and responded by saying, "I *want* to do many things but I end up feeling I *need* to do everything and it all becomes like a menu at a restaurant that has too many choices and I give up." By witnessing this line of exploration, A was also able to step out of his own phantasy state and rely less on their mutual projective identification process. He said, "I see her doing that too. She ends up feeling like a loser because she thinks I want her to do so much. I try and tell her all I need is for her to love herself and the baby and I will take care of the rest." Here, he was showing his willingness to understand what was really troubling B and in turn ask her to honor both herself and his needs, without him having to be the martyr or be in denial about the state of her mental health or the state of their marriage.

So, gradually I was able to make analytic contact with both A and B. This contact created more of an exploratory and mutative process in which we could see what was occurring internally for each of them. For A, it meant a painful mourning of wished for vision of marriage and togetherness that he wanted so much, based on the internalization of a father who worked hard his whole life, dedicating himself to the service of the family. But, A's father never really connected to his wife, A's mother. We examined how staying true to this memory as a way of being attached to his father kept A close to his now dead, beloved father. But, it also kept A chained to a sadomasochistic relationship with B in which he never felt truly recognized, loved, or appreciated.

For B, establishing more regular analytic contact with me meant facing the painful and frightening internal state that not thinking and manic denial shielded her from. It meant instead of blaming "her illness" for everything and enjoying the gain of being a sick person with no responsibilities, she had to begin to take ownership of her life. But to do so meant she had to face the cruel expectations of her superego and the feelings of failure and judgement when she didn't come close to her own demand for perfection.

In the transference, we were able to uncover many aspects of this inner world of conflict. Through projective identification, she enlisted me to be the punitive parent/superego that was there to make her do choirs, parent properly, and communicate better with her husband. Then, as the oppressed and rebellious child who nevertheless needs the nagging parent, B could "forget" to make her appointments, "just feel too sleepy" to get out of bed, and complain over having to take care of her baby, saying she "would tend to her baby tomorrow, I promise." When we analysed this projective identification system, we discovered how it protected her from the cruel and persecutory world of her superego demands that left her judged and depressed most of the time. Her life felt like a jail sentence with no parole so she succumbed to the hopeless and helpless feelings or she could temporarily deny any problems by relying of manic denial and manic delusions of success and harmony.

Part of what guided my interpretations was periodic bouts of counter-transference in which I found myself lost in that projective identification system with B. As Grinberg (1962) has noted, the analyst will sometimes be caught up in such dynamics and react as if there is a valid reason to become the patient's internal object. So, I would find myself, for a period of time, telling B that she "must get out of bed earlier so she can take care of things" and that she "needed to start acting like a mother and not neglecting her child." During such acting out, I felt justified to do so in that I thought her behavior, especially with her baby, was "so inappropriate" that "I had to make her see the light" and "start doing the right thing." Fortunately, I began to see that I was simply becoming the spokesperson for her exacting and commanding superego and inflicting the same demands on B as she usually did on herself.

This revelation helped me start exploring these internal struggles with B. We looked at how her manic states were an understandable escape from her own critical voice that left her so depressed it was hard to function. I interpreted that she probably felt so constricted by the idea of already having "been cheated" out of a childhood and a young adulthood and now "having to be a grown up, a house-wife and a stay at home mom" that she was overcome with depression. Or, we discussed, her manic episodes provided magical escapes in which she "could do it all" and "have it all" or simply be in control by denying all of the critical superego demands and any actual external demands along with it. The more I made these sorts of interpretations, the less anxious and psychotic B appeared and the more she responded in an integrated fashion, exploring some of these ideas herself.

Even though her medications had now been increased to the levels prior to having her baby, she still had times where she was frankly manic, psychotic, or unable to function from depression. However, we now could quickly trace such relapses to her being overwhelmed by superego demands and projective identification cycles of perfection, devaluation, persecution, and ridicule. Similarly, when A and B descended into periods of fighting and angry outbursts, we could trace it to these superego attacks and A's backsliding into accommodation, denial, and fear of self-expression.

B slowly revealed to both A and myself how she felt her whole life "had been wasted from day one" when she had to take care of her younger siblings while her mother was either working or laying around the house drunk. B's father was "long gone" and when B was a teen, she had to spend many long hours caring for her senile grandmother. In her twenties, she struggled to work and "barely make ends meet" without any hope of college or "a better life." I interpreted that now she was angrily claiming "back pay" by being the kid and teen she wished she could have been, being cared for and not having so many responsibilities. But, I interpreted, she now came down on herself with such superego demands that life felt as constricted if not more constricted that it had earlier.

When B married A, she felt she was again being controlled, feeling "now I have to be a housewife and have kids. What about My life? What if I want to get an education or have a career?"

Interestingly, A was always very supportive of any of these types of pursuits and encouraged B to "go for it, as long as she is taking care of the baby and is feeling mentally stable." But, B saw him as restricting her and confining her. Sadly, she felt the same about her baby.

For the first year of motherhood, B was emotionally and physically absent. She had no desire to be with the baby and neglected her when A wasn't around. A and the team of social workers took the majority of the care and when B was willing to hold her child or feed her, it only lasted until the baby did something to frustrate B. This meant that any crying, need for diaper change, or general neediness on the baby's part made B turn away. I interpreted, "you want your baby to be perfect and not cause any trouble. When she isn't and you can't figure out how to make her be perfect and content, you get angry and walk away. Maybe that is because you want to be the perfect mother instead of simply getting to know her and her needs, gradually finding ways of soothing her. So, with that kind of critical voice you must hate to be a mother." B said, "I feel exactly like you just said. I never pictured ending up like this. I feel my life is over."

I said, "if you have to always be the perfect housewife and mother, you life is over. But, you are the one who can decide if you get any wiggle room in that equation." With some patients, it is best to make a comment or question and wait for their association. For patients like B, there is usually no association, because of the lack of thinking caused by the intense projective identification they are locked into. So, technically I often made these types of more lengthy interpretations that were designed to build some bridges to B, dealing with the great distance she put between herself and her objects due to the superego struggles and persecutory phantasies she lived with. The more I made such interpretive proposals, we slowly established a stronger level of analytic contact.

While the analytic work is certainly not finished, A and B are doing much better now as a couple and each are happier as individuals. B continues to see me and is showing more and more openness at exploring her internal world, her feelings, and her conflicts. She is now "feeling like I really love my baby and want to be with her." She is motivated to change her, play with her, feed her, and B now takes great interest in "trying to figure out what her needs are." She said, "I get frustrated but I try and hang in there and see what it is she wants and then I can usually do something to make her ok. It is not as hard as I thought it would be." I added, "It's not as hard as you used to make it. You are more compassionate with yourself now so you can be compassionate with your baby too."

The case of A and B embodies many of the concepts important to psychoanalytic couple's treatment. The case illustrates matters of projective identification, problems with thinking, the concept of the container-contained, and analysis of transference issues that arise in a couple's setting. With B, Brenman's (2006) idea that the patient treats his objects the same way his superego treats him is relevant. In addition, most of the time B felt everyone treated her like her superego treated her. She was a cruel taskmaster and therefore felt overwhelmed by her projective efforts to rid herself of those superego attacks. In addition, Brenman notes that deprivation may leave the infant with no proper attachment to contradict the infant's sense of narcissistic omnipotence. I believe this was the case with both A and B. A never learned that he could not simply control, heal, and care for the object by constantly sacrificing, working, and giving into the object's desires. He did not see his father give up, become angry, or demand his own satisfaction. So, A was left with the phantasy that if he tried hard enough, he could make it all better and if he couldn't do that, he could somehow ignore what he didn't heal or fix.

For B, she was never provided with a limiting container that not only provided soothing but limiting as well. So, B remained narcissistic in her ideas of being able to manically do as she pleased, conquering all and having the world to herself. In fact, it is a vicious cycle because when left without a container object that shows you the limits of love and life, one is left to feel overwhelmed by a life that one apparently should be able to control and conquer. So, B was always searching for her life, her lost object, and her turn at happiness but this was a cruel endless journey because she didn't want the despair of realizing she had an inadequate object and that she herself was less than perfect. In fact, she was so driven by oral aggression to have a satisfying object and so hounded by her superego to be a satisfying object to others that she was always on the losing side of life. To avoid this unbearable state of mind, she used psychotic defences to blank out the reality of her life and the reality of those around her who were trying to help. She did not want to face that persecutory and painful inner reality so she tried to manically and psychotically erase the presence of those who could bring her through the despair, hopelessness, and cruel demands of her superego. To make it to the other side she had to swim through the deadly waters of her internal conflicts and it took us two years to begin that journey.

CHAPTER NINE

Optimism as a way to save the self and the object

Klein (1952) spoke of the balance between love and hate in the infantile ego being easily disrupted by frustration, deprivation, and conflicted attachments. When this imbalance predominates, greed and oral rage emerge. If the ego tries to save the object from these aggressive feelings and phantasies, several defensive systems arise, including the manic use of optimism. Klein (1952) points out how splitting of the depriving or frustrating object into good and bad is central to basic psychological functioning and often is exaggerated in cases of intense loss or abuse. When the ego experiences objects that it depends on to be unavailable, fragile, or prone to shifting into being rejecting and abandoning, the ego may try to create or reinforce a good object through manic optimism. This is a precarious approach and the object must be continuously propped up to prevent the reemergence of the bad, injured, or lost object.

Klein (1952) also writes about how the ego creates idealized, always gratifying objects in order to protect the ego from the persecutory fears it harbours regarding the bad object that can either attack, reject, or abandon the needy ego. This psychic situation can create a vicious cycle in which the bad is continuously denied and projected, leading to an over reliance on optimism and false hope as well as a continuous need to find the extra-good in the world to protect the self and the object from the extra-bad in the world.

If and when the ego is able to synthesize these divergent phantasies and feelings about the object, the depressive position (Klein, 1935) is within grasp. Just as optimism can shield the ego from paranoid threats, optimism can also be used as a primary defence in undoing or avoiding any perceived harm to the object. Optimism is also a way to make amends and reparation in that it overrides any ill feelings and replaces them with positive feelings, much like a peace offering to an angry or offended God.

If the ego feels the object is injured, offended, burdened, or even permanently overcome, the ego may over-identify with this crippled state, feeling even guiltier. This creates a need to inhibit any or all aggressive feelings, needs, or conflict and to make reparation. The resulting manic defensive system includes denial, splitting, and the over reliance on optimism to cure any potential strife between self and object. Grotstein (2000) postulates hate, resentment, or rage to be a way the infantile ego alerts the object that an imbalance in the primary attachment has occurred, which needs to be rectified. Specifically, Grotstein sees hate and aggressive phantasies as an unconscious attempt to destroy the bad object so as to clear the way to restoring the good object. However, if the ego doubts the strength or commitment of the good object, anger or hate are felt to be too dangerous and possibly overwhelming to the meagre or weakened good object. So, optimism is a safer stance to take, to bolster the sagging good object and hope it can manage to administer to the needy ego.

The view I am proposing regarding pathological optimism as a defence against paranoid or depressive anxieties is in line with what Steiner (1987) has written about pathological organizations, which the ego erects to avoid the pain, guilt, and fear of those two mental experiences.

Case 1

This first case was a brief encounter with a patient who seemed to need to rely on a pathological organization (Steiner, 1987) that included optimism and over-eating to ward off overwhelming internal experiences of loss and persecution. Stacy was asked by her company manager to seek help with her over-eating. She called me for an appointment, saying she "could never afford an opportunity like this herself, but her company was generous enough to pay for twenty visits and it looked like a great opportunity to do some self-discovery." Immediately, I was struck by her cheery, upbeat approach, which sounded scripted or fake in some way.

Stacy weighed close to three hundred pounds and was frequently distracted from her work by visits to the cafeteria or snack food vending machines. She told me, "I always bring candy to work. I can't picture being there all day without it." I thought to myself that she seemed to be describing her avoidance of something dangerous and overwhelming.

Stacy was thirty-seven and had been single for the past five years. She told me she dated occasionally, but that "most men only want to get into my pants. It is hard to find someone who is willing to work on a relationship instead of just have a one-night stand. Not that I am against that! I have been known to get frisky as well!" I was surprised by her view of herself as being pursued by men only wanting sex, as she didn't fit that physical stereotype at all. I took note of this and how she again related in this optimistic and overly positive outlook.

This same sort of discrepancy appeared in the way she talked with me about other matters. Stacy presented herself as a simple sort of woman, but then she talked philosophically, appearing to be a deep thinker. But, as we went along, it started to look like she in fact lived a rather shallow emotional life. She engaged me in various conversations that often had a self-help book or twelve-step meeting air about it, and at some point, she would lapse into a more dependent, "what do I do about it doc?" type of relationship. The seemingly important insights she might make or that I interpreted were never really pursued with much interest. She didn't seem to grasp the importance of what she was saying. More and more, I felt like I was being read to from a manual on healthy living, a positive, upbeat view of life that Stacy knew the words to, but didn't really own.

Sometimes, Stacy seemed to read from that manual for optimistic living with enthusiasm, as if she really felt it and meant it. Other times, she seemed to be just "phoning it in." I tried to bring this up for exploration, but Stacy would usually respond, "Oh no. I am just tired today" or she might answer with a self-help slogan like, "you might be down, but that doesn't mean you are out for the count" or "Oh well, tomorrow is another day!"

Approximately five years before I saw her, Stacy was hospitalized with psychotic symptoms and medicated. She had stopped the medications twice since then and had to take herself to the hospital both times, hearing voices and "feeling paranoid."

During the first few months of her treatment, we discussed her "low self-esteem" from being obese. Also, she felt depressed because she hadn't been in a relationship for quite some time. When I tried to explore the nature of her over-eating, she told me "I know it is a form of emotional eating. We can examine it and hopefully I can work through it." Again, she said this in both an engaging and optimistic manner that promised curious introspection, but also it sounded like something she had been told in the hospital and was simply repeating.

In one session, Stacy referenced the "hard times" she had growing up, where "everyone was always fighting" and where there was "often not enough food to eat since we were so poor." Then, she said that as an adult, "I often feel bored, tired, or lonely." She paused and said, "I don't know Doc, sometimes I just start eating." In the counter-transference, I felt like she had given me the first comment about her feeling bored and lonely for safe keeping, not making a link to it with the second comment about how she "just starts eating." In my own mind, I wondered if Stacy avoided putting these two states of mind together because it might result in too much anxiety and pain.

I interpreted that she may have grown up feeling the lack of a nourishing, safe object that filled her up emotionally. I said, "Maybe without that nourishing, safe feeling in your family, you were left feeling empty and lonely. If so, maybe food was the concrete answer to your emotional hunger." In response to my interpretation, Stacy began to weep and sob. After a few minutes, she told me important details about her upbringing.

Stacy's father was a chronic alcoholic who would drink until drunk and then start fighting with his wife. Stacy grew up "watching my parents beat the shit out of each other more times than not." She said the atmosphere in the home was always tense and unpredictable. Her mother had a psychotic break at some point and was hospitalized. Stacy told me, "Mom was this person in my life who would say I love you in the morning and beat me silly at night." She went on to describe the violent neighbourhood she grew up in and how she was beaten and almost raped at age twelve by members of the local gang. School was a place she remembered being picked on for her acne and shyness. Finally, Stacy told me how the one "source of warmth I had was two small cats that we found and took home. But, one day after I had them for about a year, one got sick and since we couldn't afford to take them to the vet, my father gave them both rat poison." She began sobbing again.

During the next few visits, I continued to pursue the link between emotional hunger, food, and this enormous backlog of pain and anguish. I interpreted that the trauma she suffered as a child was still alive inside of her in the sense that she felt empty, scared, and alone. She tried to find safety and soothing in food, but her deep emotional need turned this respite into another source of pain and unhappiness. She didn't like being obese, but she didn't feel she could give up her obsession with food because she would be left with overwhelming loneliness and internal chaos. In response to these interpretations, Stacy replied, "I don't know if I want to stop over-eating!" I said, "If you don't know what to replace it with, of course you don't want to stop it. Together, we need to discover how you can feel safe and strong without that." At that point, I felt we had made a small yet significant move towards understanding her unconscious motives and feelings. I also felt we had a long way to go.

My overall view of this patient at this point in the treatment was that while she was vaguely and broadly aware that over-eating was a psychological matter which probably related to environmental and emotional turmoil in her past, Stacy mainly viewed the over-eating as a quick and convenient way of eliminating boredom and loneliness. Stacy didn't really want to know the extent or depth of those feelings she was trying to eliminate, she just wanted them gone. This was understandable given the overwhelming control they must have had and still had on her inner life.

Over the months ahead, I tried to continue this method of translating what she had given me. But, she was less able and less willing to take it on. In fact, she became all the more optimistic, concrete, and prone to sharing self-help slogans with me which seemed to shield her from this psychological abyss. I tried to be careful to not go to fast or deep in my interpretative translations, so as to not overwhelm her. But, even with a carefully paced analytic approach, Stacy was reluctant to examine herself much more. This reluctance made it very difficult to explore the transference. Often at the end of a session, Stacy would say, "Wow, Doc! You really work wonders. I feel so much better. How do you do that?"

This always left me with a sense of false reassurance, a hollow optimism that felt like she needed to prop me up or prop both of us up as to avoid something profoundly difficult or unbearable. When I tried to interpret this, Stacy would not move past the concrete aspect of the optimism into deeper meanings. This spoke to a quite unmovable defensive stance that seemed to protect her from paranoid-schizoid fears as well as primitive depressive anxieties. All had to be ok and happy, or else.

It was difficult to establish analytic contact (Waska, 2006; 2007) with Stacy because this defensive optimism was such a necessary aspect of her psychological survival. O'Shaughnessy (1983) has noted that "instead of being about the patient's intrapsychic dynamics, interpretations should be about the interaction of patient and analyst at an intrapsychic level" (p. 281). While this is certainly the technically correct approach with most patients, it seems that with patients who cling to optimism as their primary defence, the transference is very difficult to access unless the central intra-psychic phantasies are explored first. If these phantasies reveal core anxieties regarding allowing dependency on the object or independence from the object as being dangerous to the self and the object, than that is a clinical porthole to gradually address the transference situation. Counter-transference feelings and phantasies can also be helpful with these difficult to reach patients. If the analyst feels kept at a distance or artificially propped up, it can show the way to making tentative interpretations that the patient may be able to tolerate.

Stacy's lack of psychological maturity was the result of her over reliance on splitting, projective identification, and the use of optimism to avoid the intense disappointment her inner life brought. Unfortunately, her overly positive stance was fragile and only seemed to work in conjunction with her reliance on food as a psychological stabilizer. The internal chaos she lived with created a paranoid experience in which she had to constantly ward off the reliving of her early family trauma by constant optimistic reassurance and constant oral gratification and soothing. I think that she was unable to forgo either defence because of this paranoid phantasy of immediately being victim to the loneliness, anxiety, and fears of her early years. Indeed, her psychotic episodes seemed to be confirmation that these paranoid phantasies easily invaded her mind and needed constant fending off with the only methods she knew or trusted, optimism and food. Therefore, optimism and food formed a rigid pathological defensive system that provided shelter from intense paranoid fears of loss and persecution. Stacy had to see the object as always good to avoid the phantasies of an unrelenting bad object that left her starving, hurt, and alone.

Case 2

Initially, Amy came to see me for help with parenting. Her teenage daughter was starting to act rebellious and there were ongoing debates and conflicts regarding choirs, homework, and curfew times. Also, Amy was having difficulty communicating with her husband about these parenting issues. As a result, they were never on the same page regarding how to respond to their child's needs and her recent behaviours. Amy told me, "My husband doesn't seem to see what I do and doesn't seem to want to pitch in to try and make things better. He seems to leave it all for me to take care of." So, Amy and I started off focusing on these problems. But, I had an initial countertransference feeling that she was acting overly nice and polite with me, when in fact she was telling me about matters that should have left her irritated or angry. I had the feeling Amy was holding back from letting loose in order to not leave me with the experience of an angry object pouring out foul waste. I felt she was protecting me or making sure not to dirty me up with this waste. Therefore, I made some initial interpretations about how she seemed to be telling me in a very round about way that she was frustrated with her husband and sometimes even angry with him about his lack of communication and lack of effort. I told her it seemed she was holding back or protecting me from these stronger feelings. She said she didn't want "to sound like a bitch. But yes. Sometimes, I am pretty fed up."

It came out rather early on that she had been flirting with a man at work and had started sending letters to him. The letters quickly became sexual in nature. Amy's husband found one of these letters and there was a long period of frosty distance between the two of them. In discussing it, Amy told me she really didn't understand "what had happened or why she had ever started writing the letters." I was struck with how unrelated she saw her resentment at home to her acting out at work. Amy was confident she would never have a sexual affair with this man, but she was very confused as to how she ended up in this situation. All she knew was "that it felt good at the time and I never really considered its effect on the marriage."

I interpreted that perhaps she was angry with the lack of communication at home and this "letter affair" was a way to get back at her husband. Amy thought about it and added, "well, my husband hadn't been interested in sex in a long time and I wasn't sure if he thought I was unattractive, fat, if he was just or bored or what. But, I felt like he was sort of ignoring me." I said, "I think you are trying to tell me that the letters were also a way of getting that attention and feeling important to him, as well as maybe getting back at him for ignoring you." In my interpretation, I was introducing the idea that she was cautious or reluctant to express any aggressive feelings or strong intent in my presence. Amy said, "I never thought of it that way. I think you are right. But, why would I do that?" I said, "It seems you are uncomfortable letting me know your stronger feelings. Maybe it's the same with your husband. Then, they come out in other ways like the letters."

This line of exploration led us to other examples of Amy's reluctance to face her own feelings when they felt in conflict with others. This knowledge, gained in the transference, helped us better understand several other situations in her life. Amy casually told me she had noticed herself very tired in the last few months and that she had discovered a lump in her breast. She told me "it is probably no big deal and I am just thinking about it too much." She had put off an examination but made an appointment after I pointed out how she was ignoring her own wellbeing. During our session and several sessions following, I interpreted that she seemed reluctant to share her worries or vulnerability with me. I said I wondered if she thought she might be burdening me. Amy told me that she "always feels like she is burdening someone." This led to a discussion of her never asking for much from her family because she didn't "want to infringe on them or cause any trouble." I interpreted that she didn't want me to have the stress of her health worries. So, she kept it to herself. She told me it "probably is not a big deal. There is a history of breast cancer in my family but there is no use in worrying about something you don't know about. Even if it turned out to be something, there are plenty of good treatments out today and ever reason to feel ok about the outcome." I thought about how she may have, through projective identification (Waska, 2004), be placing her anxiety into me and then feeling compelled to reassure me that everything was alright. Here, I was tentatively following the transference/counter-transference thread that seemed to be within the realm of the depressive position (Klein, 1935). I made this interpretation about her trying to protect me and reassure me. Amy said she was not aware of any anxiety, but "Definitely saw my point. Still, it didn't feel like a big deal."

After having a breast exam, she found out that she did indeed have breast cancer. It was considered in the beginning stages and a type that was quite treatable. However, it was still a life-threatening illness that she now had to have ongoing treatments for. Because of her use of projective identification to avoid hurting me, she put me in the role of the spokesperson for her needy, scared feelings. She thought they were too aggressive or draining to me if she owned them. Therefore, I had them for safekeeping and detoxification. But, she wasn't sure if I could handle them either. When I made this interpretation, she was quick to tell me, "I don't want to be that kind of person since it sounds selfish and too much to put on others." The combination of my interpretations and our working on these depressive phantasies of draining the object with her needs began to open the door to her becoming more expressive and able to share some of her formally hidden feelings.

Unfortunately, another catalyst to Amy sharing her feelings appeared when she received her blood test results from the initial cancer diagnosis. The blood work showed she also was diabetic and in need of insulin treatment. Besides our analytic work, the shock of suddenly having these two maladies provided some emotional push for her to start expressing herself in ways she had never done. So, Amy began sharing her fears and anxieties with me about her illness and what might happen next in her life. We also spent a good deal of time examining whether or not part of this new expressive freedom was the result of her feeling she had permission since it was a medical issue. Following this deeper avenue of exploration allowed her to bring up other situations in which she felt burdened or even angry but thought she didn't really have the right to speak out. As a result, there was a steady stream of stories about the household, her husband, their child, and various friends and how these important people in her life left her feeling used or taken for granted because Amy never felt she deserved a choice.

Instead, she tended to have an "Oh, its ok! No problem!" face of optimism and niceness that shielded her from guilt about being hurtful or aggressive. Amy's analytic treatment is in the very initial stages, but the transference is already a guidepost to her internal world. Sometimes, she wants to sugar-coat things to please me and convince me that she is coping with everything just fine. In those moments, she wants me to either not see those more hungry, angry aspects of her character or she wants me to carry them for her and be the one who has to speak about it so she doesn't have to. Other times, she is trying to please me by telling me about her anger, her despair, and her needs because she thinks that is what a good, motivated patient does. Her optimism usually gives her away. For example, Amy will be telling me something about the hardship of her cancer treatment or the difficulties of her struggle with diabetes and say, "but it isn't really all that bad! I just have to learn to manage it and everything will be fine!" At that point, I usually say, "You suddenly are anxious that I can't bear your fears and anger so now we have to put on our rose colored glasses." At that point, Amy is able to stop and acknowledge some of her anxieties and struggle to understand them a bit. Part of that is exploring how and why she feels I will be so vulnerable to her pain and how and why she imagines I might not want to or be able to help her with her anguish. So, bit by bit, Amy's optimistic defence and intense denial are diminishing and she is beginning to face her internal world by working on her phantasies regarding how she affects others.

Case 3

Andrew was in his late thirties when he came to me for help with his second marriage. He was a part-time disc-jockey at a local radio station and had been married for five years. Since his twentieth birthday, he had been on a high dosage of blood pressure medication. This factored into much of his view of himself and the way he viewed life.

I saw Andrew twice a week, when our schedules permitted, and he used the analytic couch. He was very motivated, which I slowly realized was part of an overly optimistic and compliant way of relating to people.

Andrew told me that when growing up he felt his father was "never really interested in what I had to say and didn't really take me seriously." His mother was "a volatile woman who had constant moods, always inconsistent." Andrew felt distant from his family as a result and reported that he "grew up dwelling on things outside of the family and found a focus in music and art." When he was diagnosed with severe high blood pressure, Andrew remembered one doctor suggesting that he seek psychological help as well as medical assistance, but nothing came of it. It wasn't long before Andrew was very worried about his health and began to think of "when he would die and how long he had left." He tried to bring up these terrible worries with his family, but quickly realized they "were quick to offer reassurance and get him to change the subject."

As a result, Andrew felt he "better keep these worries to himself so as to not bother or hurt others, since they seemed to need to focus on other things." However, we quickly discovered that Andrew was never able to feel free from this dread and ongoing sense of "life is short," even though he kept it to himself. As the analysis unfolded, we saw how this attempt to conceal his inner feelings led to a pattern of trying to capture life so as to not lose it. This came out in countless forms, such as Andrew always taking pictures of any person or event he thought important or special, to "preserve it and have it for memory." I interpreted this as his desire to make an emotional or mental scrapbook of his objects and his connection to them, as he felt he would soon be pulled away from them and lose them forever.

This method of scrap-booking his internal and external life was important to the analytic investigation. I interpreted that Andrew put everybody in his life, including his analyst, in a mental album, devoid of emotion or connection. He could reminisce about somebody, talk about how exciting an event had been, or discuss his last session, but it was always done in this detached manner. I told him, "I think you are giving me a guided tour of our relationship, but you are not really present as you do it. I think it must give you a sense of control and safety to be more of a docent of your life than to let yourself be immersed in it." He said, "I think I know exactly what you mean. I have always loved to take pictures of everything, every event, and then I show people them later and tell stories about the events. I do that with my camera phone now too. I have the feeling I do it because I feel the thing will or could go away so I want to sort of immortalize it." I responded, "You can freeze it in time and capture it as something or someone to hold on to, but I get the sense you don't really ever feel satisfied by that. You have to keep doing that with the next event and the one after it, as if you have a hard time finding that memory or feeling inside yourself and if you find it, it doesn't last." Andrew said, "I don't ever feel I can embrace my life in a way that would keep things intact, so I like to keep celebrating them with pictures and stories." I interpreted, "maybe you don't know if you will be around to remember all the good times." Andrew said, "I have always had a fatalistic view."

I said, "So, the scrapbooks are an act of desperation, since you don't feel you can contain those things inside yourself and share them with feelings. You have to capture them and artificially enjoy them from a distance. Maybe you don't think I would want to hear your true feelings, much like you said your father brushed off your worries and fears." Andrew said, "Well, you might be right. I always thought I shared a lot with everyone, but now you have me thinking. Maybe I do a good job at seeming to share but I really keep things to myself." I said, "Especially the negative things? You seem to cover them over with optimism pretty quick." He replied, "I coat them with sugar so I don't smell the stink?" I explored this comment and over time we found that he "didn't want to smell the stink" because he would find himself without the idealized object he phantasized about, an object that understood him and helped him with his worries and fears. Without that object, he felt scared and alone. At the same time, our exploration led to a fear that if he were to acknowledge "the stink," he would have to confront or even fight with the object and Andrew was scared he would hurt this beloved and idealized object.

This fear of harming his object and his defensive reaction of being optimistic about any problems that would engender conflict continued to come to light in several ways. With his current relationship, which was Andrew's second marriage, he described his wife as a very moody woman who wanted things her way and complained much of the time. However, when I focused on that description, he was quick to make it sound like she was "just adjusting to things at her new job" and "doing her best to deal with some communication problems with me and some stress over her sister." The more I heard him describe his marriage, I had the impression he was married to someone who was quite bossy and dominating. But, when I pressed Andrew to tell me how he viewed her, he switched to this more rosy, optimistic picture. He reported the same sort of scenario with his friends, in that they had told him his current wife "was pretty bitchy" and some of them thought she was having an affair from how she was acting. But, Andrew could only see the sunny side. So, when things in the marriage started to really deteriorate, I wasn't surprised. But, Andrew was. I suggested that he needed to shield himself from any red-flags he saw and to deny any flaws he noted in his objects. I interpreted that he needed to shield both himself and me from any worries or conflicts he felt, because he wasn't sure if I would be supportive or not or if I wanted to shoulder the burden.

Andrew was initially surprised to hear that I thought he was being overly optimistic and denying negative feelings he had about himself or others. But, as we proceeded, he began to tell me that he "saw what I meant" and he "had started to experiment with looking at things head on and then trying to draw some boundaries." This shift occurred over the course of about one year and Andrew did begin to trust his feelings as something others might value and something he didn't have to hide from. Over time, my interpretations were concentrated on how he projected his own worries and unhappiness onto others, particularly those who gave him cause for concern, and then denied there was anything wrong.

We saw that his current defensive optimism with his current wife was similar to how he related to his first wife. Andrew told me that in his first marriage he had gradually become "scared that he wasn't fully satisfying his wife's sexual needs." One issue had been the occasional impotence caused by the side-effects of the high blood pressure medication. While his wife seemed to be understanding about it, Andrew started to feel anxious that he was disappointing her. Over time, he grew so worried about disappointing her that he was too nervous to have an erection. The situation became worse and worse until after a few years he gave up altogether and his wife became frustrated and angry. This was one of the main reasons she eventually divorced him. In exploring his fear of disappointing her, it came to light that this was an intense anxiety about letting his object down and hurting her feelings. I interpreted that he must feel he holds great power over his objects and can easily hurt them by withholding his favours. This idea of him being fearful of disappointing and hurting his objects by not giving them what they wanted was certainly a major factor in his internal conflicts. However, I also interpreted that it sounded like he was possibly scared of his own desires, his own aggressive needs. I said, "Maybe your own sexual needs and wants seemed selfish or too aggressive, so you held them back to protect her." He said, "I think you are right about that, even though I have never thought of it that way. I don't want to impose my needs on anyone, it does feel selfish and it could be hurtful." So, we proceeded with that line of thought and I also interpreted that his optimism was a way to deny, cover, and negate these selfish, scary feelings and thoughts. So, we focused on his fear of harming his object and his self-destructive solution of fleeing from his own opinions and wishes as a way to avoid trouble.

In trying to understand the source of Andrew's quest to not harm the object with what felt like pushy, aggressive opinions and needs, Andrew drew attention to his childhood experiences with his father. He told me that his father "was an unbending, stubborn man who insisted that everyone always succumb to his point of view. He had to be right on anything and everything, no matter what. There was no room for anyone's ideas or opinions." I said, "It must have been tough to be close to him and find a way to express all of yourself around him." Andrew said, "I could only be close to him if I agreed with him." I interpreted that Andrew found optimism as one of many ways to adapt to his father's rigid and limited offer of love and closeness. Andrew replied by telling me he "made a decision very early in my life to always give others the benefit of the doubt, no matter what! That was my way of making sure I would never treat others like my father treated the family." I said, "You're 'no matter what' sounds just as controlling and narrow as your father's 'no matter what'. Perhaps you have gone to the opposite extreme, away from his pessimistic have to be right approach to an optimistic, maybe everyone else has to be right approach." This interpretation opened up much thought for Andrew in the next few months. He began to be more reflective about when, how, and why he chose to be so forgiving and optimistic before really allowing himself to feel whatever was going on at the moment. He started to see how he sacrificed himself to others in an effort to not hurt them or cause confrontations. This exploration led to insight around the dynamics of his first marriage.

Andrew's first wife had a temper and towards the end of the marriage was prone to yelling at Andrew and calling him a "weak man" and "a loser in the sack" after he stopped initiating sex. When I asked Andrew about how that made him feel, he was quick to avoid the shame and anger he most probably felt and instead colored it with optimism. He said, "Well, it was a tough time and we were all doing the best we could. We tried to stick together and talk it out. I can certainly see why she was so frustrated and people say things when they are mad that they don't really mean." Here, we gradually looked at why he needed to portray it to me in that way, hiding his more angry or resentful feelings. But, it was slow going because Andrew did his best to cling to his optimistic view of life.

The counter-transference with such patients can be tricky in two ways. First of all, there was a pull to become frustrated and put Andrew down for not being more of a man and for not expressing his needs more strongly. So, this would be the lecturing father telling the child to grow up and act like a man. This would be particularly bad in Andrew's case, since he felt his father was always stern and intimidating, telling him the "right way" to be. The second counter-transference trap was to be the spokesperson for Andrew's feelings that he avoided. So, it was tempting with Andrew to say, "You must be feeling angry" or "you must have really wanted to tell her off." This would be the result of a projective identification process in which the analyst takes on the patient's unwanted aspects of themselves, specifically their aggressive or assertive side. Either one of these two counter-transference pitfalls is essentially a negative reaction to the overly positive optimism these patients over-utilize.

Examples of this counter-transference struggle with Andrew came about in many ways. During the time I was seeing him, his first wife would contact him whenever she was depressed or lonely. Even though she had divorced him and consistently criticized him as someone who never satisfied her emotionally or sexually, she would call him whenever she needed emotional support. So, when she was fired from her job, when she broke up with a boyfriend, when she was fighting with her family, or when she simply was bored and wanted someone to chat with, she would call Andrew. He would tell me about this, setting the stage to convey the type of emotions he was probably feeling. But, instead of telling me he was annoyed, angry, or confused about why she would divorce him and call him a loser and then call for sympathy over her breakup with her new boyfriend, Andrew would say he "tried to be understanding and helped cheer her up." He would add, "after all, we were married for awhile and we have some history, so it makes sense that she would see me as an ally. I know she will pull through this, she is a fighter." The counter-transference pull was an urge to say, "Wait a minute! What the hell is she thinking? She dumped you and now she wants to cry on your shoulder about her boyfriend? You have got to be kidding!" So, if enacted, this would be a replay of both Andrew's phantasy of an angry father who had to have his view imposed on others and Andrew's successful projective discard of his unwanted anger onto me, using me as the spokesperson for the phantasies and feelings he did not want to bear. There were numerous events that tested these transference↔counter-transference waters, including him letting his ex-wife use his credit card to pay off a gambling debt and hiding it from his current wife. Another such test was when his mother came to visit only to tell him he couldn't sleep with his current wife while Mom was visiting because they hadn't had a church wedding. When Andrew didn't speak out, his wife was of course incredulous.

His fears of harming the object and in the process creating either an injured or enraged object were central phantasies that shaped the way he related internally and interpersonally. In the transference, Andrew saw himself as close to hurting me or offending me at any given moment. This combination was important for me the analyst to notice because it meant that Andrew was at times tittering between the depressive fears of harming the object, leading to feeling over-whelmed by guilt and remorse and the paranoid fears of causing conflict, leading to being punished and hurt by the object. Indeed, this is an internal dilemma many patients face, in which their guilt easily shifts to a more persecutory state and rather than feeling con-cerned for their injured object, they begin to worry that the injured, fallen object will rise up and seek revenge and retaliation. This is a state of primitive loss (Waska, 2002) that brings with it great anxiety and phantasies of persecution or attack, angry separation, and lack of forgiveness. For the most part, it was the depressive guilt that Andrew suffered with, but the combination of anxieties and phantasies from both arenas came through at times in the transference.

An example of this occurred one morning when I arrived for Andrew's session later than I usually did. He was already standing in the parking lot, waiting for me to unlock the front door. I was on time, but I would be walking into my office with about one or two minutes before Andrew's appointment time. As I walked up to the front door to unlock it, I said hello and Andrew responded, "Hello. I must be late." I did not respond to that comment as it was obviously something coming from a place of great anxiety. I told him to come in and we began the session. What came out rather quickly when I asked about him saying he was late, when clearly we were either on time or I was the one who was in fact late, was that he was scared of making me feel bad and causing any conflict. He said, "One of us has to be right and that means the other has to be wrong. And, out of the two of us, you have to be right." I interpreted that this phantasy involved two equally frightening states. Andrew felt I was demanding to be right so he had to sacrifice his identity to save himself from any angry conflict. Also, he sacrificed himself to save me from being wrong, which might leave me hurt and ashamed. So, Andrew related to me from this dual place of fear and guilt. The guilt was prominent but certainly colored by the secondary paranoid fears.

Another example of the transference, in which his optimism gave way to expose deeper feelings that the optimism defended against came up in the way Andrew paid me. Each time we met, he brought me three twenty-dollar bills. This fee had been decided on how often we met and his ability to pay. I noticed that Andrew made a great effort to always bring new bills and he always unfolded them and pressed them nice and flat in his hand before handing them over. So, each one looked fresh and free of wrinkles. The whole feeling in the moment was of a respectful servant handing over an offering to his master in a very humble way. I made this interpretation to Andrew who said he "had never given it any thought but when I pointed it out, he could see what I meant." He went on to say, "I guess I feel like I need to make sure everything is ok and to not give you any problems or hassles. I don't want to inconvenience you or make trouble."

Here, I had interpreted the dual threats Andrew experienced of hurting me and burdening me along with the threat that he could make trouble that could lead to me being angry with him. Again, the leading anxiety was guilt, but it was mixed with some paranoid fears.

He went on to say "I always try and keep things clean and tidy and I think you deserve a fresh bill, not a messy, old bill." After our discussion about the money and the meaning of his approach to me, he began to simply take money out of his wallet and hand it to me without bothering too much with making the bills just so. I pointed that out and he said, "Well, I thought about what we talked about and decided that if you have a problem with it, you will tell me." I said, "So you must be trying to trust that if I am upset with you or if I feel hurt, I will be able to tell you and we could figure out the problem together and make it right." "Yes, I think we can, at least with the money," he replied. "And, hopefully we are working on the rest of it," I answered.

This type of gradual growth and change occurred in other areas of Andrew's life, as we worked on his use of optimism to cover his guilt and anxiety. He reported how his new friend from work was turning out to be a selfish person who always borrowed money, only talked about themselves, and "had to be right in all matters without the consideration of anyone else." Several weeks went by with Andrew putting up with this and repeatedly denying any anger on his part. In fact, I pointed out how he felt guilty about his anger and used optimism to cover it up. He would tell me about examples of how this person was rude and manipulative and then say, "But, I am sure I haven't gotten to know him well enough yet to realize his good side. I am sure he will grow on me. I just need to be patient. Everyone is a good person below the surface, so you just have to know how to find the gold!" However, Andrew was able to take in my interpretations about this optimism and gradually allow himself to face his independent thoughts, face his angry feelings, and then make a healthy separation from this person. He said, "I realize I don't need to be part of that person's bad behavior. It is ok for me to turn away from him and turn towards my own thing. That doesn't mean I am being mean, I think it just means I am starting to respect myself and see that it is ok to have my own life."

CHAPTER TEN

Why won't the voices leave me alone: Patients who live in a world of persecutory anxiety

S ome patients demonstrate a rigid internal cycle of demand, hatred, and expectation of not only the self but of the object, for idealistic levels of performance, acceptance, and love. Love, acceptance, and success should be around every corner and therefore these patients find flaw and failure in most aspects of their lives. Often, emotional hunger and cautious distancing combine in the transference to make for a sense of demand, disappointment, and hopelessness. A profile of idealism, devaluation, demand, and depression emerges, mobilized by defences of projective identification, denial, and splitting.

Transference interpretation is essential in these difficult cases, but often hard to do when the patients hold such strong convictions regarding these phantasies of longing, dread, judgement, and hopelessness. For many of these patients, there is a complicated oscillation between the paranoid (Klein, 1946) and depressive positions (Klein, 1935), never really reaching an integrative stance in which whole objects exist. Negotiation, compassion, or understanding is not available to counteract the judgemental demands.

The patients I am highlighting are trapped in an endless search and quest for the approval, reassurance, and affection of the object, but this frantic search is based on two elements of internal pathology. First, the patient is critical, attacking, or hateful of themselves and needs the object's love to counterbalance, heal, or reverse this cruel sensation. Second, the object's love is sought out in a sure to fail manner that speaks to the fundamental doubt of the object's love in the first place. It is not an experience of unconditional love. It is an unconditional doubt of love. This leads to regular attempts to please the object, combined with cruel and rigid demands of the self that force the patient to feel like an unlovable failure and fundamentally bad person. By employing drastic levels of projective identification to eject and deny these feelings, they are left paranoid or in the case of the patient presented, at times psychotic.

When feeling the object is unwilling to love them, they feel left with nothing. They say, "I am nothing without your love" or "now I am nothing" or "now I have nothing." There is a psychic collapse, a dark inner void. They are left with their own self hatred and become overcome with attacks on the self. One patient said, "I always hate myself. So, I need your love to counterbalance that."

The phantasy world that these patients live in is the investigative aim for all analytic work. Unless their core phantasies regarding the search for love, the constant lack of love, and the dreaded abandonment or rejection in place of love are all uncovered and resolved, their psychological suffering goes on. One main phantasy centres around objects that are experienced as easily angered or hurt and easily prone to being rejecting, unavailable, and retaliating. So, the end result is a state of primitive loss that combines strong paranoid feelings with severe states of persecutory guilt and rejection. These patients present with a combination of desperate desire and chronic disappointment. They are constantly in need, wondering why they are not loved and what they have to do to win the object's approval. In some cases, these feelings are defended against with narcissistic denial and omnipotence, but this shield is brittle and crumbles easily.

Harsh superego states are part of this cycle in which self and object are judged mercilessly. These states of high expectations and incessant demand are more directly aimed at the self in terms of "what am I not doing that causes them to not love me" and more indirectly at the object in terms of "why aren't you paying attention to me and rescuing me?" When the superego attacks are prominent in the analytic setting, there is often a pull for the analyst to become reassuring, forgiving, and rescuing. This can take the form of a counter-transference acting out in which the analyst sides with the patient against whatever persecutory phantasy they have. The patient seems to want the analyst to tell them, "Oh no, you aren't all those bad things. In fact, you are lovable and likeable in many ways." To this clinical dilemma, Feldman's (2007) recent study on interpretation is relevant. However, I will mention later in this paper why I also disagree with or deviate from some of his principles when working with this type of patient.

Diagnostically, these patients are in the borderline spectrum (Kernberg, 1967) and operate with primitive phantasies of loss (Waska, 2005; 2006) that point to paranoid-schizoid levels of functioning as well as very brittle depressive experiences. Indeed, this fragile hold on the depressive world seems to shatter very easily and shift into more persecutory experiences of attack, betrayal, and abandonment.

This Chapter will explore some aspects of such patients with one case report and in doing so it will illustrate the technical approach of establishing analytic contact (Waska, 2007). Analytic contact is the consistent exploration of the transferences, defences, phantasies, internal conflicts, and interpersonal methods of relating that the patient utilizes in their relationship to her objects, especially the analyst. Criteria such as use of couch, frequency of visits, level of pathology, length of treatment, and method of termination are all considered significant, but are also viewed as secondary in clinical importance compared to the analysis of phantasies, transference, and internal conflict states. Phantasy is in itself the primary destination of all analytic activity as that is the source of the patient's suffering. Transference interpretation and exploration is the most direct vehicle to this goal.

However, part of this interpretive quest often involves an ongoing need for containment, by the analyst, of previously unknowable and unbearable states of mind in the patient. Gradually, the analyst translates these warded off, acted out, and projected states in his own mind, coming to an understanding of what might be the underlying conflict. This is then offered to the patient as tentative translations of what is actually occurring in their internal object relational world. As this approach of cushioned interpretations is offered, the analyst pays close attention to the patient's reactions and responses, which then need to be further contained and translated. When the patient seems able or ready to bear a more direct exploration of these phantasy states, then a more direct line of transference interpretation can be pursued. This particular analytic stance also allows for some degree of enactment, often unavoidable, but vital and valuable for understanding the core elements of the patient's conflicts.

Case material

As with all case presentations, this patient only embodies some aspects of this paper's theoretical focus and not others. But, I believe this case well illustrates the core persecution that emerges when there is excessive projective identification of aggressive judgement, demand, expectation, and disappointment.

Paul came to me because he was "tired of feeling depressed." He felt "worried that he wasn't doing enough at work, leaving him burnt out and wondering why no one ever noticed how hard he worked." While he was describing his ongoing stress with long hours and tight deadlines, Paul casually mentioned he was "bothered by voices. He told me that "for the last year or so I hear voices in my apartment and I am pretty sure the neighbors have put some kind of listening device or camera in the wall."

I asked him about the nature of the voices. He said they were "always critical, mean, and accusatory." The voices "blame me for things I never did and accused me of being a bad person. Sometimes, they call me a conceited person." The judging voices were very specific about things Paul had done "wrong" and things he "should" have done but hadn't. Paul said he was sure there was some kind of listening device in the wall because "how else could they know all these details about my life?"

I asked Paul if he had considered that the voices could be his own. He was "pretty sure they were coming from the upstairs neighbors, who might be in league with the landlord." During the first six months of his analytic treatment, Paul was reluctant to think that the voices might be the result of his own internal struggles. Here, it was important to remain in close contact with his inner experiences and phantasy state then to try and force my opinion on him. Indeed, by forcing him to look at himself, I would be duplicating his psychotic superego experience of the neighbours looking at him in a judgemental way. I think this form of holding is part of the analytic contact that must be established with patients who are not immediately able to share their phantasies or let the analyst into their mind just yet.

Sometimes, the scope of Paul's persecutory delusions widened. Paul would look out his window to the other side of the street and noticed people "looking at him and talking about him." He thought they must be "part of the game being played on him." Paul was not so much scared of these voices as bothered and perplexed as to why they would want to put him down for things he felt were false.

Most of the time, Paul looked like he hadn't slept for days and was extremely anxious. He talked nonstop and seemed to both look to me for guidance and help but also ignored me except for when he asked for immediate solutions to the voices and his work stress. His mannerisms and way of speaking were somewhat aloof and superior and he readily spoke of himself in rather grandiose ways. He had broken up with his girlfriend about the time the voices began but he didn't see any correlation. According to Paul, things were going well until she cheated on him and then she decided to leave him. He said he had "been sad but was now mostly over it." This was an example of how I had the impression he was acting rather aloof or superior about something which must have been devastating and probably still left him sad and angry. Indeed, she still called him on a regular basis and wanted to be friends, telling him about her troubles with her new boyfriend. When I remarked that this must leave him angry and hurt, he was quick to deny it and almost insisted that he was "open to being friends and helping her through a difficult time even if it meant revisiting some of his prior sad feelings."

This optimistic, I don't have a problem with anyone or anything attitude was pervasive in Paul's life. I interpreted that he might need to have such an outlook if he had feelings that he felt overwhelmed by. He said he "felt fine, but he would think about what I said." There were other ways in which he kept his distance from me with this "I will think about it" transference, only letting me in a bit at a time if at all. So, when I wondered if he was trying hard to avoid his feelings about the breakup, Paul said he was "over it" but "could see why I might think he was still affected." Even though he seemed narcissistic and self-absorbed, I considered this stance to probably be related to the anxiety and psychotic persecution he felt from the voices.

Paul's overall demeanour was so riddled with anxiety that he seemed to be constantly fighting off intense feelings of attack, ridicule, and shame. The nature of the voices Paul heard gave me insight into this anxiety. The voices were always "picking on him and putting him down." Within a short time, it became clear that this was a projection of his judgemental, demanding self. However, he was completely unaware of those feelings.

For example, the voices would tell him, "You are so vain. All you ever do is work out at the gym and look at your muscles in the mirror. How pathetic." Indeed, Paul went to the gym religiously and it was very important to him to "look buffed." He said, "I don't get it, I like looking good and I want to have muscles, so why are they putting me down for it? I am tempted to ask my landlord if they installed any cameras or devices recently. If they did, it would be illegal to spy on me!" I said, "I wonder if you enjoy looking buffed but sometimes judge yourself for being too into it as well." He said, "Well, I know others have told me I am really into looks and how I dress, but I am fine with it." So, this type of conversation went on for several months. The voices were only taunting him on the weekends and he played loud music and wore headphones to try and ignore them. He tried to record them to show me "evidence," but when he played back silence he was sure "they had some kind of technological scrambling device." I interpreted that he felt responsible and diligent during the week but perhaps felt he was being too indulgent on the weekends so his conscious was punishing him.

Paul said he understood what I meant and was "considering it because sometimes he could be hard on himself." Here, I think my steady, persistent but patient manner of offering interpretations without any retaliation if he refused them let Paul gradually trust my presence in his mind. He slowly took the small offerings of analytic food and occasionally tasted them, sometimes eating one and other times spitting it out.

The voices made fun of Paul's way of dressing, his lack of a girl-friend, his obsession with being the best worker at his job, and the way he liked to keep his apartment neat and tidy. When he came home at night after working late and decided to not call and check on his elderly mother, which he did almost every day, the voices yelled at him for "being a bad son" and a "lazy, spoiled brat." Paul wasn't sure "why would they know if I called or didn't call my mother unless they had put a listening device in the phone." I interpreted, "I think you might be feeling bad about not calling your mother so the voices are really you attacking yourself for being a bad son."

Paul said he thought I "could be right and that he did feel guilty about it, even though he is normally very diligent about it and does think he is a very good son. So, that part doesn't exactly fit." I said, "Maybe there is a way you try so hard to be a good son and live up to your own expectations that when you fail, you attack yourself." Paul said he "was aware that he has high expectations. Maybe there is something to that. I am not sure."

A similar situation occurred when he told me the voices had started "an ongoing campaign" to "put him down and accuse him of things he would never do." For several months, the voices would say "we know Paul is a lazy alcoholic and we are going to tell his boss and his family. All he does is sit around and drink. He is a lazy boozer." Paul would try and drown the voices out by wearing his headphones. I interpreted that "part of you judges yourself if you don't do things in a perfect way. I think you put yourself down quite a bit. You don't speak of it here but I think part of you is judgmental and irritated when things don't go the way you want. So, when you sit around relaxing with a glass of wine instead of being social or doing something productive, I think part of you gets very judgmental and that is where the voices come from."

Feldman (2007) has studied the ways in which interpreting different aspects or parts of the patient's personality can in fact feed into a manipulative transference and become a mutual acting out, a fearful avoidance of the aggressive sides of an emotional conflict by reassuring the patient of the other more positive or healthy aspects of their conflict. I think this is a helpful insight into how some patient's manipulate the analyst to reassure them and side-step their depressive fears of overwhelming the analyst. However, with patients like Paul, who suffer with the results of severe denial, splitting, and projective identification, it is helpful to reintroduce them to these foreign and aborted aspects of themselves by addressing them as they surface in the analytic setting.

So, I found it helpful to speak to Paul about how he was hiding a more hostile or demanding side of himself from us and perhaps needed to protect me from that part of his personality. I interpreted that he might not feel confident that we could cope with that pushy side of him. He felt more in control and more confident in his self image if he made sure I only saw a more acceptable side of him. I said it was probably confusing and frightening to share, expose, and accept all of himself, "the whole package." In this way, I was not downplaying, as Feldman cautions, the more negative or unhealthy aspects of Paul's personality, but instead I drew attention to how Paul played a very active role in dividing, denying, and fragmenting his mind in order to not face the shameful, painful, and punitive stance of his own superego.

In the counter-transference I was pushed by Paul's projective identification to see him as perfect, nice, and without blame. I found myself momentarily thinking, "Maybe the neighbors are playing a joke on him and have installed speakers and cameras in his apartment." When I realized I was drifting into that psychotic realm, it helped me to see how he desperately tried to expel and destroy that side of himself. Therefore, I began to interpret how he must want and need me to see him as beyond reproach and how this must be a great emotional burden on him to live up to.

In my approach with Paul, I was doing the opposite of Feldman's notion of interpretive collusion. I was identifying the hostile and aggressive parts of Paul that he was projecting and expelling as an important aspect of his personality that he actually needed to function. Although that part of him was currently made rigid and severe by excessive projective identification and splitting, it was still an important piece of him that needed to be integrated. In other words, it would, with modification, be a useful and helpful layer of his internal world.

Paul replied to my comment about needing to have me see him a certain way, "Well, I know I can be judgmental and I do like things to go a certain way, but I never thought I was judging myself like that. I will give that some thought!" Indeed, he was now thinking more about my comments. This was a sign of significant progress. With less reliance on pathological projective identification, he was able to think for himself and to allow me into his mind without feeling as persecuted. In the beginning of our analytic work, Paul would return to tell me he thought I was wrong because he wasn't drinking enough to be an alcoholic so he couldn't be judging himself for that." In other words, he first took me in a very concrete form. I would explain that I meant it more emotionally. Then, later into the treatment, he was able to return and say, "I gave that some thought and I think you are right about how I might be judging myself. I am open now to the idea that the voices might be me. I know I can judge others, but I try not to. So, I will work on that because I don't want to be like that. I like people and I don't want to see myself as putting anyone down, including myself. I think I am a good person so I don't see why I would put myself down in the first place."

Paul would often bring up examples of how he felt mistreated by his boss, his neighbours, and sometimes family members. I told him I had the sense that he felt he tried very hard to always be the best worker, best friend, and best neighbour but always felt underappreciated, unheard, or unloved. He took my observations about his feeling hurt or ignored by others as a concrete suggestion to start being assertive interpersonally, which he did and reported great success and a better sense of himself in those situations. However, he was slow to understand how I meant that he felt underfoot or unlovable and that might be the reason he wanted to be strong, in shape, dress right, work hard, and feel superior.

During this period of the analysis, Paul began to date again. This was another major change for him in that he was almost housebound when we started. Except for going to work, going out to buy food, or going to the gym, he was a recluse. He dated a woman for about a month but started to feel ignored. From his description, it did sound like she was not very demonstrative with him and possibly aloof in some ways. However, it was the sharp rejection that Paul felt which stood out. He felt she was "icy and mean." After one week in which she changed plans with him twice and didn't return his phone calls immediately, he felt angry and dismissed. Also, he was put off that she didn't want to have sex immediately. He confronted her and told her that "I now realize you don't have the same feelings for me as I do for you and that is fine. But, I need someone who respects my needs and doesn't brush me off. If you aren't into me, that is fine. But, I need someone who understands me and treats me accordingly. I hope you have a good life and I appreciate meeting you, but obviously this isn't working out so I must move on."

She responded with surprise and told him that she felt they had just started to get to know each other and things were "just warming up." She said she liked him and just wanted to take it slow and was surprised to hear that he felt so rejected. When I proposed that while she may have been standoffish, he might have taken that very personally and felt cast aside in a way that was important to understand, Paul brushed me aside and said it was simply a case of "no connection and two people on different paths." He said he "was glad to have noticed it and taken care of himself before it went any further." I commented that he seemed to shut down the possibility of us thinking about it together and he was adamant in his concrete dismissal of it.

This difficulty in exploring Paul's transference, phantasies, and conflicts was a theme in the treatment. I felt he used me to feel better but kept at arms-length and didn't want to reveal much of himself. However, over time, I came to understand this impersonal stance to be more a part of the severe splitting and narcissism he maintained between his need for perfection, striving to always be likeable and upstanding and his real feelings that he felt were wrong and fallible. So, to protect himself from my scrutiny, he had to be operating on an intellectual, aloof level at all times or I might detect his real self and find it offensive. I made this interpretation periodically. Initially, Paul would say it wasn't so and continue on with another topic. But, over time he began "to consider it" and slowly said he thought "it might be right sometimes."

I would routinely make the observation that Paul looked extremely exhausted, anxious, and scattered. I tried to engage him to be curious about what might be causing him such distress. In my mind, I thought he was constantly on the run from his own cruel judgements and expectations, which left him tired and always on guard. At one point, Paul said he took my comment about him being anxious and "now has started to try and relax and not see everything as a deadline." I interpreted that he partially took my comment in as a concrete judgement that he is too hyper so now he is doing the opposite. I said that because he felt so on guard and not good enough that it was difficult for him to realize I was commenting on how he seems to be anxious and running away from something in his mind, such as an internal deadline or standards to follow, not external deadlines. Paul reflected a bit and said he "now understands and is starting to see what you mean. It is starting to make some sense and it helps." This seemed more sincere and he seemed less anxious as he spoke. So, we were now more able to directly address the transference.

At one point, Paul reported he heard voices that said, "you needy baby, you need mommy. You are a sissy. You are so weak. It was so pathetic when you fell down at the gym." Paul said he tried to reason with the voices but they wouldn't stop so he used his headphones again. He told me it was strange that the voices said what they did because he had in fact fallen down at the gym and he had not called his mother the day before. But, Paul said he didn't see any correlation between those events and why the voices were "on his case again."

I interpreted that he was strict and demanding of himself and saw himself as weak when he fell down, literally or figuratively, from those expectations. He said "you finally made sense and I see what you mean. That is the way I see myself from the inside, even though I am not usually aware of it." This was a great shift in Paul's ability to be more reflective and engaging with me in the transference. Rather than quickly dismissing me or refusing to contemplate anything emotional that didn't fit into his rigid, concrete way of thinking, he now was willing to permit more of a link (Bion, 1959) between himself and me, between my thoughts and his thoughts, between his conscious and unconscious, and between his logic and his emotions.

Another example of Paul being more receptive to my interpretations was when he told me that the voices are only on the weekends or holidays. We had discussed that before and I made my same interpretation. I interpreted that when it is a workday, he might be feeling he has done his penance by working as hard as he could all week to be perfect, nice, and right so he is forgiven by the voices and they don't punish him. I added that "the" voices are his voice. I interpreted that he is very harsh about any time he feels he has fallen below the strict standard he has. Paul replied, "I think you might be right, but I still wonder if someone drilled a hole in my wall and is listening to me. So, we tracked both ways of thinking for awhile.

Another inroad to his internal conflicts came about when Paul discussed his new friend at work and how nice she was to him. He followed up those remarks with telling me several times how he "doesn't want to take advantage of her kindness." I interpreted how in making this cautionary comment he must feel like he has to prevent himself from becoming selfish and predatory. Paul said, "I totally agree. But, isn't that normal?" I replied that he must be afraid that if he doesn't always monitor himself about what he wears, says, or does, he will "be this bad guy who can hurt others or be selfish." Paul said, "I am amazed at what you are saying. I feel incredibly enlightened. I think you have been saying that before but now this makes very clear sense." Paul went on to tell me how he does see himself that way and is always trying to be perfect. He said he is now going to try and relax and be more carefree with himself without that type of judgement.

After a pause, Paul said, "what if I now start being someone who doesn't care about others and start being cruel to others? I don't want to turn into a selfish person that just goes around doing as they please, using others!" I interpreted that in his mind he now has to let go of controlling himself in front of me and the result is a scary descent into being a bad, selfish monster, someone I will not like. I interpreted that he is used to working very hard to convince me and others, but mostly himself, that he is nice and kind and genuine. But, now that he stopped making that great effort in the session, he felt in the grip of great anxiety over being judged and punished. Paul said, "I see what you mean. I certainly don't want to see myself that way. I feel like the minute I let go of trying to be good, I became bad."

This dramatic breakthrough in Paul's treatment continued, slowly but consistently. Over time, we were more and more able to understand how his borderline (Kernberg, 1967) functioning led to extreme reliance on pathological splitting and projective identification. He lived in a world of always striving for perfection and convincing himself he was kind-hearted and loving when he also had other feelings that felt very dangerous and needed to be denied and destroyed. However, this created a psychotic cycle of projective identification in which his harsh judgement of self and others had to be expelled. This led to a return of internal persecutors in the form of voices. Paranoid-schizoid experiences of loss were always looming, in which love was ripped away and replaced with rejection. Compassion, understanding, and patience, all the virtues Paul tried to constantly convince himself that he had, were in fact elements of an internal object he couldn't find. So, he was left to fend for himself in a weakened state, doubting his own worth and unable to find soothing or support from his internal other. This was a psychological state that would take much time for us to understand, repair, and change. But, Paul had already begun that journey.

Discussion

Summers (1988) and Kernberg (1967) are among many writers who cite the borderline patients' struggle with splitting. Kernberg (1967) also identifies a "predepressive idealization" that is more paranoid in nature. Rather than a simple good versus bad, one particular aspect of this paranoid-schizoid splitting is a chronic conflict between idealized objects and devalued objects. In fact, due to the mechanism of projective identification, there is a constantly shifting cycle of idealized aspects of the self and/or object competing with, in conflict with, and generating opposing devalued aspects of the self and/or object. This more primitive state of idealization fragments the aggressive feelings and denies any guilt or fear or retribution. Paul was entangled within this divided world of denial, self idealization, and persecutory devaluation. His use of splitting and projective identification was so severe that he was subject to psychotic delusions.

Lindon (1966) has described how Melanie Klein, as well as her contemporary followers, made clinical contributions to understanding how over reliance on projective identification and splitting create paranoid and psychotic states that then lead to even more drastic defensive postures. Reparation, forgiveness, or compassion is impossible to find due to the stringent, cruel standards and the resulting "take no prisoners" approach to self and others. If such cruelty is rigidly projected, there can only be blame and a sense of persecution. To find healing and change, Paul gradually and painfully had to reclaim this aspect of himself and to examine his view of the object in order to slowly rework it and sort out his angry and unforgiving feelings that coloured that phantasy. Part of Paul's internal struggle had to do with how rigid his idealization of self was. If there was any hint of some feelings or thoughts that interfered with this profile or seemed different than his wished for self portrait, he panicked and had to rally his defences again.

Sacksteder (1990) describes the relationship of narcissism and manic defences in which no grief is associated with the contempt, rage, or disappointment in an object. The splitting and projective identification are overwhelming to depressive phantasy states and pull the ego into more of a paranoid state where consideration, reparation, or forgiveness is unavailable.

Regarding depressive anxieties, Sacksteder states, "the primary anxiety is that anger and hate will become overwhelming and lead to total destruction of the loved object or the loving relationship. This motivates the individual to repress anger, hate, and all other aspects of relatedness to the loved object that would threaten the continuity of the relationship. In this context, individuals come to experience guilt and concern when their anger does, in fact, hurt someone they love and these affects motivate them to undo the effect of the aggression through acts of reparation" (p. 23).

For individuals like Paul, they are afraid of the "total destruction of the loved object or the loving relationship" but they do not have the capacity for guilt, reparation, or forgiveness as they are still in the grips of paranoid phantasies in which the object or the self is unrelenting in its attack and the object or the self is without aid or relief from this attack. Therefore, narcissistic and manic defences are commonly used to deal with dependency, loss, and separation. Since reparation or forgiveness is not available in the psychic experience, the "total destruction of the loving relationship" is indeed total and this creates a frightening paranoid phantasy in which survival is the only issue and any and all defences are attempted to escape the annihilation of self or object. In this sense, Paul was constantly struggling with phantasies of primitive loss (Waska, 2002; 2005; 2006) and alternated between feeling completely self-sufficient and desperately in need. These paranoid-schizoid states create borderline and narcissistic levels of functioning that centre on the conflict of valuing and depending on others and the dread of helplessness, need, and dependency that can result. Vicious cycles of projective identification and splitting create intense paranoia and persecutory anxiety leaving the ego subject to brittle reliance on idealization and devaluation of self and object.

In interpreting these dynamics, I found it helpful to refer to the opposing aspects of Paul's mind, but as I mentioned previously, only in regard to how he was trying to prevent me and himself from seeing feelings and thoughts he was shameful and frightened of. In other words, I stayed in the realm of the transference and his phantasy experiences rather than more intellectual or experience distant remarks.

De Masi (1997) has noted that the regressed patient maintains a relationship between a primitive sense of morality and intimidation. This is similar to Klein's (1929) idea that the primitive superego is a core issue in psychosis. My interpretations of Paul's voices, his auditory hallucinations, were in line with Klein (1929) and Rosenfeld (1965) in that I interpreted the voices to be the punitive words of the superego. To do so, one is drawing the patient's attention to how the superego is as punitive as the ego is destructive (De Masi, 1997). This destructiveness is at the heart of the psychoanalytic treatment.

During my work with Paul, the psychological healing took place in the realm of the transference. By exploring, facing, and enduring his destructive and judgemental feelings and thoughts, Paul discovered the survival of both of us (Little, 1966), without retaliation or complete and infinite loss. Slowly, he learned that we could survive his aggressive phantasies and feelings and in the process we could begin to understand them. This understanding gave him the new freedom to either allow them to exist as an acceptable part of him or to change them in accordance to his now fuller self-knowledge.

In working to establish analytic contact with Paul, I had to contain and tolerate his narcissistic manner of non-relating, his desire for control and immediate gratification, and his aggressive urges for love and affirmation. I think Paul benefited from my overall efforts to neither judge him as his savage superego did nor try and placate him as he hoped his idealized object would. By trying to stay out of these two major aspects of his pathology, I think I provided him the vision and hope of a new self and a new object that could exist in a much less persecutory and less exacting way. This was only possible by keeping a constant lookout on my counter-transference experiences. I began to drift into thinking that it might be true that Paul's neighbours were spying on him and they were part of some conspiracy. These feelings and thoughts left me frightened. That fear and confusion alerted me to my counter-transference. Just as Paul was focusing on the external to escape the demanding and frightening internal, I was now projecting to distance myself from Paul's emotional state. This working through of my counter-transference paved the way back to the transference and his immediate phantasy state, where I was able to say, "I think it is easier to think about the neighbors and their possible conspiracy than to face the frightening and confusing emotions you have inside. But, perhaps if we both try and focus on your inside world we will not be so overwhelmed by the outside world."

I think Paul was able to slowly make psychological changes and find a less critical experience of his own values and expectations by using me as a translator for his unbearable and unacceptable feelings about himself. Bit by bit, he was able to take over this function from me and begin to translate, understand, and master his own inner world. This shift went hand in hand with a new trust in letting me into his mind, rather than simply projecting and expelling. A sense of curiosity and welcoming began to replace his automatic judgement and defensiveness. While certainly a small shift in a larger rigid system, these changes bode well for Paul's continued growth and integration.

PART III

COUNTER-TRANSFERENCE AND THE ESTABLISHMENT OF ANALYTIC CONTACT

Using the counter-transference: Analytic contact, projective identification, and transference phantasy states

In the course of some psychoanalytic treatments, the analyst may find themselves puzzling over where the patient's transference lies. Often, this is a situation where the patient talks primarily about current external situations in which they are depressed, angry, or anxious. These situational symptom-based scenarios invite the analyst to ignore the transference and focus on everything but the relationship in the consulting room. Within this atmosphere, both parties can begin to collude to avoid exploration of the transference.

How to find the trail back to the transference can be very confusing and difficult. The counter-transference provides a valuable aid to this task.

In our efforts to establish an understanding of the transference and to be able to consider the value of our counter-transference, the dynamics of projective identification must be addressed. It is the opinion of this author that most patients utilize projective identification as a psychic cornerstone for defence, communication, attachment, and aggression in their relationship to the analyst. As such, projective identification constantly shapes and colours the transference and counter-transference. For analytic contact (Waska, 2007) to be established, these three aspects of the clinical situation must be constantly explored, investigated, interpreted, and worked through.

By analytic contact, I mean that the analyst should always attempt to engage the patient in an exploration of the patient's unconscious phantasies, their transference patterns, style of object relations and defences, and internal experience of themselves in the world. Regardless of frequency, use of couch, length of treatment, or style of termination, the goal of psychoanalytic treatment is always the same: the understanding of unconscious phantasy, the resolution of intra-psychic conflict, and the integration of self↔object relations, both internally and externally. The psychoanalyst uses interpretation as their principal tool with transference, counter-transference, and projective identification being the three principal elements of those interpretive efforts.

Interpretation of the transference is always central to establishing analytic contact. But, the clinical unfolding of analytic contact includes a valued place for the total transference situation, the complete counter-transference, and both genetic and extra-transference states. Taken in total, the goal of analytic contact is to make therapeutic contact with the patient's unconscious phantasies and the conflicts that surround them. To make the optimal interpretations towards this goal, Segal (1962) states,

> Melanie Klein has enriched and expanded our concept of transference. Through paying minute attention to processes of projection and introjection, she showed how, in the transference relationship, internal object relations are mobilized by projection on to the analyst and modified through interpretation and experience as they are reintrojected. Similarly, parts of the ego projected on to the analyst undergo modification in this new relationship. Thus, what had been structured is again experienced as a dynamic process. The role of the analyst is to understand this process and to interpret it to the patient. A full transference interpretation—and though we cannot always make a full interpretation, we aim eventually at completing it—a full interpretation will involve interpreting the patient's feelings, anxieties, and defences, taking into account the stimulus in the present and the reliving of the past. It will include the role played by his internal objects and the interplay of phantasy and reality.

She adds,

> (i) Insight is therapeutic because it leads to the regaining and reintegration of lost parts of the ego, allowing therefore for a normal growth of personality. The reintegration of the ego is inevitably accompanied by a more correct perception of reality. (ii) Insight is therapeutic because knowledge replaces omnipotence and therefore enables a person to deal with his own feelings and the external world in more realistic terms. (pp. 212–213)

How the patient interacts with us within the envelope of analytic contact is the best therapeutic assessment for understanding and possibly bringing about the specific change that patient is seeking. Indeed, if the patient's interpersonal and intra-psychic reaction is to push the treatment into something less than analytic, this is important information in assessing their psychological struggles.

I think that the patient's phantasies, transference, and defences all work together to shape, distort, enhance, or influence the therapeutic encounter into being a particular form of relationship. Similarly, the analyst's counter-transference can create various states of acting out, collusive enactments, and role responses that further distort the treatment into something less than analytic. Therefore, the definition of what is psychoanalytic is often the sum total of the clinical atmosphere: how the patient/analyst pair negotiate, analyse, work out, or act out the phantasy states that come alive in the treatment setting. How is analytic contact proceeding and what is getting in the way of it forming and unfolding are some of the technical questions we must constantly ask. Consistent examination of transference, counter-transference, and projective identification cycles can help to keep analytic contact within reach and eventually established in a firm enough manner for the successful resolution of unconscious conflict.

Spillius (1983; 1994) has noted the value of understanding the intersection of transference, counter-transference, and projective identification in contemporary Kleinian practice. Much of this understanding and the manner in which to interpret such clinical moments comes from Rosenfeld's (1983) discovery of the different forms of projective identification. He has noted the projective dynamics that are used for communication and those which are for getting rid of unbearable states of mind. When the patient uses projective identification for communication, the analyst is not perverted or distorted by the process. They are simply utilized as a container for non-understandable elements of phantasy and feeling until the analyst can process those states into a new and more tolerable experience conveyed by interpretation. This also gives the patient the experience of being accepted and understood, which provides stability and repair to an otherwise weak ego.

More destructive are the efforts to deny, eject, and annihilate unwanted aspects of the self by projecting them into the analyst. Interpreting this type of evacuation is experienced by the patient as an assault and a refusal to take what has been given. Persecutory phantasies are increased by this attempt to eliminate unwanted feelings and thoughts only to then have to fight off the return of the dreaded unwanted. Rosenfeld added the important point that this narcissistic evacuation can either be to forever rid the self of toxic elements and bury them in the analyst or it can be an aggressive dumping of unwanted psychic debris with the faint hope that the analyst will share the painful internal suffering and maybe find a better solution to the problems than the patient has done.

This behaviour is frequently misunderstood and misinterpreted as being entirely aggressive and as a result the patient feels even more rejected, misunderstood, and alone. At the same time, this patient may feel overwhelmed by guilt in that they know they have forced the analyst to endure and contain that which they hate and suffer with.

Grinberg (1962) has studied the intersection of transference, counter-transference, and projective identification in detail. He speaks of the more ideal scenario in which the analyst selectively introjects the patient's verbal and non-verbal material, together with their corresponding emotional charges. Then, after containing and working through the material, the analyst (re)projects the translation of the patient's experience by means of interpretations. Grinberg (1962) outlines two other possibilities. First, the analyst may respond through his own conflicts or anxieties, intensified or reactivated by the patient's material. This would be a helpful way to understand the enactments that sometimes become consistent and profound in the course of an analytic treatment. In such a vein, Feldman (1997) has clarified the universal presence of enactments between both patient and analyst as the result of projective identification mechanisms.

The second possibility Grinberg (1962) discusses is one in which the patient, actively and unconsciously, projects his inner conflicts upon the analyst, who acts in this case as a passive recipient of the more intense or even violent projections of the patient. This intensity is often the result of exaggerated emotional charges resulting from internal conflicts and from the violence with which this same mechanism was imposed on the patient during childhood.

Whenever the analyst is related to with such violent projective identifications, he may react in a more balanced way, interpreting the patient's material. Doing this can help the patient realize he has not damaged or destroyed his object. Sometimes, however, the analyst may be unable to tolerate this forceful message, and he may then react in several other less helpful ways. Grinberg (1962) outlines these more pathological counter-transference reactions as a thought-less, immediate, and reactionary rejection of the patient's projection.

By denying this reactionary feeling, the analyst can try to control the reaction, but it will leak out and contaminate the treatment at a later point. Finally, the analyst may attempt to suffer the effects of such a violent project and take on the role of the bad or unwanted object or aspect of self. Again, many enactments occur in this situation, with the analyst justifying their actions in a variety of manners.

Throughout all analytic treatments, there is a strong pull, especially with some more disturbed patients but even with more integrated ones as well, to act out the counter-transference. Containment is a vital element in preventing excessive acting out or the outright demise of analytic contact. LaFarge's (2000) idea of containment and interpretation on the counter-transference experience is helpful. She is using her concept to discuss the careful technique of working with certain action-oriented transferences. I am applying her idea to the counter-transference.

In a similar way, I am using Steiner's (1984) ideas about containment but with a twist. He points to the two types of interaction seen in analysis, the more action-orientated form and the more symbolic form. While all patients communicate in both manners, the more action-orientated patient elicits affects and reactions from the analyst. Therefore, they shape the counter-transference by their particular use of projective identification-based actions. There actions can be silence, stubbornness, hostility, seduction, and so forth. They can be both passive and active types of action. Steiner (1984) states,"

> I find it important to try to characterize the mood and then link it to the patient's verbal communications and to any observable or inferable external events, which make up the total situation of the transference. Often, the mood is helpful in orienting the analyst to the patient's utterances, and these, in turn, help to illuminate the mood. If the analyst can contain the action and express the meaning of it in verbal and symbolic terms, the patient may eventually be able to enlarge his own capacity for containment. Of course, some action is part of every meaningful communication and is what gives the communication depth and resonance. What I think develops in a successful analysis is that the verbal and symbolic elements that accompany the action become more able to contain it and to be in harmony with it." (p. 461)

I am taking Steiner's ideas about the patient's actions and the need to contain them and applying it to the analyst's counter-transference. This then provides a reminder to the analyst to contain their impulses to act out and instead search for the meaning within, eventually attempting to interpret that understanding or incorporate it into his therapeutic approach. So, in the complete counter-transference situation, the analyst is always noticing or reflecting on their own mood, utterances, and reactions to the patient's material or other external factors. By containing these feelings and phantasies, the analyst can hopefully put them into some type of helpful symbolic expression (an interpretation) that can guide the patient and analyst further towards their goals.

In containing volatile feelings and phantasies that have been projected, the analyst has a chance to sort out what he is really experiencing and how best to utilize it in the treatment. Part of this gradual exploration is coming to a sense of the nature of what has been communicated or thrust upon us. Knowing from what developmental level the patient is coming from or pulling us towards is important. So, in the counter-transference, we may find ourselves operating at either paranoid-schizoid (Klein, 1946) or depressive (Klein, 1935) levels of experience. Understanding the nature of the counter-transference allows for greater containment and eventual symbolic expression.

Regarding the paranoid position and depressive positions, Stein (1990) states,

> In the paranoid-schizoid position, the guilt is fear of revenge from the object, a fear which results from projected aggression and destructiveness which becomes persecutory anxiety. In the depressive position, the guilt consists in the sense of one's own responsibility for badness or harmfulness and is ineluctably accompanied by reparative urges to re-create the lost or harmed object. Anxiety is about the survival of the ego (which in Kleinian theory is not distinguished from the self) in the paranoid-schizoid position and about the wholeness of the object in the depressive position; guilt is, inversely, fear of an object in the paranoid-schizoid position and fear of oneself in the depressive position (p. 505).

Elaborating on the depressive position, Joffe and Sandler (1965) state,

> In contrast to the anxieties of the paranoid-schizoid position (where the child feels that his ego is attacked by his own projected hostility), the main anxiety is now that the infant will destroy the object he loves and upon which he is dependent. The child is at the mercy of feelings of despair, guilt, and hopelessness when he feels that he has destroyed his external or internal mother. (pp. 400–401)

Discovering the paranoid or depressive function of the counter-transference feelings and phantasies the analyst is struggling with can provide more of a compass to determine what therapeutic direction to take. Part of understanding the depressive or paranoid essence of the counter-transference is to untangle the relational climate of the of self↔object phantasy. So, sorting out, in the counter-transference phantasy, who is doing what to whom and why and how they are doing that and how the other is reacting or contributing to that way of being is essential. This, in turn, leads to a better understanding of the transference and the projective identification dynamics at play. "Exactly what are the relational specifics of my phantasies" is a question the analyst must continuously ask himself.

Case material

Steve had been seeing me for almost three years and had made much progress working on his sense of failure and self-hatred. However, his tendency to shift internal and external relationships into sado-masochistic interactions was still very prevalent. His sister had been an unstable woman who used a variety of drugs and engaged in very erratic relationships for years. About two years ago, she started talking about how the FBI was chasing her and how the mafia had hit-men out for her. She thought there was a grand conspiracy that she had been a part of and now was on the run from. Some of this seemed like the result of certain strong drugs she took but more and more it became obvious that she was exhibiting signs of schizophrenia. Steve had a very hard time accepting this and blamed himself for his sister's condition. She has been in a locked ward for over a year now, diagnosed with schizophrenia. We have spent much time exploring how he tries to control her, rescue her, and fix her by blaming himself and seeing himself as the only person who can make her right again. Also, he sees his family to blame in how they raised her. Steve feels he should have stepped in and prevented that. He has clung to this masochistic vision of power and it has been in the transference work for some time.

In a recent session, Steve came in very distraught. He told me that he was "very upset because he had confided in a friend at the gym about his sister. The friend told him something new about his sister's condition." Steve said, "He informed me that her condition is the result of using too much speed and smoking too much pot. Apparently, when the drugs wear out of her system she will be ok. He told me the current medical thinking is out of date and doesn't account for that type of thing. So, it isn't a mental problem after all. It is a drug problem."

Steve elaborated for awhile and I started to feel very irritated and even a bit outraged. My counter-transference reaction became overwhelming, perhaps due to a more violent form of projective identification in which Steve was forcing me to be part of a particular internal phantasy. This caused me to act out in the moment. I said, with a slight tone of distain, "Well, what type of medical training does your friend have?" Steve replied, "None. He is a cook." I noticed myself getting even angrier and realized something important was happening in the clinical moment that I need to contain and understand before acting on. So, I "sat on it" which was quite difficult. My urge was to put Steve and his friend down and question Steve's intelligence. My discomfort eased as I realized I was in the grips of a projective identification response in which I was the irritated authority ready to be dismissive and angry with my uneducated child who could be so naïve or stupid. In other words, I was very disappointed in my patient/child and wanted to scold or punish him. This knowledge led me to see that what set the transference/counter-transference trap was the bait of my patient's conviction. He seemed so easily and stubbornly convinced of what he had been told.

So, as the result of containing and exploring the projective iden-tification challenge and beginning to examine the nature of my counter-transference phantasy and the exact type of object relational roles within it, I was able to make an interpretive remark. I said, "You seem to be so convinced, like you want to believe what he told you no matter what." In response, Steve said, "My family and myself. We are to blame for my sister's condition. We should have done something to help her. I am sure I could have done something to prevent her from ending up like this. This is my fault. I should have been there for my sister. I failed her. I hold myself responsible for her wreaked life."

I now realized the motive behind Steve's conviction and the resulting projective identification that made me want to tell him his was a failure in my eyes for believing his friend at the gym. In other words, by holding that conviction and taking that stand with me, I was pushed into almost treating him like he was already treating himself, like a failure and a bad person. So, I interpreted, "you quickly grabbed onto what that person said to you because it is ammunition for your cause against yourself. You want to con-vince me that you are bad and have wreaked your sister's life. You expect me to hate you and see you as neglectful and irresponsible. This is easier in some ways than to accept your sister as having her own troubles separate from you and that you could be your own person, responsible and happy separate from her. This makes you uncomfortable and guilty so you don't want to show me that side of things. It is easier to be the bad boy who causes trouble." Here, I was using what I discovered in my counter-transference and the dynamics of Steve's projections to make an interpretation of his depressive phantasies and conflicts.

Steve responded, "I am sure that if I were to simply be me and not try and make sure everyone is always happy and ok, I would be of no value or worse. I am afraid you would just be angry with me and not want me around. So, I have to be on alert at all times." I answered, "And, you have to control me and your sister and blame yourself ahead of time so we don't have the freedom to either love you or hate you in our own right. You have to come to the end of the story right away because it feels scary to just see how it will turn out. Will we be ok and will I accept you? Will you sister work through her troubles? It makes you very anxious to let us be separate and see if we end up together. You feel more in control by pulling us apart in this blaming way than to see if we can be separate and be happy together."

Steve said, "I am terrified to be separate like that. I feel like everyone is broken and I am to blame." So, we were now deep into his core phantasies and how they played out in the transference. Part of how we found our way there was by my struggling within the counter-transference and working with his projective identification dynamics.

Case material

With this next patient, I was pulled into a depressive desire to take care of and protect. In addition, I felt there were far less controlling or intrusive projections that shaped my counter-transference as compared to the last case. Therefore, my thinking was less muddled and I was less prone to slip into any sort of acting out.

Tom was raised by his parents until the age of nine when they announced they were divorcing. Tom said, "This was so out of the blue I was floored. I never saw it coming. Everything in my life changed and was never the same again. But, then I went about trying to adapt to it and do the best I could. Tom reported being a latchkey child before and after the divorce and remembers the "empty afternoons waiting for someone to come home."

During the second year of his analysis, Tom was recalling his childhood. He told me how he was prone to obsessive behaviours such as needing to touch the bushes as he walked home from school "for some strange reassurance or security." We had made a great deal of progress in working on his fear of loss and his pattern of never depending on others so as to not cause them any burden or heartache, a projection of the childhood experience of wanting to depend on his parents and feeling he was a forgotten burden who would exhaust his fragile, weak objects. We had discovered his transference conflicts of wanting my care and attention and guidance, but feeling guilty for wanting it and reacting by trying to be self-sufficient and overly focused on other's wellbeing.

As a boy, Tom had a rock collection of "all the rocks that looked sad and lonely." He said, "I felt the need to save them or rescue them and give them a home." I made the interpretation that he was the sad homeless rock in need of help and he was hoping I would help him just as he tried to save the rocks. But, I added, he put so much sadness and hopelessness into the rocks that it was a terrible task to save all of them. I said, "Given how much sadness and hopelessness you may feel sometimes, it makes sense you doubt if we can do much to change you. But, I also have the sense that you are somehow anxious of what it would be like if we did find hope and create change." Tom said, "Sometimes I don't know if I deserve to do better, it almost feels like I am asking for too much. The last thing I want is to be greedy. Maybe, I should just realize I am fine and learn to like the way it is. Maybe what I feel is normal." I said, "Sounds like you are still trying to adapt to the painful divorce and the feelings of being out of control and wanting help." Tom began to cry and said, "Sometimes I feel like it will never get any better. I feel so small and useless."

During his analytic treatment, tom became aware of a lifelong pattern of worry and anxiety. He would find himself spending time with his wife and three small children and begin thinking of different scenarios in which he would be separated from them, they would be taken away or attacked, or some other type of tragedy would befall them all. He would become overwhelmed with panic and try to figure out the best way to prevent such catastrophe. This lead to elaborate precautions, first-aid kits, disaster planning, and many sleepless nights.

For quite some time in his analysis, Tom insisted these dangers were real and he was simply being a good husband and father by trying to keep everyone safe and together. These anxieties seemed to come in two camps. One was when they came to him "out of the blue." When I heard him use that phrase, I immediately pictured his experience of his parents divorce and how helpless he must have felt to control this "out of the blue" disaster. At this point, my counter-transference feeling to his concrete resistances was more paranoid in the sense that there was nothing I could do against this outside force surrounding me. I made the interpretation that he felt surrounded in this helpless way and added that he was looking to me to find an anchor, a reassurance that he didn't have to be on guard all the time. Tom agreed immediately and added, "That would be like magic. A huge weight would be taken off my shoulders, like some kind of responsibility would finally be gone."

This was a clue to the other aspect of his worries. I pointed out that when the disaster worries were not "out of the blue," they were thoughts he had when he or the family were having fun. They might be out to a movie, camping, at the park, or on vacation and he would start to envision some type of terrible disaster where they would be separated or killed. So, I interpreted that his "responsibility" to make sure everyone was always ok was part of a vicious cycle in which he felt unworthy and somehow to blame for things. Therefore, having fun and enjoying the bond of the family was not right and had to be punished by some out of the blue disaster. Tom said that "while the whole thing sounds crazy and makes no logical sense, he never heard it put that way and it felt like a light went on in his head about it all." So, this interpretation was based more on my depressive feeling of counter-transference in which I pictured love, pleasure, conflict, guilt, and punishment. This was more of an oedipal, depressive counter-transference interpretation. For several months now, we have been working on this theme of paranoid tragedy, depressive loss and guilt, and the desire for a parent (myself) to take charge and reassure him so he can go back to being a carefree child instead of an anxious on-guard watcher waiting for trouble and desperately trying to prevent it and control for it.

In a recent session, Tom came in and said, "Wow. You had your old sports car. Now, you have your new one. I noticed they are coming out with a really super-charged version of the new one next year. Maybe you can get that one too!" My immediate counter-transference feeling was that I could have it all. I was able to take the pleasure I wanted and even some more. But, the way he said it also left me feeling a bit guilty as I thought I was too indulgent. I was not sure what to do with this feeling in the moment, so I chose to contain it and attempt to understand it. It seemed like probably a projective identification move on his part, putting his desires and confidence into me and then attacking it with guilt. But, it felt like if I immediately interpreted this to Tom, I would be closing down a pathway of communication and closeness. In other words, I felt it was a communication type of projective identification rather than an effort to discharge something toxic or an outright attack.

So, I chose to contain my feelings and ideas for the moment and see what came up next. In fact, in the past Tom has made other comments about my car and I have made these more immediate types of direct transference interpretations. They have been helpful and he has associated to wanting more in his life but doubting his capabilities and "not feeling right about wanting more." On this occasion, I was struck by the increased intensity of his message, in that both the urge for pleasure and the guilt that followed was more in the counter-transference than ever before. To me that indicated a deeper level of projective identification than before and I wasn't sure what the difference was yet so I held off rather than instantly trying to control it by labelling it, which is what Tom did so often.

So, Tom proceeded to tell me about his weekend. He told me how he was watching television and on the news there was a story about a child being abducted from a family's home and the search to find the child. Tom was overtaken by worry that this could happen to his family too. He said, "I was overwhelmed for awhile. But, then because of what we have been doing here, I was able to step back and think about it. I didn't have to do anything. I was still upset and worried for awhile, but I didn't find myself racing to protect the family or coming up with a plan to protect everyone. So, it was different."

Here, I thought to myself, "He did it. He was able to take care of himself and help himself though the anxiety. He didn't have to project as much of his fear and anger from the past into the present. He was able to have the sports car." Before I could interpret any of the victory he was conveying, as an equal not as a passive child hoping for reassurance or rescue, Tom changed his tune. He told me, "When I think about it though, I am not sure if I did it the right way. We talked about how I operate in those moments and I am left with two ideas about what happened. On one hand, I think I did what we have been working on because I thought about it enough to realize what was going on and then I stepped back and didn't get sucked into it. But, I wonder if I still thought too much about it in general and gave it too much power. On the other hand, I wonder if I didn't think enough about it. Did I just ignore it and go into some kind of denial about the whole thing? That wouldn't be good either. So, I am not sure if I really went about this in a very helpful way." Tom went on like this for another five or ten minutes with his dialogue becoming more and more convoluted and obsessional. It soon became, to me in the counter-transference, an urgent cry of a child looking for reassurance and guidance.

I interpreted, "You started out telling me about your victory. You found yourself in that familiar scary place and then you found a way out of it. But, as soon as you shared that victory with me, you had to change your tune. Instead, you are doubting yourself and intellectualizing everything to the point of confusion and meaninglessness. At the end of all that doubt, you are looking to me to reassure you or set you straight. So, maybe it is easier to be passive and under confident with me than to share your victory."

Here, I used my counter-transference reactions to make a projective identification-based transference interpretation. Tom associated to basketball, which he loves to play and is quite good at although he is reluctant to admit that to me. He told me how he sees the basketball team as a unit and that "no one person can ever stand out in glory." And, he added, "If one person tries to be the champion, they are easily put in their place by someone else right away." He told me this for a few minutes and in the counter-transference I felt like I was being taught a lesson. By this, I mean I felt both I was being instructed in the proper way of living and also given a warning that I should not ever think too highly of myself or I would be put back in my place. Given that I thought this to be a communication in projective identification in which he wanted me to grapple with a conflict he was struggling with and provide some direction, I made an interpretation. I said, "You are warning me about how easy it is to be punished if you get too proud of yourself. You told me about your victory and how our work together led to an important change. But, you are worried you are feeling too confident and that out of the blue I could take you down a peg. So, you are playing it safe and waiting to see what I say. It is almost like you need my permission or someone's permission to feel more confident."

Tom was quiet and started crying. "This is so hard. I am trying my best but it is sure hard." He said this in a way that meant "Yes, I agree. I am trying and I am scared of being punished. I am willing to keep trying but it is very scary." This was a fruitful point in Tom's analysis. It is slow going and he has considerable resistance to change given the anxiety he feels about it. However, he slowly tries to push forward and is making important progress.

Case material

Kim had been hospitalized for suicidal thoughts and a long-term depression. After being released, she sought help with me. She had a history of feeling "like she had screwed up every job and every relationship she had ever had." She was quick to blame herself for things and apologized ahead of time for the grief or frustration she imagined I would suffer under her hands. The first two years of her analytic treatment were taken up with how much she hated herself and how she invited me to constantly confirm her negative self-image. Kim was sure I merely "tolerated her." Having done some online reading about psychiatric conditions, she became convinced she was a borderline personality and constantly beat the drum of "I am a borderline, a hopeless case, aren't I?" I found myself pulled into this web, sometimes thinking she was simply working hard at understanding herself and her mental dynamics. Mostly though, I felt she was debating with me and bullying me for a worst diagnosis possible. So, the counter-transference helped me in exploring and interpreting this sadomasochistic transference. In turn, this led to a gradual decrease in Kim's anxiety, her acting out, and her depressive feelings.

During Kim's third year of analytic treatment, twice a week on the couch, this sadomasochistic frenzy and panic had greatly lessened but her depressive phantasies and fears still shaped much of her thinking. Now, we focused more on how she could never be good enough for me to love her and how she kept trying to meet my expectations but always felt behind. So, there was less pleading for me to "be honest and tell her how fucked up she was" and more subtle forms of worry and anxiety over our relationship. How she affected me was the focus of many sessions. For months, she embarrassingly told me about "her crush" she had on me and how I showed up in dreams and her thoughts during the day. Part of my investigation into this "crush" was her fear of "crushing" me with her desires, needs, and sexual wishes.

Kim's former outright shotgun approach to apologizing for everything and anything changed to more complicated stories that started out with a few pieces of pride, excitement, or joy and then shifted to mistakes, remorse, and self-recrimination. In the counter-transference, I noticed the curious sensation of being led down one path, beginning to share her pride, joy, or achievement, only to be then convinced that she didn't deserve it for a whole host of reasons. To myself, sometimes I would become fairly lost in the complex details of how and why she "messed it all up again" and lost sight of her original point, that of being happy about her life or happy to be with me. So, I was able to use this counter-transference insight to point out her projective identification recasting of events and of her true feelings. My counter-transference pointed the way to understanding her defensive warding off of her conflicts and the resulting mental confusion she felt.

Along the way, as part of her "crush," Kim wanted to make me a series of music tapes of all her favourite songs and that way I "would be able to really understand her and the deeper emotional places she sometimes goes to." We talked about this idea and her fond feelings for me for quite awhile. It was clear she was nervous about the idea, was sure I would hate it, and "realized it was a huge violation of the rules of therapy."

At one point, she was talking about the type of music she was including on my gift tape and how it was taking so long because there is "so much for me to fill you in on." In the counter-transference, I noticed I was more and more drawn into thinking about the music tape gift and what types of songs would be on it and if I would like the music or not. What struck me was that in my mind, I was more and more involved and relating to the vision of the music tape and less and less in touch with Kim. I was now ditching one object in this triangle for the other object, who seemed so intriguing and exciting. Kim was now this forgotten bland object of the past compared to my shiny new object of the future. In other words, I began to see that through projective identification, Kim was constructing an oedipal situation in which I choose the other, not her. And, she had directed my attention away from her being a lovable object over to this other more lovable thing, the tape. So, I interpreted these ideas.

I said, "you are engaging me in a lot of detail about the tape, the songs, and whether I will like them or not. But, it seems that might be a way to hide from the feelings you have about making the tape, the meaning the songs have for you, and the message you want to give me by offering the gift. In other words, you are getting me to have a relationship with the tape and veering away from revealing and sharing your actual feelings to me. You want the tape to be the middleman instead of directly singing your songs to me." Kim said, "I get it. Yes. I am reluctant to tell you how I feel and I would rather let the tape do the dirty work for me." I interpreted that this was the problem, that Kim felt her feelings were dirty and her wanting to be with me and teach me about herself was dirty work that should be hidden and disguised.

In response to my interpretation, she said, "I want to try and be more open. Let's see. I will try and tell you about one of the songs and why it is important to me. It is a song about a couple on a beach and their connection with each other. It makes me feel so good to listen to. I like it because it reminds me of this time I was traveling and I went down to Mexico. I met a wonderful man there and he took me to all the sites and treated me so nice. I really had a great time. The song reminds me of that and in particular we went to this one beach at sunset and no one else was around. We were naked, the sun was bathing us, the sun was setting, and we were drinking wine, and making love as we looked out onto the ocean. It was this perfect moment in my life. That song brings it back to me. I keep it as a special and wonderful time. Of course, that was also around the time I had been dumped by this other guy that I knew. We were never getting along but then it got worse and we were fighting all the time. Finally, he just told me he wanted to break it off. Even though I saw it coming, I felt really hurt. But, I also felt like it was partly my fault. I thought I wasn't a very reliable girlfriend and I didn't communicate very well. I had decided to quit my job before I started traveling because I didn't feel like what I was doing was meaningful and I never felt I was any good at it either. I met a few interesting men along the way in my travels but just about every one of them seemed to treat me nice in the beginning and then just throw me away. I felt very used and stupid. I should have seen it all coming. I feel like a really stupid loser most of the time."

I noticed in the counter-transference that I had initially felt very soothed and pleasured by the beach scene. But, now I was pulled away into an increasingly depressing and scattered series of failures. I felt I was being robbed of my beach time. So, I interpreted, "you shared this special magical memory with me where everything felt fine and full of pleasure. I think you are worried it is too much to have, that I will be judgmental of you feeling proud and happy. So, the next thing you just did was to cover your treasure with lots of failure and disappointment. You must feel guilty to tell me you are a sexy, romantic girl with memories of wonderful adventures. You have to dirty it up and make excuses for it, to apologize for it."

Kim said, "Ouch! That is right, it hits the target hard. But, I can't imagine letting myself think of me in that way. It seems too selfish or arrogant, just waiting for a fall. Sharing those kinds of happy feelings with you? That feels really dangerous!" So, we were now in the heart of the transference and at the core of some of Kim's more conflictual phantasies. The counter-transference provided a way to comprehend her projective identification process.

Another situation occurred that was similar in some ways but also showed Kim's increased integration and ability to separate from her object without feeling she had destroyed it. Kim told me about her new mentor in the management training programme at work. They had been meeting for several months. In the beginning, Kim told me she was "intimidated and often sure that she would see Kim as a failure and a joke. I am sure it is only a matter of time before she is sick of me." I thought to myself that this is exactly how Kim has felt about me, on and off during the analytic treatment. Kim went on to say that "over time, I was able to feel safer and let my guard down and begin to trust her a bit. I still looked up to her and greatly admired her, but it felt less dangerous and fragile." Again, I thought that this was a parallel reference to us but I elected to be silent so I could find out more and get a better sense of what Kim was really communicating to me. In the past, I have made such interpretations, and they proved helpful. But, in this moment, it felt like they would be incomplete.

Kim went on to describe her feelings towards her mentor in the present. Kim said, "I feel so good talking with her and learning things with her. I feel our time together is become very special and important. I learn so much from her. She takes the time to truly listen to me. I used to feel intimidated around her but now I notice that she will sometimes smile at me and suddenly all seems right with the world. It is very soothing."

In the counter-transference, I noticed myself in two modes. Intellectually, I was ready to make the "you are talking about us" interpretation. But, I noticed that emotionally, I was feeling a bit jealous. Kim seemed to be describing an erotic attachment and idealization of this mentor and I felt left out. I wondered if I was still important. I realized that if I made the "you are talking about us" interpretation I would be defensively reacting to my oedipal discomfort. This helped me see that Kim was probably testing me through this interpersonal aspect of projective identification to see if it was alright to be independent without hurting me or enraging me.

I interpreted that idea and Kim replied, "Yes. I am aware of consciously hoping you will be ok. The word test is interesting because I do feel like I am testing you and hoping the outcome will be ok. I am hoping you will allow me that happiness on my own without getting hurt or misunderstanding it. But, the more we talk about it, the more I feel a little worried. Are you ok?" I said, "you felt strong enough to trust that we were going to make it through the test and that I would be ok sharing you with someone else and letting you have your own life. But, being strong like that makes you anxious and guilty so now you are trying to take it all back and make me ok. But, the way we are talking about this makes me also think you are a bit worried but not hanging on the edge of the cliff like before. I think you can see I am still in one piece even though you are your own person." Kim said, "You are right. I think I just had to check, or double check. You know, old habits die hard!" I said, "You just want to make sure I don't die if you pick up some new habits." She said, "You got me there!"

CHAPTER TWELVE

The counter-transference and analytic contact

In working to establish analytic contact, I employ a combination of classical and contemporary Kleinian approaches to better reach the patient at his current internal experience of self and object. This involves the consistent exploration and interpretation of all conflictual self↔object relational states and the struggle between phantasies of love and hate and life and death. Counter-transference is vital to finding the often jumbled threads of transference and to understand the nature of projective identification communications or attacks that are so frequent in most treatments.

Just as Joseph (1985) spoke of the total transference situation, I think we need to also be clinically aware of the "complete counter-transference" situation. By this, I mean the awareness of not just the basic "I feel x so patient must be projecting that feeling into me" method of understanding counter-transference. Instead, we must be alert to the overall atmosphere of mood, action, thought, sensation, urge, and emotional climate that exists within the treatment setting. The complete counter-transference situation is elusive and fleeting in most treatments, not something easily formulated. But, if the analyst is paying equal attention to the counter-transference and transference as well as the dynamics of projective identification, analytic contact is possible. With this therapeutic contact, a clinical process in which the patient's core phantasies will be revealed, understood, interpreted, and worked through is possible.

The complete counter-transference situation is difficult to manage at times for a variety of reasons. Gill (1979) has pointed to the dual difficulty in analysing the transference in which he cites the patient's resistance to the acknowledgement of the transference as well as the patient's reluctant to let go of the transference experience. The counter-transference can bring about similar hardships for the analyst. The analyst may resist acknowledge of the counter-transference because of various anxieties, shame, guilt, or loss of control. And, the analyst may not want to give up those feelings and phantasies out of anger, pleasure, paranoia, anxiety, or a sense of loss, envy, or jealousy.

O'Shaughnessy (1992) has noted how analysts can go to two incorrect extremes in their interpretation, either to enclaves or to excursions. Thinking about the source of these enclaves and excursions, I think that counter-transference acting out of either not acknowledging the counter-transference roles and feelings one is in or unconsciously refusing to give up those feelings and roles can both lead to a crippling or a perversion of the treatment.

Another reason the counter-transference can be challenging to monitor, manage, or understand, let alone utilize, is the clinical and technical challenge that occurs through the various forms of projective identification that emerge from the transference. Through analytic exploration, what is often found at the core of our most vexing, confusing, or difficult patient's troubles is a vicious cycle of projective identification in which the ego's demands and expectations are relentless and exaggerated. For example, the need for constant love, reassurance, and approval can be intense. These feelings are partly the result of an identification with a demanding, exacting object combined with the ego's own projected aggressive desires. When these exacting demands are projected, the ego feels faced with a vicious, rigid, picky object reluctant to love or care. The ego is left feeling angry and alone and is even more desperate and aggressive about wanting love and attention. This creates the phantasy of retaliation, through detachment or attack. Then, the ego feels abandoned or persecuted.

Or, some patients feel they are disturbing a violent, angry object with their needs so they do everything they can to avoid conflict by not engaging with the object. Often, all these internal situations parallel past external circumstances. Many of our patients come to us with a history of unavailable, demanding, or fragile objects that both generated and reinforced these internal feelings and phantasies. Now, in their adult lives, these memories and phantasies are acted out interpersonally.

Quinodoz (2003) thinks the reason this type of patient is

> difficult to understand is that he sometimes resorts to non-verbal means in order to communicate with the analyst and that he makes frequent use of projective identification; the analyst then experiences a specific form of countertransference that, following Grinberg (1962), I shall call 'projective counter identification'. In my view, knowing how to use this specific type of countertransference forms an integral part of the language that touches (Quinodoz, 2003). For the psychoanalyst, it is first a case of perceiving what the patient is unconsciously communicating to him without words and then of interpreting what he thinks the patient has thus conveyed to him. Some analysts who do not use the term 'projective identification' make use of this concept by another name, or by theorizing similar phenomena differently. The term and the references that are used are not very important; I have chosen to use the name that Klein gave to this mechanism because she was the first to discover it (p. 1474).

Projective identification is a universal dynamic that confronts all analysts in the course of their treatment journey with each patient. The unpredictable nature in which the mechanism unfolds within the transference demands a variety of interpretive approaches (Waska, 2004).

Many of our more difficult to reach patients (Waska, 2006) are struggling with intense phantasies of primitive and persecutory loss (Waska, 2002) and find the change and the learning that analytic treatment provides to be a dangerous risk to their internal safety. As a consequence, they utilize defences such as projective identification on a regular and intensive level.

Projective identification is often the trigger of powerful and confusing counter-transference reactions and unless understood, contained, and used as a guide to working with the patient's transference and phantasy states, it becomes part of a mutual acting out process. As mentioned, there are various forms of projective identification and therefore a variety of interpretive approaches regarding their translation and resolution. In attempting to establish analytic contact, projective identification and counter-transference are valuable and essential tools in the clinical process.

With more disturbed narcissistic and borderline patients, the intensity of projective identification defences is stronger, the pull for counter-transference enactments is higher, and the need for containment and careful interpretation is greater. In this volatile setting, the analyst must struggle and grieve over the reality of day-to-day clinical practice in which many of our cases act out, resist our help, and terminate abruptly. These unstable and difficult cases also bring out the most enactments and counter-transference confusions. While the private practice psychoanalyst will always have to face these hard if not impossible treatments as part of their caseload, the careful use of counter-transference to better work with projective-based transferences can increase the change of establishing analytic contact and hopefully maintaining it as well.

Case material

In seeing Mark, I was struck by his extremely logical way of relating. It was really a way of non-relating. Mark was a scientist and I felt like part of his laboratory in which everything was sterile, exacting, and procedural. He came to me for help with his constant insomnia and was worn down by feeling exhausted for the last year. Almost immediately, it was obvious that the new job he had taken on almost two years ago was the culprit. From everything Mark said, I felt it was apparent he hated his job and wanted out. So, I interpreted that there must be something that keeps him from that awareness and the action he would have to take if he was more aware. Mark told me he wanted to keep this job because it meant he was "the superstar of his field and he would be respected from then on out and be able to get any job he ever wanted." I asked him if he was happy at the job. He said he "had never actually thought about that." I interpreted that his inability to sleep might be his inner conflict about hating the job but not wanting to give up his superstar status. He was very interested in this idea and we explored it over the next four months.

However, Mark's narcissistic transference stance was what dominated the treatment and led to its early termination. He wanted to "be better" and wanted me to "tell him what procedures he needed to follow to find the cure and make the necessary changes." He was there to find the problem, find the solution, and go. The way he went about that and the attitude he held left me feeling used and even bullied. When I interpreted this, Mark heard me saying he was "deviating from proper procedures" so he immediately vowed "to adjust his behavior" in order to "be better," "if it would facilitate the treatment." So, I felt he related to me in this narcissistic, artificial, and sterile manner in which he was trying hard to obtain the necessary potion for his ailment without much regard for the two human beings in the room.

Mark was so obsessive, controlling, and narcissistic that he could only see me as someone he had hired to give him instructions from a manual on how to eliminate the wrong and replace it with the right. I interpreted his desire for superstar status at work as the emotional bind he was in. I said it was difficult for him to get out of that bind without feeling like a failure. Mark seemed to become more present with me and less anxious when I said this. We discussed this in detail over the few months we met. He was able to use logic to see my interpretation as "accurate" and therefore he needed to spring into action and "make changes to eliminate the stress that prevented him from sleeping."

But, as soon as Mark felt better, was sleeping more regularly, and started to look for a better job, he terminated. He told me he was doing better, sleeping most every night, and was job hunting, plus it was too difficult to find time from his work schedule to come in since the peak season at his job just started. I interpreted that he had taken what we talked about and was able to give himself permission to make changes without feeling like a failure. He could give up rock star status without feeling overwhelmed with shame or anxiety.

During this brief analytic treatment, I felt as if I was on a shifting bank of sand. I was with a friendly comrade doing important lab work together and suddenly I was with a cold, calculating stranger who saw us as tubes of success or failure. When Mark asked in one session how my vacation had gone and I explained that it would be helpful to explore his feelings and thoughts about my vacation, he took it as an "exercise to better our progress" and began to artificially answer.

Part of how my counter-transference helped me help Mark was the cold, dismissive scientific response I had to his sleep problem. I found myself thinking how obvious the problem was and how simple the fix would be, "just quit your job you dumbbell!" I realized I was in the grips of a projective identification reaction to his overuse of logic, control, and narcissistic distancing. My lack of empathy gave me a clue to Mark's state of emotional stagnation. I used this information to interpret his possible fear of emotions, his anxieties around being more in touch with his own needs, and his fears of failure and shame. This seemed to be helpful, at least temporarily. He was able to explore these chocked off aspects of himself for a bit, found a way to begin relaxing his control over himself, and become a bit less judgemental. Was his progress situational? Probably, but that may be the best analytic outcome in this particular clinical instance.

Case material

In the beginning of her analytic treatment, Sally was hard to reach. For awhile, I was left feeling like I didn't know how to interpret the transference. Strangely, this was even after she told me she "had a reputation for being controlling, a person who turns off men," and has been told by boyfriends she is "way too demanding." Sally told me she had a reputation for being "bitchy" and self-centred, and that she "is really into appearance, kind of to the point of being shallow." In addition, she had been "put on notice" at work for "her attitude" and told by her boss to "be less bitter and sarcastic." While this all should have left me feeling an easy inroad to exploring how she felt with me or interpreting how she acted with me, I was more bogged down in the counter-transference.

So, instead of being able to reflect on how I felt like another recipient of her "bitchiness" and "self-centeredness," I was more caught up in feeling put down and reacting to her air of superiority and bitterness. I think this was the result of constant and often violent and provocative projective identification attacks. In other words, she tried to discharge or expunge those disappointing and ugly views of herself into me so she would not have to suffer under their weight.

In this initial counter-transference confusion, I thought of Sally as an uptight controlling woman who could be quite conceited and "bitchy." I felt that even though she was quite pretty, I felt her appeal did not go beyond her body. In trying to understand my feelings I came to realize that this was exactly how Sally saw herself. Thus, it made sense how Sally spent hours putting on her makeup, was always shopping for a better outfit, and had several cosmetic surgery procedures in the last few years. In other words, on some level, she felt she was only as loveable as she looked but that if anyone got to know her past skin level, they would not be interested. So, this new counter-transference knowledge enabled me to make those types of interpretations. These comments seemed to help Sally begin to look at herself in a deeper manner and begin to consider what internal struggles kept her feeling so unlovable and prone to acting so unlikable.

During one session, Sally lay down on the analytic couch and told me she "sometimes is not honest with others." She told me a few examples of times she was not honest with friends. I asked about us and she said she had some secrets. Sally revealed she felt we weren't getting anywhere and she was disappointed with our progress. After listening awhile, I interpreted this to be the same feeling as she reported having with all her dates. She agreed and continued to tell me that "she gets disappointed easily and just wants things to go her way and she doesn't like it when they don't."

I interpreted that in the past she had told me before that she "was getting a lot from me, saw the value of our work, and could tell there had been a few changes in her life as a result of therapy." But now, this hungry expectation for things to go her way had created a scorched earth policy in which the satisfying progress she had before is now gone and she left herself angry with nothing. Sally replied, "I know. And, I know I need to change that. But, I still feel like I am not getting what I expect."

The next night Sally walked in the office carrying several large bags from her shopping errands and said, "Twice a week on the couch is not enough, I am moving in!" In the counter-transference, I felt a mix of emotions and took a minute to sort it out. I think it was a bit confusing for me because she was projecting and enacting her core phantasy conflicts and I felt shoved off balance by both love and hate in the same interaction.

Roth (2001) describes the different layers of transference interpretation open to the analyst. I think there are similar levels of counter-transference interpretation possible. There are the interpretations one makes to one's self, as part of a containing and self-stabilizing process. These silent interpretations may lead to eventual interpretations of the particular projective identification dynamics that triggered the counter-transference. Or, if the initial containment failed and the analyst becomes aware of some sort of enactment, the counter-transference may lead to an interpretation of that enactment. If this is purely an issue of the analyst's psychology, I do not advocate disclosures of personal problems but rather an honest expression of the awareness of making a mistake. Otherwise, the analyst can attempt to explore and interpret the mutual analyst-patient relational meaning behind that acting out.

Sometimes, counter-transference shows the way to a more genetic or even extra-transference interpretation. As Blum (1982) points out, there are different dimensions within the analytic relationship, which include the intra-psychic, the interpersonal, and the interactional. The counter-transference can be a reaction or a guidepost to which level the patient's transference, phantasies, or projective identification aim is directed to at any given moment.

So, returning to that particular clinical moment with Sally, I felt my counter-transference was directing me to the intra-psychic level and a focus on the here-and-now transference situation. Therefore, I interpreted that she was struggling with a difficult mix of demand for what she expected out of me, a hunger for warmth and closeness, some sense of remorse, and a general feeling of gratitude for our time together. Sally said I was "on the money" and that she "is always full of mixed up feelings like that, but mostly the big one is frustration." This led to us exploring how painful it is for her to be herself with me and others without constantly managing and controlling how I see her. She said, "I am worried about being rude and looking ugly." I said, "So you have to make sure I am always seeing you in a certain way by censoring yourself, monitoring how I see you, and controlling the both of us. You are on constant duty. You must feel like you could easily fail and I will see all that ugly, rude side." Sally replied, "And then you won't like me and won't want to be with me!" I interpreted, "you have to always maintain this perfect picture with me or you might fall into the gutter." Sally nodded and said, "Oh, yeah. That is how it feels!"

Later in the session, she told me how she had spent some time deliberating and "feeling really anxious" when she found herself wanting to watch television instead of doing a pile of audits she had brought home from the office. I said it was a great victory that she let herself watch television as it meant she could have felt in the gutter with me looking down on her, yet she took the risk to allow herself the pleasure of the gutter in watching television and the risk of letting me know she doesn't like maintaining the perfect picture all the time.

In response, Sally associated to a story about how a while ago she had gone out on a date for the first time with a man and she spent hours getting dressed up "just right" and putting on the "perfect blend of makeup." She tried to be calm and relaxed and give off "the right vibes and be cool and nice." But, he never called her back afterwards. She was sad but "used to it." A month later she had gone to the gym with a couple of girlfriends and during her workout there was a fire alarm and everyone had to clear the building and no one was allowed back in for almost an hour. So, her girlfriends suggested they all go next door to a bar for a drink while they waited. Sally was mortified and refused. She was panicked that she was "exposed" without any makeup, nice dress, or her hair done right. But, her friends dragged her into the bar anyway.

There in the bar, Sally was "shocked" to see the man she had gone on the date with. He came over to say hello. She told him she felt like "a pig" and apologized for looking "so ugly." He looked her over and replied, "Baby, if you had looked this hot when we went out, I would have called you back!" While we both agreed he didn't sound like the best choice in town for a long-term relationship, he nevertheless helped Sally see her intense self scrutiny and how little it means to others. Sally said, "It was a real lesson. But, I am still not convinced and definitely not comfortable feeling that exposed."

Another example of the Sally's disturbing transference reactions that often prompted complex counter-transference phantasies came about during a session about a month later. Sally came in looking ready for battle and after lying down said, "I have decided to come in less. I don't really see the point of coming in so often. I want to have some free time and this is in the way. I see no change, coming here only leaves me frustrated."

Many clinicians have extended Klein's (1946) intra-psychic concept of projective identification to include the interpersonal and interactional aspects of the analytic situation. Joseph (1988) and other contemporary Kleinians have noted the patient's unconscious ability to stimulate and provoke the analyst to pair up with the specific object relational phantasy embedded within their projective identification process.

With Sally, her way of talking and acting with me in that moment was very provocative, leaving me angry and dismissive. I began, rather quickly, to feel "I could care less and if she doesn't want to come in, so be it. In fact, she could leave right now if she wanted. I am done with this crap!"

It was the narcissistic, abusive quality of her tone as well as the content of what she was saying that left me very defensive. I noticed this and immediately did what I could to contain myself and try and understand what was going on. She went on, in a rather demeaning and caustic way to tell me, "I don't see what I get from you. I expect certain things and I never get them. I feel I don't really get anything from you. It is a big disappointment. In fact, I think I could get the same or even more from just sitting around talking with my girlfriends."

At this point, I felt like telling her to go see her girlfriends and leave me the heck alone. I thought to myself that my wanting to throw her out at this moment was probably similar to how she describes a history of "getting fired by her friends and boyfriends."

Sally went on like this for awhile and I did my best to contain, process, and understand this attack and communication. I say communication because I held out hope that this was something that had meaning, not just something destructive. Also, in the countertransference, I tried to contain myself and find some understanding rather than outright attack Sally. So, I wondered if she could find some understanding and containment of herself after outright attacking me. This is another way to see Rosenfeld's (1983) idea about narcissistic attacks through projective identification that can sometimes contain a communication as well. In fact, his idea of certain patients who unconsciously have the dim hope that the analyst will realize they are attempting to communicate behind their attacks fits Sally's case quite well.

So, after my efforts at self-containment and gradual interpretation, Sally finally revealed that she felt "overwhelmed by the pressure to change and really tired of the demands to find the answers and make sense of my badness. All I ever do is come here and look at how bad I am. I want to spend less time looking at what a loser I am so if I come here less I will feel better." I said, "Or, we can try to understand why you need to attack yourself here and demand so much from both of us. Just being yourself with me must feel very risky, like it is not good enough." Sally replied, "It has never been good enough." One of the difficulties with a patient like Sally is that her reply was simultaneously a reflective insight and a literal, declarative statement with no room for negotiation.

This more concrete, non-symbolic view of herself surfaced towards the end of the session. Sally returned to saying how "therapy was disappointing" and "a waste of her valuable time." I was left feeling she might indeed terminate altogether and if so, it would be a playing out of her "getting fired" by friends and boyfriends but in reverse. I wondered what our next meeting held.

Sally came in for her next session and said she "had been thinking quite a bit about last night." She told me she had thought a great deal about her family and her upbringing. She said her father was always angry and demanding, always on edge. No one could predict when he would lash out and "now I am like him." She went on, "Over the years, I just got used to it. He was mean all the time so it just seemed normal." After a bit, I interpreted that she was looking at how she has identified with her angry, bitter father and in telling me about that I could tell that she is also apologizing for her lashing out last session. Sally agreed but added that she is "still under-whelmed by her progress compared to what she expected to get out of it." I interpreted that her way of lashing out at me and putting our progress down is perhaps a reflection of how mean and demanding she is of herself. In other words, she is projecting the sense of personal failure she has onto me and onto the analysis.

In response, Sally associated to a story about a friend who was also in analysis but who recently "graduated." Sally said, "I couldn't believe she had graduated already. She started after I did and I think she is much more screwed up than I am. I asked her if she had told her therapist about x, y, and z. She said she hadn't. I thought that if she had she would certainly still be in treatment. There is no way she would have been able to graduate if she was honest."

I said, "It sounds like you envy your friend, as if she managed to be paroled before you did. Are there things you hold back on with me, things that you think its better to not mention?" Sally said, "Well, I used to talk to you quite a bit about the married guy I am having the affair with. But, ever since you called me pathetic, I decided I would stay quiet about it." She said this in a very bland, nonchalant manner but I felt shocked and concerned.

I thought, could I have ever possibly called her that? If so, how could I have been so cruel and inappropriate? So, I thought back to the last time we had discussed her relationship with this man and I realized what had happened. I said, "This is very interesting and important. I remember that time we talked. What I said was that given how you were describing your feelings, you sounded like you thought it was a painful and pathetic situation you were in." Sally responded, "I think you are right because I remember saying if a friend told me the same story, I would tell them it is pathetic and they should dump him and get on with their life." I said, "So, you judge yourself for many things including that, but you also push some of that judgment onto me and others, which makes you feel like we are all evaluating you all the time." Here, I was interpreting her projective defences.

I added, "What seems to be so important about you thinking I called you pathetic is that it seems like no big deal to you. Of course, you don't want me to call you names so you will be silent about the topic if you think I am being abusive. But, you are almost in agreement with me the way you downplay it so much. I wonder if it is like you told me you became used to your father being angry and mean. Now, you just assume I am angry and mean too so it almost seems like no big deal for me to call you pathetic." Sally said she understood what I meant and "had never thought of it that way, that I might be numb to the idea that other people are putting me down."

I added, "It may have started with being numb to your father's meanness, but now you are the one numb to your own insults and demands." A few minutes later, I said she is also numb to insulting me and demanding so much of me. So in affect, we are both her punching bag. Sally, said, "I feel black and blue most of the time. But, if I stop fighting, I think no one will notice me." Here, we were able to gain an important foothold in a core phantasy Sally held, that she must constantly prove herself and look good or she will be rejected and abandoned by her objects.

Case material

Beth, a patient I have written about before using a different disguised name, came to see me after "things didn't work out with her other therapist." She told me that after seeing a therapist for two years and discussing her feelings about a man who didn't want to make a full commitment to being with her, the therapist told Beth "she should move on" and "get a life and forget that guy." Beth told me, "I realized that I had gone to this therapist to try and resolve my messed up relationship or non-relationship I have with Stan. I talked about it every week for two years and then she comes out and tells me what I should do. But, it felt like that was based on what she wanted me to do. From that moment onwards, I knew this therapist was biased. It was never the same. I think she must have gotten sick of me talking about this guy and how he never wants to be with me. Also, there is this other woman that he seems to like more than me, but he claims they are just friends. I can't ever get her out of my mind. She is like the obstacle between me and him. She is this crazy, weird person who is madly in love with him but he claims he only likes her as a good friend. Anyway, I always talked about how I was sure that in time, he would see the light and want to be in a fully committed relationship with me. But, my therapist told me I was just fooling myself and I should move on. I could see her point, but it didn't feel right. So, I stopped seeing her and here I am." In the counter-transference, I noticed myself thinking what a poor therapist this other person was and how much she had missed the boat by not listening to the real story, the multiple aspects of Beth's conflict with this relationship had not been explored but instead something became acted out in the therapeutic relationship. At the same time, I was aware that the particular way Beth told me this story was part of a transference relationship in which she was, via projective identification, tugging on me to feel certain ways about her and about her prior therapist. I tried to take these ideas and my feelings into account before making my next comment.

I said, "And you are hoping for a different result. You are hoping I will be able to listen better and accept you better without reacting like that?" Beth said, "Yes. I hope you will stay unbiased." This was important information of course as it gave me a reference point to watch out for in my counter-transference. Indeed, within six months, I could understand how and why this last therapist had acted out in that way.

Overall, Beth was very polite and somewhat passive in the way she related to me. She was motivated to tell me everything that was on her mind, but she also needed me to ask her questions to prime the pump. I commented on this and she said, "Well, I don't want to just say any old thing, you might think I am crazy or not following the rules." We explored this aspect of the transference and found she had phantasies regarding my reaction to her being more independent and having more of her own identity. Over time, we came to understand this as a way she felt she had to be passive and helpless in order to one day win my approval and love.

I interpreted that this meant she kept two versions of us alive in her mind. There was the meek and scared little girl who kept her feelings and needs to herself in order to not rock the boat and waited to see if the superior object would one day notice her, appreciate her, and accept her for having her own thoughts and desires. And, there was the vision of us combined in a happy unity where there was no conflict and she had the freedom to be herself and I was accepting and understanding. This was the golden reward for all her waiting and suffering.

When Beth told me about her family history, I immediately noticed how it felt like a tragic tale of great proportion. I felt like I was settling down in my seat at a darkened movie house and taking in an epic tale. Here, I noted to myself that there was another triangle happening in the room, with her once again on the outside of it or drifting in the middle. There was me, her, and the epic tale. In the counter-transference, I was more drawn to the tale than her in the room. So, I commented that she seemed to keep herself out of the story by keeping certain feelings to herself. I said certain feelings because she was sobbing through most of the retelling, but I noticed I was unmoved by her, yet moved by the imagery and plot of the story. So, I thought she was projecting her truest affect into the story and leaving us with a more controlled and modulated account of her life.

Beth's grandparents lived in a remote Caribbean location and her grandfather was a famous political figure and extremely successful businessman. Both grandparents were very superstitious and regularly sought the counsel of local fortunetellers and mystics. After the birth of their first child, they consulted the mystics about the future of their new baby. They were told he would be a rich and powerful man and a positive influence on the family heritage. When they had their second child, my patient's mother, they also consulted the mystics. This time, they were told the child was a curse to the family and should be removed from the family after birth to minimize the risk. Specifically, they were told the child would cause sickness to the mother and financial ruin to the father. So, when my patient's mother was five, her parents sent her to relatives on another island. When Beth's mother was ten years old, her parents decided to take her back because the relatives could not care for her anymore. Within a year of her return, the political climate in their country changed, drastically affecting Beth's grandfather's fortune. His money was lost and he was reduced to a managerial job that was an embarrassment to the entire family. So, the mystic curse came true.

Interestingly, during the analysis, Beth "confessed" to me that she was consulting psychics. She was trying to keep the hope alive that her old boyfriend would transform himself from uncommitted and unavailable to focused and devoted. And, Beth was hoping the other woman he seemed to be interested in was out of the picture and not able to be a barrier between Beth and him. So, she consulted the psychics for word about these matters. She finally told me "she knew she needed to be honest if this therapy was going to work" and revealed her regular appointments with the psychics.

I interpreted this situation, focusing on the elements I thought to be the foundation of her phantasies and internal conflicts that were now emerging in the transference and often relayed thought projective identification. I interpreted that she longed for an ideal union with her distant object but when I made my interpretations they made her feel she was losing this ideal union and I brought her into an unbearable state of loss. By not being honest with me she could keep her hope alive. I was put in the position as the one who kills the hope, leaving her abandoned and lost.

As far as the transference, I interpreted that I was the harsh voice of reality, another obstacle that kept her from her beloved phantasy of transformed objects. I stopped her broken, unavailable, distracted ones from being turned into focused, committed caring objects. Beth could not look directly at her relationship with the man and see it for what it was, a disappointing, sad affair. So, instead she distracted herself by paying attention to the woman. I commented that my voice of reality took that protection and denial away. Therefore, she didn't want to tell me about her feelings and instead spoke to the psychics whom she hoped would tell her that her wishes were coming true. Finally, I pointed out that Beth wanted the psychics to tell her the other woman was bad and was no longer in the picture, shipped away like Beth's mother was after the psychics said she was a curse.

After Beth's grandfather lost his fortune, the family felt Beth's mother had led them into a life of shame. So, Beth's mother was considered the outcast. She lived under this shadow till she was eighteen and met a man whom she would marry a year later. Once married, Beth's mother had two daughters.

From what Beth told me, her parents got along fairly well before Beth was born but that they started drifting apart soon after Beth's birth. I pointed out that Beth's unspoken belief was that she was a curse to them much like Beth's mother was a curse to her family.

When Beth was five years old, she walked into her father's office and found him dressing up in women's clothes. Her father yelled at her to get out of the office as if she had done something wrong. Over the next few years, her father would walk around the house wearing makeup and women's clothing as if nothing were odd about it. Also, Beth remembers her parents fighting and yelling more and more. During this time, her father was drinking to excess almost everyday.

When describing her relationship with her mother, Beth told me, "I wanted to be able to go to my mother for comfort, but she was often more rejecting then my father. It felt like I could never do enough or be good enough for her. She found fault with everything I did. I could play with my sister when I was really young, but as we got older, she seemed to go her own way so then I felt completely alone."

Beth told me that once she was nine or ten she "began realizing what was going on around the house much more clearly." Being an alcoholic, her father lost several positions at his accounting firm before he was fired. He was then reduced to low-paying jobs as a contract worker to fill in when others were sick or on vacation. Beth said, "no one respected him anymore and our family was filled with shame. We couldn't afford to stay on the island so we moved to the States and my father found odd jobs with various firms but never really got back on his feet. The whole time, when he was home he was dressed up like a woman and was either drunk or walking around enraged and yelling at us. I felt like I could never be close to him. I kept waiting for him to change and be my father but it never happened." When Beth stopped crying after she told me this, I pointed out that this was her current state with her ex-boyfriend, waiting for him to change but feeling she could never be close to him.

Beth told me she knew from age eight that her mother was a drug addict and relied on the local doctor to supply her with pills that she took everyday. These were mostly narcotics and she spent many a day in bed, high on pills and "depressed about her marriage." This was "another way I could never rely on my parents or feel I could get close to them. My mother seemed to love her pills more than she loved me." When Beth was in her late teens, her mother killed herself. Her father died of cancer five years later. Many of the analytic sessions were filled with Beth's terrible sorrow, sense of betrayal, and loss over never "really having two normal parents who cared about their kids. They just cared about themselves."

Beth was truly overwhelmed by grief, but it was unresolved grief due to the many emotional conflicts she felt over her connection or lack of connection with her objects. When I noticed myself not very moved by her frequent sobbing, I was able to use my counter-transference indifference to make a provisional interpretation to Beth about her sense of both loss and angry rejection of her parents that left her emotionally conflicted. She was sad and angry about the indifference they showed her and the care she so desperately craved. Her sobbing was the desperation and my indifference was her projected anger as well as her view of her object's cold distance.

When I noticed how unengaged I was with Beth as she is sobbing and as she told me her family stories, I also noticed I was more interested in the stories than her and her affect. I realized that once again there was another triangular situation involving Beth, myself, and her history. Specially, I was more interested in the stories than her, thus feeling in the counter-transference the indifference towards her and the stories being the obstacle between me and her. This repeat of her historical experience of always wanting to get to one or both of her parents and feeling it impossible to get thought the obstacle of their desire (the drugs, the cross-dressing, the alcohol, the anger), and instead being left with their indifference was now a part of the transference and counter-transference through the dynamic of projective identification. Bit by bit, I was able to notice these feelings and phantasies and interpret them to Beth. As a result, she was slowly able to re-own these unwanted psychological experiences and begin to work through her conflicts about them.

So, as Beth's analysis progressed, we were able to identify more and more of these projective identification-based transference situations and make better sense of them. My counter-transference continued to guide the way. One important discovery was Beth's lifetime wish to have the unavailable object transform into the ideal, caring parent she longed for. I interpreted that to reach this ideal she had to strike a bargain in which she passively suffered with a broken, unavailable, or angry object. This included her subtle assault on me with ongoing tales of missing her ex-boyfriend. Just like her last therapist, I ended up wanting to tell her to move on and quit whining. If I fell into this, I would shift into the angry, uncaring object. I interpreted that she hoped I could tolerate this and one day be transformed into the understanding, caring object instead. But, to achieve this, she had to wait in pain and be a victim and give me a taste of her anger and frustration in the meantime.

These triangulated projective identification-based transferences emerged rather frequently in the treatment. In these phantasy states, Beth viewed me as the helpful parent who could help her, instruct her, or give her permission to find happiness and transform the unavailable object. However, as I have outlined, this meant she had to be my inactive, helpless, and scared little girl waiting for the time when, maybe, things would get better. Until then, she had to live with the obstacles in the way to her feeling strong, loved, and happy.

Examples of this transference phenomenon were abundant. Beth told me how she had been loosing sleep for years because of her toilet running all the time. I felt a pull to step in and ask her why she didn't fix it and give herself a decent night's sleep. When I did ask her, she responded by saying she was worried the landlord would be angry since she already paid such low rent. At this point, I realized the projective identification pull on me to become the rescuing, caring parent who would stand up for her against the angry, non-caring landlord and provide her with an average expectable living situation. I interpreted that she so wanted someone, me, to intervene for her and transform the unhappy situation into something better. But, in the meantime, she had to be the passive victim who longed for a transformation but had to endure the lack of comfort until this magical moment occurred. So, I interpreted her wish for me to be a certain way, her positioning herself between me and the landlord, and her bargain in having to be the victim waiting for the elimination of the obstacle to her desires.

Almost the same exact situation occurred when Beth revealed she had used a small portable heater for the five years she had lived in her apartment. I found this out when Beth was telling me about how she was more able to "separate and draw some boundaries between her and her disappointing boyfriend who was never really a boyfriend." In allowing herself to feel disappointed and take a stand for her own needs instead of dutifully waiting for him to come around and be a boyfriend, Beth was making progress in separating from her phantasies of a broken, unavailable object for whom she was eternally waiting for their magical transformation and special wished for union. Instead, she was now able to bear the thought of pursuing her own needs and obtaining what she wanted on her own even if it meant saying goodbye to the disappointing object. This marked a significant move forward in her psychological growth and was a shift towards healthy mourning of her prior disappointing and neglectful objects.

In exploring how she gave her power over to others in the hopes of being loved, Beth told me she hoped her "boyfriend" would one day decide he wanted to marry her and buy a home together. This was part of her painful on-hold life that had brought her in to see me, wanting change but also fearing and resisting it. As a result of our analytic work, Beth was now able to enjoy the vision of "buying her own cozy home that she could call her own and be happy in, instead of being lonely in a broken down shitbox of an apartment." She told me "One day I will have a heater to keep me warm. I may not have Mr. X to keep me warm at night, but I will be ok."

I asked Beth about her "having to make due with a small portable heater for five years." I told her I was pretty sure it is illegal to rent a dwelling without heat so I was interested in why she would put herself through that sort of torture. She told me "I never thought about it much, I guess I am used to being without. I think that is about my family, my past. I grew up having to be without, to be cold all the time emotionally." In investigating this, we discussed the same type of triangulation transference in which, via projective identification, she tried to enlist me as the rescuing, soothing parent who would either stand up on her behalf against the unavailable, cold, and neglectful landlord/parent or to help her remove the obstacle in the way of finding warmth and care.

Another example was later in the analysis when Beth told me she had decided to "get rid of her old, broken down television, so blurry it was hard to tell what you were watching." She had endured this "piece of junk" for years and now for her birthday, decided she "deserved something that would give her pleasure." She went out and bought herself a nice big new television. We discussed how this symbolized her new ability to throw away, grieve, and move past her former unavailable, disappointing, and broken objects and to not put obstacles in the way between her and her desires. So, bit by bit we worked through these primitive oedipal situations that became part of the projective identification-based transferences that in turn activated my counter-transference. We worked through the analyst/patient/internal phantasy triangle formed by splitting and traced it back to her mother/grandmother/internal phantasy triangle. Also, we worked on the internal triangles present in the patient/unavailable ex-boyfriend/other woman, the patient/father/father's cross-dressing, the mother/patient/mother's drug habit, the mother's suicide/patient/patient's success and separation, analyst/patient's adult independence/cared for child feeling loved and rescued. These were just some of the internal sets we discovered and worked on.

Today, Beth is still working hard to understand, accept, and change many of her internal feelings and phantasies regarding herself and her objects. She had made remarkable progress and no longer sees herself in the same narrow and confining manner. Nor does she feel as captured and weakened by the historical links with her parents and her deep and painful disappointments with them. Finally, she is much less inclined to want to wait for a lacking, rejecting, or unavailable object to finally notice her and be transformed into a loving, caring object committed to her. Beth is now able to accept that she lost out on fundamental important experiences with her family but that she can still find strong, meaningful bonds to others in her life that she can share reciprocal, rewarding relationships with.

SUMMARY

Analytic Contact is a therapeutic process that holds the transference as the primary vehicle of change, but also considers the elements of containment, projective identification, counter-transference, and interpretation to be critical to therapeutic success. Dreamwork, genetic reconstruction, analysis of conflict and defence, and extra-transference work are all seen as valuable and essential. The concept of analytic contact is not so much tied to external factors such as use of couch or frequency of visits as it is in building a clinical forum for the understanding and modification of the patient's deepest phantasies. Analytic contact is about finding a foothold into the transference and as well as into the core phantasy states that are having the greatest impact on the patient's feelings, thoughts, and actions.

Many of our hard to reach patients exhibit a cruel sense of judgement and expectation that they project and then feel surrounded by. While they crave a loving, soothing object that can rescue them from their internal torment, they also work against the union with a good capable object unless it is ideal and fully capable of providing all at all times. Therefore, they tend to maintain a degree of separation from the analyst, wanting contact but forcing distance and preventing union. Brenman (1982) has described this in terms of primitive superego functions that cancel out guilt and concern, finding contempt in any possible mutuality or understanding. Because of this aggressive stance against accepting regular, non-ideal attributes of the self or object, the patient is unaware of what they do obtain from the analyst or of what they are capable of achieving themselves. Brenman (1982) thinks it is important to continuously interpret the lost good parts of the relationship to provide the experience of bearing the loss and aggressive attacks from the superego. This cycle of interpretation, I think, will also help the patient achieve a new faith in recovering those lost objects and aspects of the self as well as to begin to value them. However, this line of interpretation is only useful if all aspects of loss, destructiveness, and anxiety are explored. This means a consistent following of the transference and the patient's phantasies as coloured by excessive projective identification.

Klein (1948) notes that one source of the infant's anxiety derives from the phantasy that the beloved mother has been destroyed by his sadistic impulses or is in danger of being destroyed. Klein calls this fear neurotic anxiety, in which the ego perceives the mother as an indispensable external and internal good object that will never return. However, this depressive phantasy includes the notion that there is someway to retrieve, restore, or repair that loving object, enabling the good to return. The patients highlighted in this paper certainly have phantasies of injuring or destroying the needed and loved objected. But, they do not have the stable or enduring capacity for faith, hope, and trust in the recovery, reconstitution, and reunion with the lost or destroyed object.

Part of this problem is the patient's sadomasochistic commitment to the dominating, rejecting, or absent object. They wait for the reward that never comes, the love that never unfolds, and the attention they never get. This creates a negative therapeutic reaction where the patient consciously or intellectually feels, "I should seek better, I can be independent" but emotionally they feel it is dangerous to sever their connection to the hoped for rescuing object.

Making analytic contact with such patients can be difficult and fraught with setbacks. In treating these individuals, the internal struggles with persecution, primitive loss, and fragmentation emerge quite quickly and need to be addressed as they unfold. The patients highlighted in this paper certainly have phantasies of injuring or destroying the needed and loved objected. But, they do not have the stable or enduring capacity for faith, hope, and trust in the recovery, reconstitution, and reunion with the lost or destroyed object.

This is part of a state in which the patient waits to be reassured, parented, or guided. Of course, this means they have to be weak, lost, and confused to be rescued and reassured. As I interpreted to one such patient, "you have to be a servant to receive the guiding hand of a master." Of course, this is one element that emerges in the transference of such patients and often becomes a point of struggle in that logically the patient wants to change and become more independent and self-soothing. But, emotionally, they don't want to give up the dream of finally being under the loving wing of a guiding parental object. Therefore, one common complication in such treatments is the patient's view of any strong, independent, or unique expression of themselves as dangerous, arrogant, or poisonous. It is seen as potentially offensive to the object and a way love could be lost and conflict could occur. It would mean they have to give up the dream or wish of a guiding, ideal object. Therefore, all personal strength, thought, skill, and opinion must be censored or devalued. This too becomes part of a masochistic transference that is difficult to resolve. Pride and hope are hidden, change is very frightening, and love must be constantly captured from the object to ward off feelings of isolation and fragmentation.

Analytic contact is the therapeutic process in which the analyst attempts to assist the patient in getting in touch with and gradually reaching an emotional and intellectual understanding of their warded off unconscious phantasies regarding the relationship of self and object. This insight provides the vehicle for subsequent working through and change, but does not solve the issue of resistance to that change. This is the arena of the ongoing analysis of transference, defences, anxieties, and internal gratifications.

Regarding the concept of analytic contact, more and more clinicians within the psychoanalytic field are concluding that this is the more honest definition of what is psychoanalysis in that it is about the clinical process. Fossege (1997) believes there is no real distinction between psychoanalysis and psychoanalytic psychotherapy and therefore proposes that the best definition of psychoanalysis is that it is an investigatory science searching for the best understanding of the patient's experiential world. This is in line with my concept of analytic contact being the therapeutic process of clarifying and modifying the patient's core conflictual phantasy states. And, analytic contact contents that the transference→projective-identification→counter-transference→interpretation climate is the best possible venue to achieve that goal.

The focus of analytic contact is the working through of phantasies and the multiple manifestations of love, hate, and knowledge that involve anxiety towards self and/or other. Projective identification is very often the primary climate in the analyst situation. The interplay between projective identification and transference can be intense and constant in particular treatments, regularly triggering counter-transference feelings and thoughts.

Therefore, it is crucial for the analyst to be willing to examine himself throughout the course of treatment for counter-transference information that could help shed light on the patient's here-and-now struggle with manifestations of love, hate, and knowledge. In today's world of psychoanalytic technique, it is widely acknowledged that counter-transference is a valuable and indispensable tool. Indeed, Gabbard (1995) points out that counter-transference is part of the emerging common ground among analysts of a wide and diverse theoretical persuasion. He sees this as the result of the now common theoretical conviction that projective identification and counter-transference exist in an overlapping dynamic that is always linked to the patient's transference phantasies. Accordingly, Baranger, Baranger, and Mom (1983) speak to the necessity of interpretation in projective identification-based transference states and the intensity of counter-transference reactions to such transference states. If unnoticed and not resolved through containment and/or interpretations, these types of counter-transference states can also become a state of pathological fusion with the patient's phantasy world (Baranger, Baranger, and Mom, 1983). This creates an atmosphere of mutual acting out and fragmenting enactments taking the place of resolution and integration. Of course, a certain degree of counter-transference enactments is to be expected in all treatments (Joseph, 1983), especially those with projective identification-based transferences. However, if these moments of enactment can be monitored, contained, and understood, they can serve as guideposts to learning about what the patient's current state of anxiety or desire might be. This is what Grotstein (1994) has remarked of as the "analytic instrument" that helps to illuminate the patient's deeper struggles, conflicts, and communications.

In closing, I think the concept of analytic concept enables the field of psychoanalysis to step back into the heart of its original goal, to help those suffering from unbearable psychological despair and conflict and to restore the individual's view of self and other to one of choice, trust, and hope. By defining psychoanalysis by its clinical elements rather than external criteria, analytic contact becomes the optimal clinical technique in exploring the mind and utilizing the transference and phantasy world to promote learning and change.

This view of analytic contact as the best method of practicing the art of psychoanalysis is echoed by Hayley (1990) when he said, "When I first qualified, and I was trained as a Kleinian, I used to accept for treatment only those who could come five times a week. This had been insisted upon by Melanie Klein, as by Freud. I was astonished when I was offered a patient by Bion, who said, 'He can come only once a week, but you just do psychoanalysis once a week'. My conclusion was that Bion believed that whether it was psychoanalysis or not depended not on the number of times, but on whether it was an interpretive procedure leading to the revealing of psychic truth and relying very much on the understanding of the phenomenon of the transference." (p. 8)

BIBLIOGRAPHY

Akhtar, S. (1996). Someday and if only fantasies: Pathological optimism and inordinate nostalgia as related forms of idealization. *Journal of the American Psychoanalytic Association, 44*: 723–753.

Alvarez, A. (1992). *Live company*. London: Routledge.

Bartner, R. (2007). Repairing the reparative instinct, news and notes. *The Psychoanalytic Institute of Northern California, 13*(1): 17–19.

Bass, A. (2007). The as-if patient and the as-if analyst. *Psychoanalytic Quarterly, LXXVI*: 365–386.

Bicudo, V. (1964). Persecutory guilt and ego restrictions—characterization of a pre-depressive position. *International Journal of Psychoanalysis, 45*: 358–363.

Bion, W. (1959). Attacks on linking. *International Journal of Psychoanalysis, 40*: 308–315.

Bion, W.R. (1962a). A theory of thinking. *International Journal of Psychoanalysis, 43*: 306–310.

Bion, W.R. (1962b). *Learning from Experience*. London: Heinemann, Pg. 128.

Bion, W.R. (1963). *Elements of Psycho-Analysis*. New York: Basic Books; London: Heinemann.

Blum, H. (1982). The transference in psychoanalysis and in psychotherapy: Points of view past and present, inside and outside the transference. *Annual of Psychoanalysis, 10*: 117–137.

231

Brenman, E. (1982). Separation: A clinical problem. *International Journal of Psychoanalysis, 63*: 303–310.

Brenman, E. (2006). Separation: A clinical problem. In: G.F. Spoto (Ed.), *Recovery of the Lost Good Object* (pp. 22–33). London: Routledge.

Britton, R. (2001). Beyond the depressive position: Ps(n+1). In: C. Bronstein (Ed.), *Kleinian Theory: A Contemporary Perspective* (pp. 63–76). London: Whurr.

Burch, B. (1989). Mourning and failure to mourn—an object-relations view. *Contemporary Psychoanalysis, 25*: 608–623.

Charles, M. (2006). Precocious illusions: Re-constructing realities. In: M.K. Revisited (Ed.), *Other Banalities* (pp. 77–104). London: Jon Mills, Karnac.

Clarkin, J., Yeomans, F. & Kernberg, O. (2006). *Psychotherapy for Borderline Personality: Focusing on Object Relations.* Arlington, VA: American Psychiatric Publishing.

Couch, A. (1995). Anna Freud's adult psychoanalytic technique: A defense of classical analysis. *International Journal of Psychoanalysis, 76*: 153–171.

De Masi, F. (1997). Intimidation at the Helm: Superego and hallucinations in the analytic treatment of a psychosis. *International Journal of Psychoanalysis, 78*: 561–575.

Espasa, F. (2002). Considerations on depressive conflict and its different levels of intensity: Implications for technique. *International Journal of Psychoanalysis, 83*(4): 825–836.

Feldman, E. & Paola, H. (1994). An investigation into the psychoanalytic concept of envy. *International Journal of Psychoanalysis, 75*: 217–234.

Feldman, M. (1997). Projective identification: The analyst's involvement. *International Journal of Psychoanalysis, 78*: 227–241.

Feldman, M. (2007). Addressing parts of the self. *International Journal of Psychoanalysis, 88*: 371–386.

Fine, R. (1979). *A History of Psychoanalysis.* New York: Columbia University Press.

Gabbard, G. (1994). *Psychodynamic Psychiatry in Clinical Practice: The DSM-IV Edition.* London: American Psychiatric Press.

Gabbard, G. (1995). Countertransference: The emerging common ground. *International Journal of Psycho-Analysis, 76*: 475–485.

Gill, M. (1979). The analysis of the transference. *Journal of the American Psychoanalytic Association, 27*: 263–288.

Gorkin, M. (1984). Narcissistic personality disorder and pathological mourning. *Contemporary Psychoanalysis, 20*: 400–420.

Grier, F. (2005). *Oedipus and the Couple.* London: Karnac.

Grinberg, L. (1962). On a specific aspect of countertransference due to the patient's projective identification. *International Journal of Psychoanalysis*, 43: 436–440.

Grinberg, L. (1963). Relations between psycho-analysts. *International Journal of Psycho-Analysis*, 44: 362–367.

Grinberg, L. (1964). Two kinds of guilt—their relations with normal and pathological aspects of mourning. *International Journal of Psychoanalysis*, 45: 366–371.

Grotstein, J. (1994). Projective identification and countertransference: A brief commentary on their relationship. *Contemporary Psychoanalysis*, 30: 578–592.

Grotstein, J. (2000). Some considerations of "hate" and a reconsideration of the death instinct. *Psychoanalytic Inquiry*, 20(2): 462–480.

Grotstein, J. (2007). Personal communication.

Hayley, T. (1990). Charisma, suggestion, psychoanalysts, medicine-men and metaphor. *International Review of Psychoanalysis*, 17: 1–10.

Hinshelwood, R. (1991). *A Dictionary of Kleinian Thought*. London: Free Association Books.

Joffe, W. & Sandler, J. (1965). Notes on pain, depression, and individuation. *Psychoanalytic Study of the Child*, 20: 394–424.

Joseph, B. (1981). Towards the experiencing of psychic pain. In: J. Grotstein (Ed.), *Dare I Disturb the Universe* (pp. 81–90). Beverly Hills, CA: Caesura.

Joseph, B. (1982). Addiction to near death. *International Journal of Psychoanalysis*, 63: 449–456.

Joseph, B. (1983). On understanding and not understanding: Some technical issues. *International Journal of Psychoanalysis*, 65: 291–298.

Joseph, B. (1985). Transference: The total situation. *International Journal of Psychoanalysis*, 66: 447–454.

Joseph, B. (1988). Object relations in clinical practice. *Psychoanalytic Quarterly*, 57: 626–642.

Joseph, B. (1989). Psychic equilibrium and psychic change: Selected papers of Betty Joseph. In: M. Feldman & E. Bott Spillius (Ed.). London: Routledge.

Kernberg, O. (1967). Borderline personality organization. *Journal of the American Psychoanalytic Association*, 15: 641–685.

Klein, M. (1928). *Early Stages of the Oedipus Complex, in Love, Guilt, and Reparation and* Other Works 1921–1945, Volume 1. London: Hogarth, 1985.

Klein, M. (1929). Personification in the play of children. In: *Contributions to Psychoanalysis 1921–1945* (pp. 215–226). London: Hogarth Press.

Klein, M. (1931). A contribution to the theory of intellectual inhibition. *International Journal of Psychoanalysis, 12*: 206–218.

Klein, M. (1935). A contribution to the psychogenesis of manic-depressive states, The Writings of Melanie Klein. In: *Love, Guilt, and Reparation and Other Works 1921–1945*, The Writings of Melanie Klein Volume 1 (pp. 262–289). London: Free Press.

Klein, M. (1940). Mourning and its relation to manic-depressive states. *International Journal of Psychoanalysis, 21*: 125–153.

Klein, M. (1946). *Notes on Some Schizoid Mechanisms, The Writings of Melanie Klein, Volume 3*. New York: Hogarth Press.

Klein, M. (1948). A contribution to the theory of anxiety and guilt. International Journal of Psychoanalysis, in envy and gratitude and other works 1946–1963. In: M. Masud & R. Khan (Eds.), *The International Psycho-Analytical Library*. London.

Klein, M. (1948). A contribution to the theory of anxiety and guilt. *International Journal of Psychoanalysis, 29*: 114–123.

Klein, M. (1952). The origins of transference. *International Journal of Psychoanalysis, 33*: 433–438.

Klein, M. (1952). On observing the behaviour of young infants. In: R. Money-Kyrle (Ed.) *Envy and Gratitude and Other Works* (pp. 94–121). London: Hogarth, 1975.

Klein, M. (1952). Some theoretical conclusions regarding the emotional life of the infant, in envy and gratitude and other works 1946–1963: Edited By: M. Masud & R. Khan, 1975, *The International Psycho-Analytical Library, 104*: 61.

Klein, M. (1957). Envy and gratitude, in envy and gratitude and other works 1946–1963: Edited By: M. Masud & R. Khan (1975). *The International Psycho-Analytical Library, 104*: 1–346.

Klein, M. (1963). On the sense of loneliness. In: Roger Money-Kyrle (Ed.) *Envy and Gratitude and Other Works* (pp. 300–313). London: Hogarth Press, 1975.

Klein, M. & Riviere, J. (1964). *Love, Guilt, and Reparation*. New York: Norton.

Kubie, L. (1955). "Say You're Sorry." *Psychoanalytic Study of the Child, 10*: 289–299.

Lachkar, J. (1992). *Narcissistic/Borderline Couples: A Psychoanalytic Perspectives*. New York: Brunner Mazel.

LaFarge, L. (2000). Interpretation and containment. *International Journal of Psychoanalysis, 81*(1): 67–84.

Lamanno-Adamo, V. (2007). Aspects of a compliant container: Considering narcissistic personality configurations. *International Journal of Psychoanalysis, 87*: 369–382.

Lindon, J. (1966). Melanie Klein: Her view of the unconscious. In: F. Alexander, S. Eisenstein & M. Grotjahn (Eds.), *Psychoanalytic Pioneers* (pp. 360–372). New York: Basic Books.

Little, M. (1966). Transference in borderline states. *International Journal of Psychoanalysis, 47*: 476–485.

Nathans, S. (2007). *Psychoanalytic Couples Therapy*. Corta Madera, CA: Workshop in Corte Madera.

O'Shaughnessy, E. (1981). A clinical study of a defensive organization. *International Journal of Psychoanalysis, 62*: 359–369.

O'Shaughnessy, E. (1983). Words and working through. *International Journal of Psychoanalysis, 64*: 281–289.

O'Shaughnessy, E. (1992). Enclaves and excursions. *International Journal of Psychoanalysis, 73*: 603–611.

Quinodoz, J. (1993). *The Taming of Solitude: Separation Anxiety in Psychoanalysis*. London: Routledge.

Quinodoz, D. (2003). Words that touch. *International Journal of Psychoanalysis, 84*(6): 1469–1485.

Rangell, L. (1995). Psychoanalytic realities and the analytic goal. *International Journal of Psychoanalysis, 76*: 15–18.

Rey, H. (1994). *Universals of Psychoanalysis in the Treatment of Psychotic and Borderline States, Edited by Jeanne Morgagna*. London: Free Association Books.

Riviere, J. (1936). A contribution to the analysis of the negative therapeutic reaction. *International Journal of Psychoanalysis, 17*: 304–320.

Rosenfeld, H. (1962). The superego and the ego-ideal. *International Journal of Psychoanalysis, 43*: 258–263.

Rosenfeld, H. (1965). *Psychotic States: A Psychoanalytical Approach*. New York: University Press.

Rosenfeld, H. (1971a). A clinical approach to the psychoanalytic theory of the life and death instincts: An investigation into the aggressive aspects of narcissism. *International Journal of Psychoanalysis, 52*: 169–178.

Rosenfeld, H. (1971b). Contributions to the psychopathology of psychotic patients. The importance of projective identification in the ego structure and object relations of the psychotic patient. In: P. Daucet & C. McLaurin (Ed.), *Problems of Psychosis* (pp. 62–79). Amsterdam: Excerpta Medica.

Rosenfeld, H. (1983). Primitive object relations and mechanisms. *International Journal of Psychoanalysis, 64*: 261–267.

Rosenfeld, H. (1987). Impasse and interpretation: Therapeutic and anti-therapeutic factors in the psychoanalytic treatment of psychotic, borderline, and neurotic patients. *New Library of Psychoanalysis, 1*: 1–318.

Roth, P. (2001). Mapping the landscape: Levels of transference interpretation. *International Journal of Psychoanalysis, 82*(3): 533–543.

Ruszczynski, S. (1993). *Psychotherapy with couples: Theory and practice at the Tavistock Institute of Marital Studies.* London: Karnac.

Sacksteder, J. (1990). Psychoanalytic conceptualizations of narcissism from Freud to Kernberg and Kohut. In: E. Plakun (Ed.), *New perspectives on narcissism* (pp. 1–70). New York: American Psychiatric Press.

Safa-Gerard, D. (1998). Bearable and unbearable guilt: A Kleinian perspective. *Psychoanalytic Quarterly, 67*(3): 351–378.

Sandler, J. (1988). Psychoanalysis and psychoanalytic psychotherapy: Problems of differentiation. *British Journal of Psychotherapy, 5*(2): 172–177.

Searles, H. (1973). Some aspects of unconscious fantasy. *International Journal of Psychoanalytic Psychotherapy, 2*(1): 37–50.

Searles, H. (1982). Separation and love in psychoanalytic therapy. In: P. Giovacchini & B. Boyer (Eds.), *Technical Factors in the Treatment of the Severely Disturbed Patient* (pp. 131–160). New York: Jason Aronson.

Segal, H. (1952). A psychoanalytic approach to aesthetics. *International Journal of Psychoanalysis, 33*: 196–207.

Segal, H. (1962). The curative factors in psycho-analysis. *International Journal of Psychoanalysis, 43*: 212–217.

Segal, H. (1973). *Introduction to the Work of Melanie Klein* (2nd ed). London: Hogarth Press.

Segal, H. (1977). Psychoanalytic dialogue: Kleinian theory today. *Journal of the American Psychoanalytic Association, 25*: 363–370.

Segal, H. (1981). *The Work of Hanna Segal.* New York: Jason Aronson.

Segal, H. (1994). Paranoid anxiety and paranoia. In: J. Oldham and S. Bone (Eds.), *Paranoia: New Psychoanalytic Perspectives* (pp. 17–26). New York: International University Press.

Segal, H. (2001). Memories of Melanie Klein: Part One, Interview with Hanna Segal, The Melanie Klein Trust.Org.uk.

Segal, H. (2007). *Yesterday, Today, and Tomorrow, Edited by Nicola Abel-Hirsch, New Library of Psychoanalysis.* London: Routledge.

Selon, E. (2006). The newspaper reader: On the meaning of concrete objects in a psychoanalytic treatment. *International Journal of Psychoanalysis, 87*: 1629–1647.

Spillius, E. (1983). Some developments from the work of Melanie Klein. *International Journal of Psychoanalysis, 64*: 321–332.

Spillius, E. (1994). Developments in Kleinian thought: Overview and personal view. *Psychoanalytic Inquiry, 14*(3): 324–364.

Spillius, E. (2007). Encounters with Melanie Klein: Selected papers of Elizabeth Spillius. In: P. Roth & R. Rusbridger (Eds.), *New Library of Psychoanalysis* (pp. 183–198). London: Routledge.

Stein, R. (1990). A new look at the theory of Melanie Klein. *International Journal of Psychoanalysis, 71*: 499–511.

Stein, R. (1991). *Psychoanalytic Theories of Affect.* London: Karnac.

Steiner, J. (1979). The border between the paranoid-schizoid and the depressive positions in the borderline patient. *British Journal of Medical Psychology, 52*: 385–391.

Steiner, J. (1984). Some reflections on the analysis of transference: A Kleinian view. *Psychoanalytic Inquiry, 4*(3): 443–463.

Steiner, J. (1987). The interplay between pathological organizations and the paranoid-schizoid and depressive positions. *International Journal of Psychoanalysis, 68*: 69–80.

Steiner, J. (1989). The psychoanalytic contribution of Herbert Rosenfeld. *International Journal of Psycho-Analysis, 70*: 611–616.

Steiner, J. (1990). Pathological organizations as obstacles to mourning: The role of unbearable guilt. *International Journal of Psychoanalysis, 71*: 87–94.

Steiner, J. (1993). *Psychic Retreats: Pathological Organizations in Psychotic, Neurotic, and Borderline Patients (New Library of Psychoanalysis, Vol. 19).* London and New York: Routledge.

Steiner, J. (2007). Interpretive enactments and the analytic setting. *International Journal of Psychoanalysis, 87*: 315–320.

Summers, R. (1988). Psychoanalytic therapy of the borderline patient: Treating the fusion–separation contradiction. *Psychoanalytic Psychology, 5*(4): 339–355.

Tarnopolsky, A. (2000). Normal and pathological mourning. *Canadian Journal of Psychoanalysis, 8*(1): 19–40.

Torras de Bea, E. (1989). Projective identification and differentiation. *International Journal of Psychoanalysis, 70*: 265–274.

Tuch, R. (2007). Thinking with and about patients too scared to think. *International Journal of Psychoanalysis, 88*: 91–111.

Ury, C. (1997). The shadow of object love: Reconstructing Freud's theory of preoedipal guilt. *Psychoanalytic Quarterly, 66*: 34–61.

Usher, S. (2007). *What is This Thing Called Love: A Guide to Psychoanalytic Couples Therapy.* London: Routledge.

Vaughan, S. & Roose, S. (1995). The analytic process: Clinical and research definitions. *International Journal of Psychoanalysis, 76*: 343–356.

Waddel, M. (2002). *Inside Lives: Psychoanalysis and the Growth of the Personality: The Tavistock Clinic Series.* London: Karnac Books.

Waska, R. (2002). *Primitive Experiences of Loss: Working with the Paranoid-Schizoid Patient*. London: Karnac.

Waska, R. (2004). *Projective Identification: The Kleinian Interpretation*. London: Brunner/Rutledge.

Waska, R. (2005). *Real People, Real Problems, Real Solutions: The Kleinian Approach to Difficult Patients*. London: Brunner/Rutledge.

Waska, R. (2006). *The Danger of Change: The Kleinian Approach with Patients who Experience Progress as Trauma*. London: Brunner/Rutledge.

Waska, R. (2007). *The Concept of Analytic Contact: A Kleinian Approach to Reaching the Hard to Reach Patient*. London: Brunner/Rutledge.

INDEX